AF594545

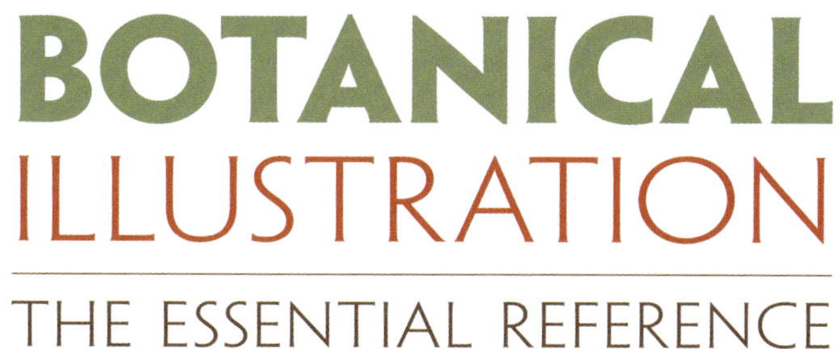
BOTANICAL
ILLUSTRATION
THE ESSENTIAL REFERENCE

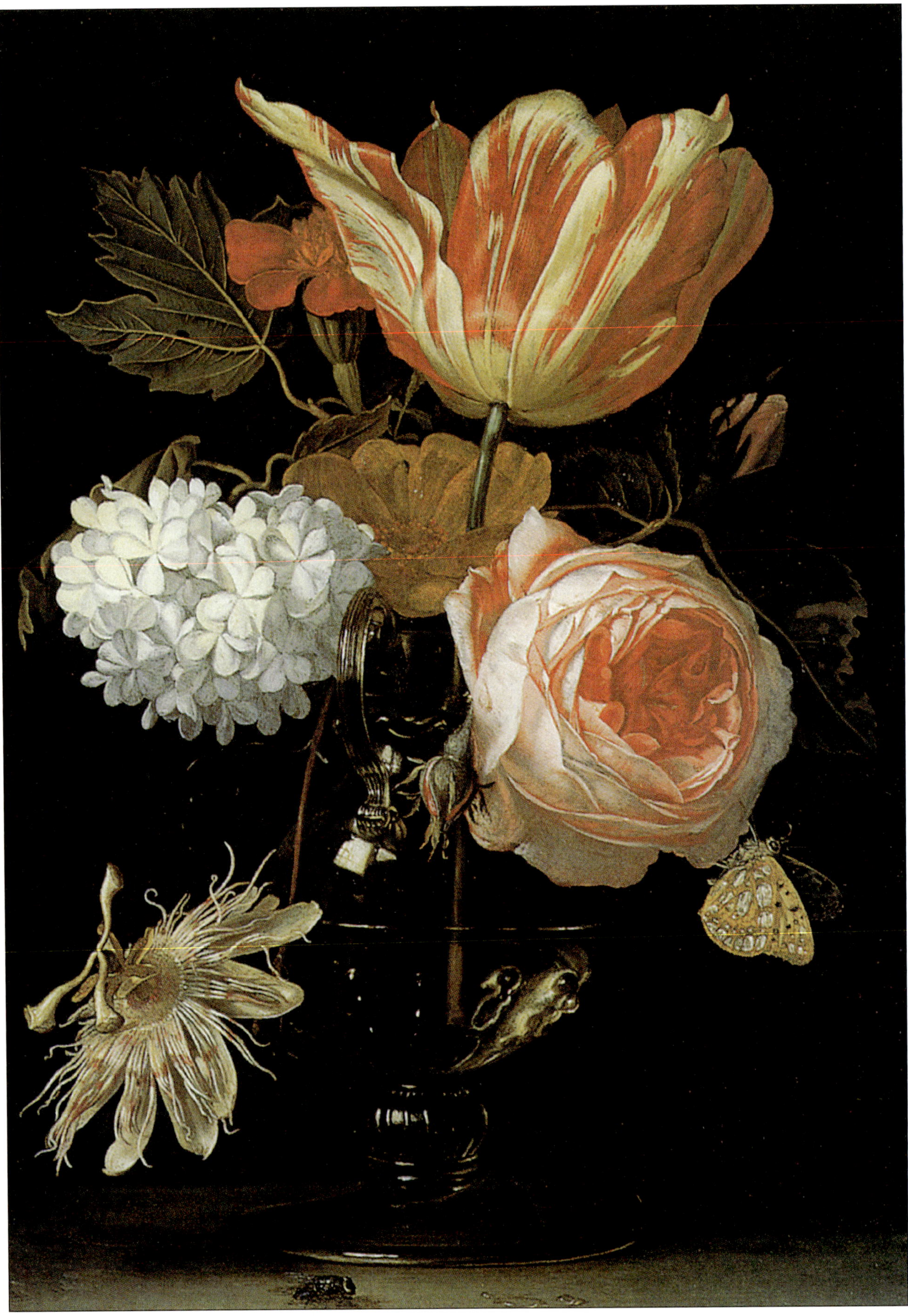

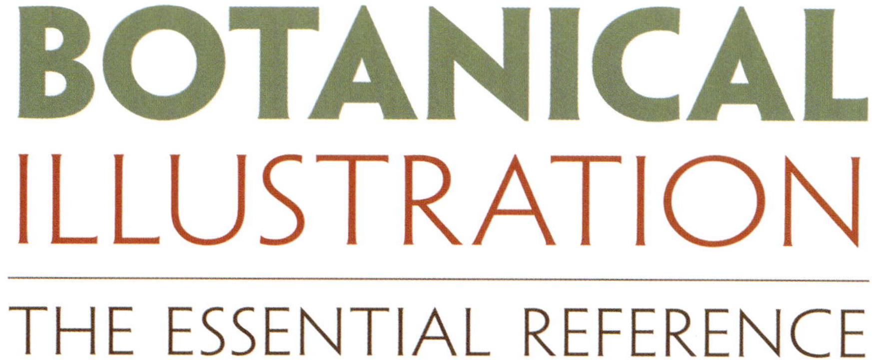

BOTANICAL ILLUSTRATION

THE ESSENTIAL REFERENCE

CAROL BELANGER GRAFTON

DOVER PUBLICATIONS, INC.
MINEOLA, NEW YORK

Frontispiece: HENDRICK FROMANTIOU (1633–94)
A Tulip, a Rose and a Passion-Flower in a Glass Vase, 1668

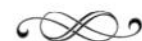

Bibliographical Note

Botanical Illustration: The Essential Reference, first published by Dover Publications, Inc., in 2016, is a new compilation of images reprinted from authoritative sources. For detailed source information see pages 135 and 136.

International Standard Book Number

ISBN-13: 978-0-486-79985-8
ISBN-10: 0-486-79985-9

Manufactured in the United States by RR Donnelley
79985901 2016
www.doverpublications.com

INTRODUCTION

The watershed event in the history of botanical illustration, like the history of so many other aspects of Western life and culture, was the invention of printing in the 15th century. Before printing, artists were of course interested in the botanical world, and depictions of plants, trees, fruits, and flowers were common enough in Medieval illuminated manuscripts, whether as elements of the historical or religious scenes depicted, or for ornamental and decorative purposes.

The invention and spread of printing after the time of Gutenberg both reflected and stimulated an explosion in the spread of knowledge and information, including botanical information, about the physical world. Few subjects demanded more insistently to be illustrated when written about. Some of the greatest artifacts ever created concerning the botanical world as a result of this information explosion are the subject of this book. The literature of botanical illustration is so vast that what is presented here is a minute fraction of it, but it does at least point out a number of the most memorable signposts to be found along this fascinating road.

Gerard's Herbal was certainly one of those signposts. John Gerard (c. 1545–1612), English botanist and herbalist, compiled and published the first edition of his massive *Herbal* (1,454 pages) in 1597. With hundreds of woodcut illustrations borrowed mostly from other books previously published on the continent combined with Gerard's lively descriptions and vast amounts of esoteric information, including a great deal of entertaining Elizabethan folklore relating to the plants depicted, also appropriated from many sources, the *Herbal* was a huge success into the next century and beyond. In 1633, Thomas Johnson, a London apothecary and botanist, acting under a commission from Gerard's heirs, published an expanded and corrected second edition of the *Herbal* with about 800 additional species and 700 new illustrations included—this edition contained descriptions of 2,850 plants and included 2,700 woodcuts. Whatever its flaws, it represented a massive step forward in botanical publishing and is a cornerstone of any library of botanical literature.

Even before *Gerard's Herbal* was published in its second edition in 1633, the world of botanical illustration was undergoing a massive shift brought on by the development of hand-colored copperplate engraving which would inevitably take over the place formerly occupied by woodcut art. Hand-colored copperplate engravings produced much finer and artistically pleasing detail, infinitely better than woodcuts both for the purpose of presenting botanical information and for displaying beautiful images. In 1613 one of the first and greatest of copperplate botanical works was published in German, the *Hortus Eysttensis* (Gardens of Eichstätt) of Basilius Besler.

Besler (1561–1629) an apothecary and botanist from Nuremberg, became the curator of the gardens of Johann Konrad von Gemmingen, Prince Bishop of Eichstätt in Bavaria, one of the greatest gardens of his era. It took Besler and his group of writers and engravers 16 years to complete the great *Hortus,* and the Bishop died before it was finished. The massive *Hortus Eysttensis* represented something new in botanical art. It was not limited to culinary and medicinal herbs, but included plates of garden flowers, herbs and vegetables, and exotic plants which were highly sought after and prized by collectors such as the Bishop. In the *Hortus,* plants were depicted often almost life-size, and of course were beautifully hand-colored in the most lavish editions. The first edition of 1613 included 367 engravings with about three images to a page, for a total of 1,084 species. Later printings were made in 1640 and 1713 from the same plates. Miraculously, most of the copperplates were found intact in the Albertina museum in Vienna in 1994.

Another 17th-century work illustrates very well the influence of copperplate engraving on the development of botanical art, the *Hortus Floridus* of the Dutch artist Crispin van de Pass (1589–1670). The *Hortus Floridus* was produced at the height of the Dutch tulip craze of the 17th century. Tulips had been introduced to Europe from Turkey in the 16th century and relatively quickly became very popular and a highly prized luxury item. Because they are grown from bulbs, and it was a slow process to grow flowering bulbs from seeds, bulbs were soon in great and continually increasing demand and the prices of them—even speculative prices for contracts to produce and deliver future bulbs—escalated well beyond anything which was reasonable. In the later 1630s, the tulip 'bubble' inevitably crashed with consequences for the Dutch economy which economic historians still debate.

Seeing the interest in tulips all around him, Crispin van de Pass made the drawings for the *Hortus Floridus* which were, as the text in the original edition said, produced with great effort and drawn true-to-life. He included engravings of other bulbous and tuberous plants and also fruit trees, fruits, and medicinal plants. The engravings themselves are considered the equal of any ever produced for a botanical work.

It was in a very different world that Robert John Thornton, born in the 1760s, created the most magnificent English botanical book of his era, *The Temple of Flora*, published in parts in England between 1799 and 1807. Thornton had an interest in natural history since his childhood and when he came into a substantial inheritance, the idea of *The Temple of Flora* started to develop. He employed the best artists and engravers he could find, and they produced plates generally considered of unequalled quality, each a magnificent example of the Romantic Art of his era, with each plate showing a brilliant flower set in an imaginative Romantic landscape. The printing techniques were the most up-to-date, employing aquatint, mezzotint and stipple engraving, partly printed in colors and then finished by hand. The greatest of English flower books was also a commercial disaster. Thornton lost a great deal of money on the project, which had to be abandoned when it was half completed because it never captured the necessary public support to see it through to completion. But the plates which were completed are today the treasures of any library or collector fortunate enough to own them.

Many great artists' work is depicted in these pages, but we'll complete this brief overview with a note about Pierre-Joseph Redouté (1759–1840), often described as the greatest flower painter of all time, based on the brilliance of his talent, the immense size and consistency of his output, and his ability to survive and flourish in tumultuous times under three different political regimes. Born in present-day Belgium, Redouté came from a family of painters, including his father and grandfather, but had little formal education. At the age of 13 he made his way to Paris where an older brother worked as a painter of theatrical scenery. His talent brought him into contact with men and women at the French Court at Versailles who became patrons and mentors, encouraging him to specialize in the art of painting flowers for which he early on demonstrated his unique aptitude. Finding safety in this niche, he painted on through the French Revolution and the Reign of Terror which followed, into the age of Napoleon, painting his pictures under the auspices of various institutions and giving lessons to aristocrats. Redouté contributed to over 50 books during his career, had many patrons including Napoleon's Empress Josephine, and his death in 1840 certainly marked the end of the Golden Age of French flower painting. In his lifetime, Redouté produced about 2,100 botanical paintings, including 486 for his multi-volume work on lilies *(Les Liliacées),* and another 168 for *Les Roses.*

The art of botanical illustration continued to flourish into the Victorian period and beyond with many fine books and periodicals devoted to this genre regularly appearing in England and on the continent of Europe, often with outstanding color reproductions of botanical paintings produced through the new medium of lithography, which made it possible for the first time to print authentic and subtle color reproductions relatively inexpensively for a much larger audience than the few hundred who subscribed to the first printings of books like *The Temple of Flora* early in the 19th century. While flower painting as such certainly continued as a genre, and is alive and well today, legions of graphic artists took the idea of using botanical forms and shapes into the new worlds of Art Nouveau and later decorative styles, proving over and over again that the fusion of the worlds of botany and art is truly inexhaustible.

John Grafton
Princeton, NJ
February, 2016

CONTENTS

15th–16th CENTURIES

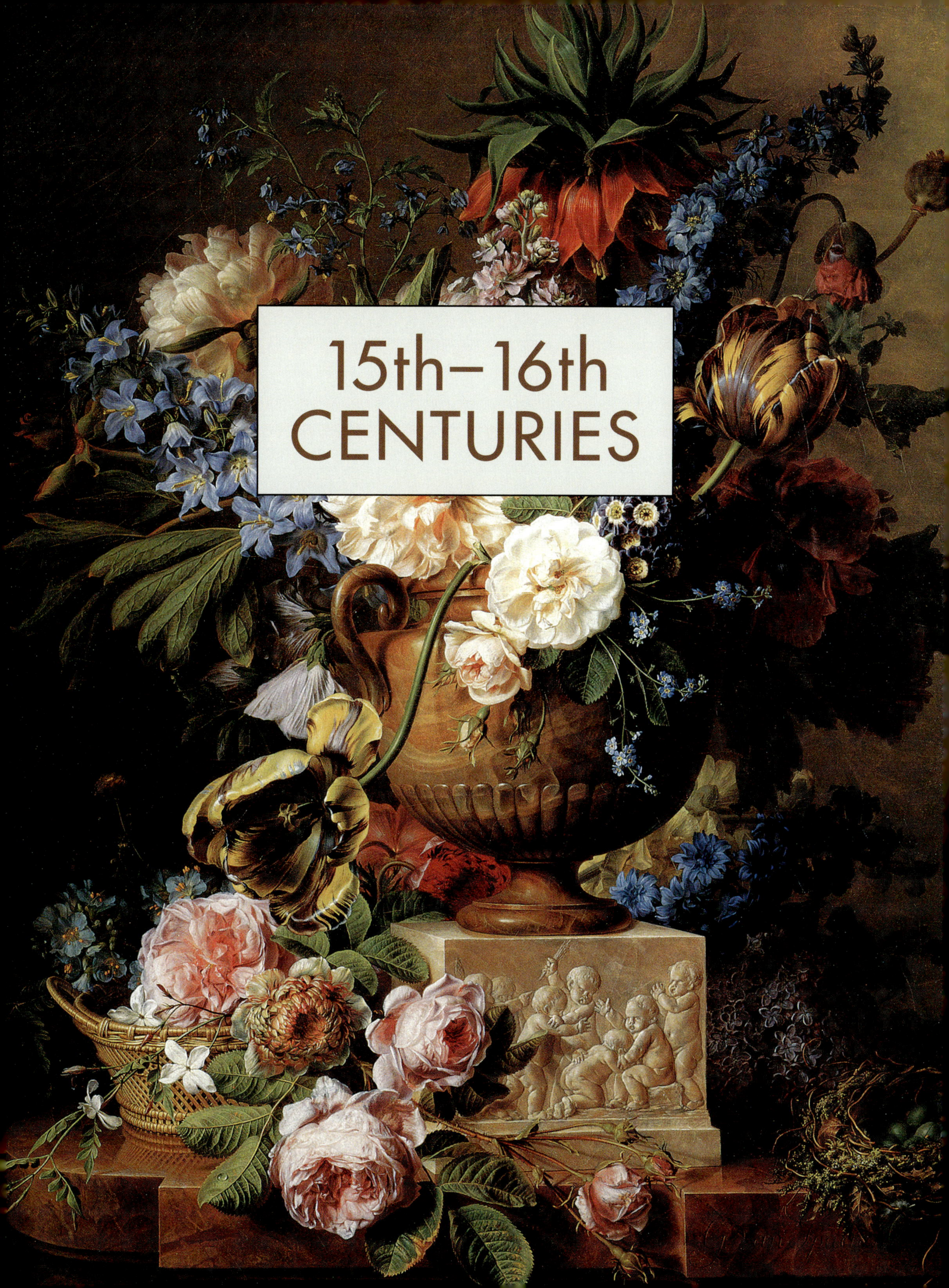

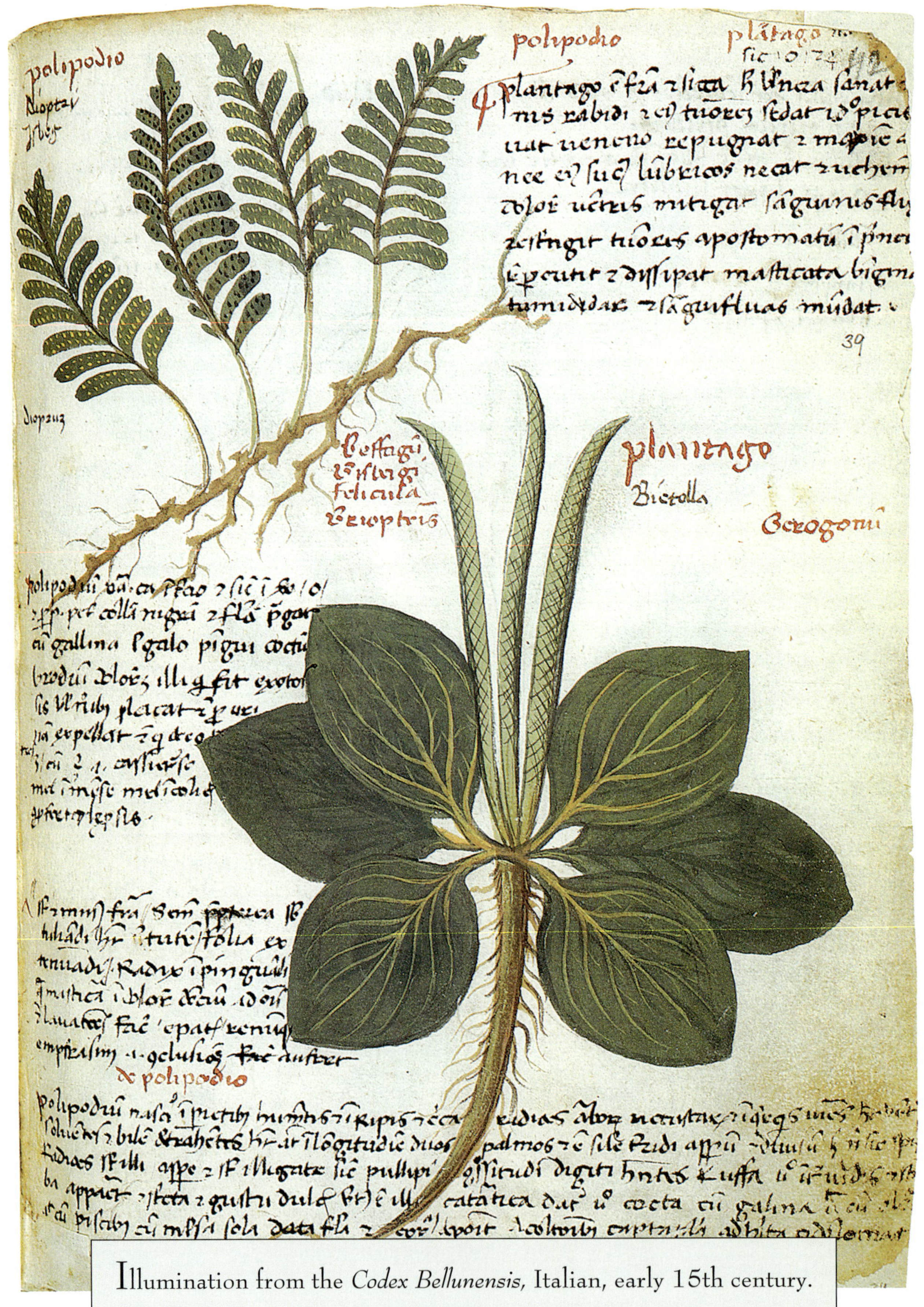

Illumination from the *Codex Bellunensis,* Italian, early 15th century.

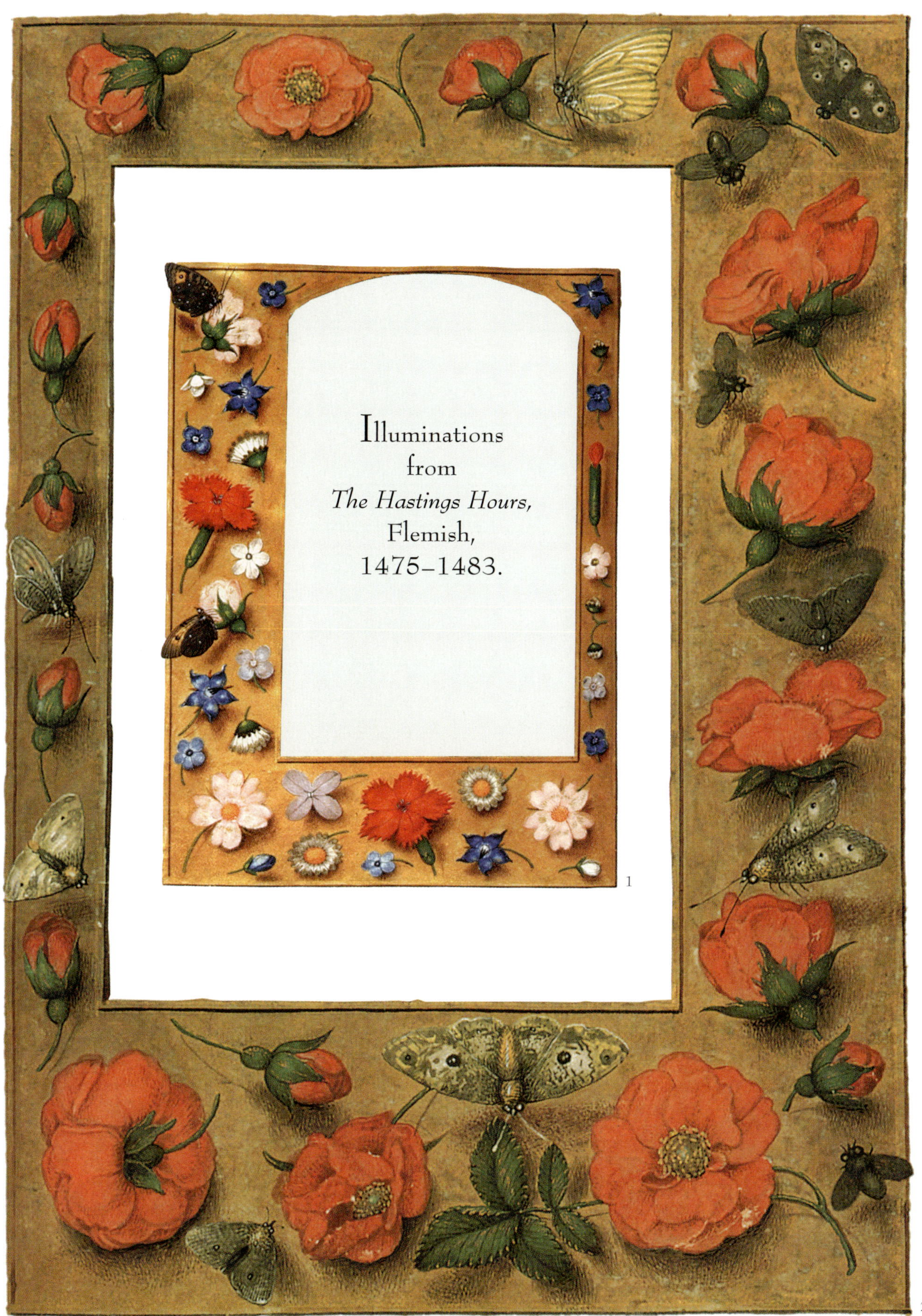

Illuminations
from
The Hastings Hours,
Flemish,
1475–1483.

1

2

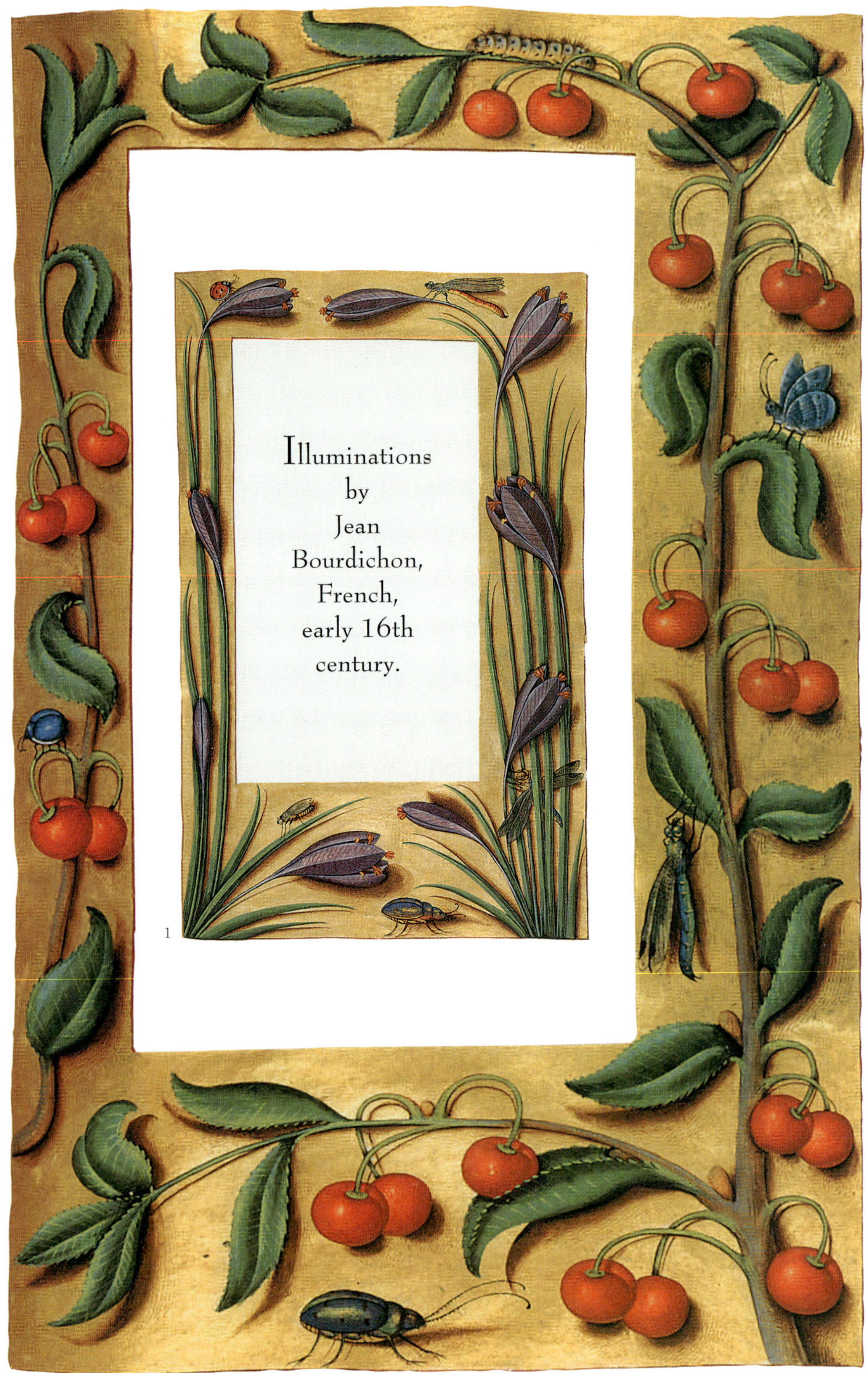
Illuminations
by
Jean
Bourdichon,
French,
early 16th
century.
1

2

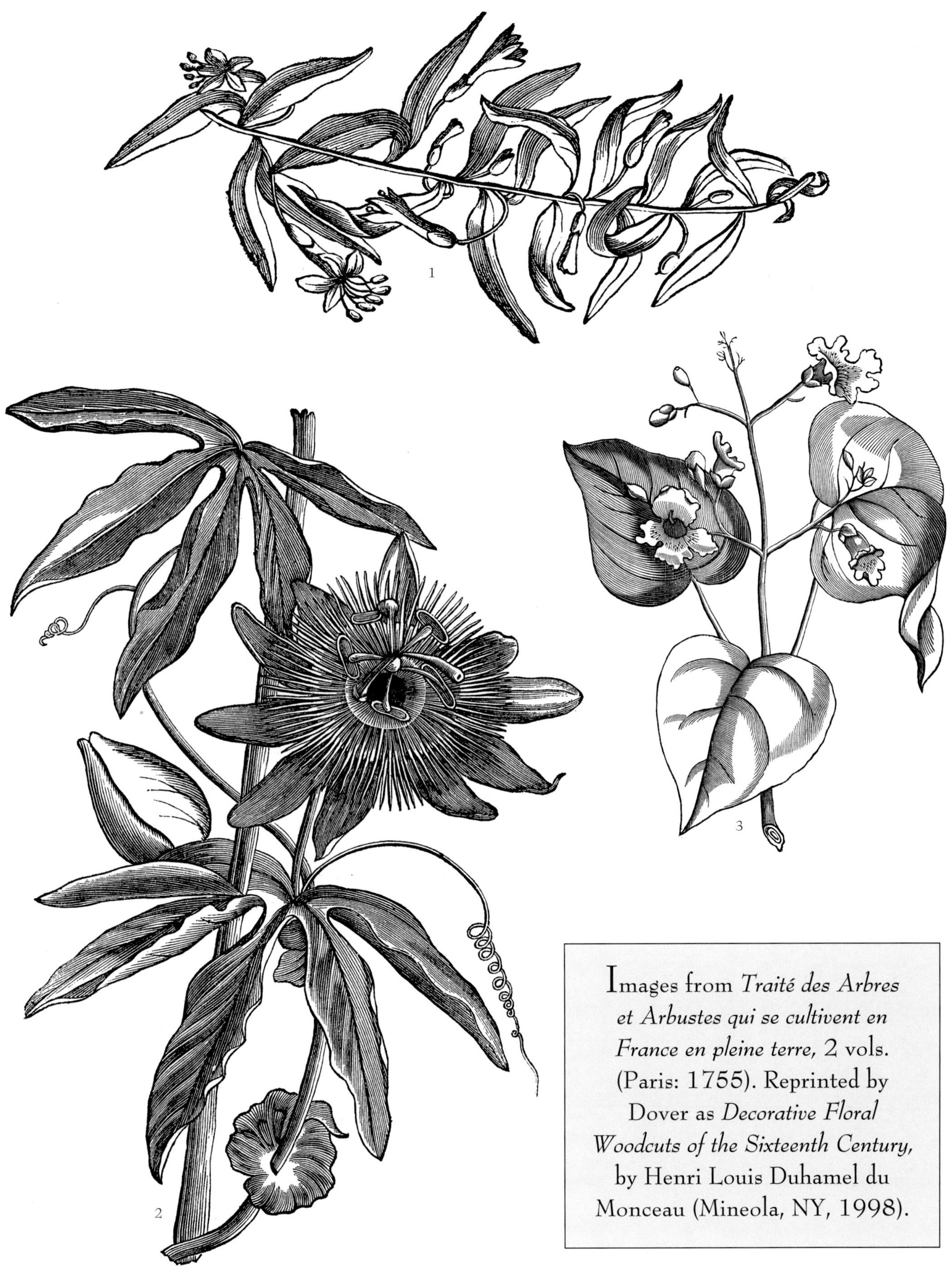

Images from *Traité des Arbres et Arbustes qui se cultivent en France en pleine terre*, 2 vols. (Paris: 1755). Reprinted by Dover as *Decorative Floral Woodcuts of the Sixteenth Century*, by Henri Louis Duhamel du Monceau (Mineola, NY, 1998).

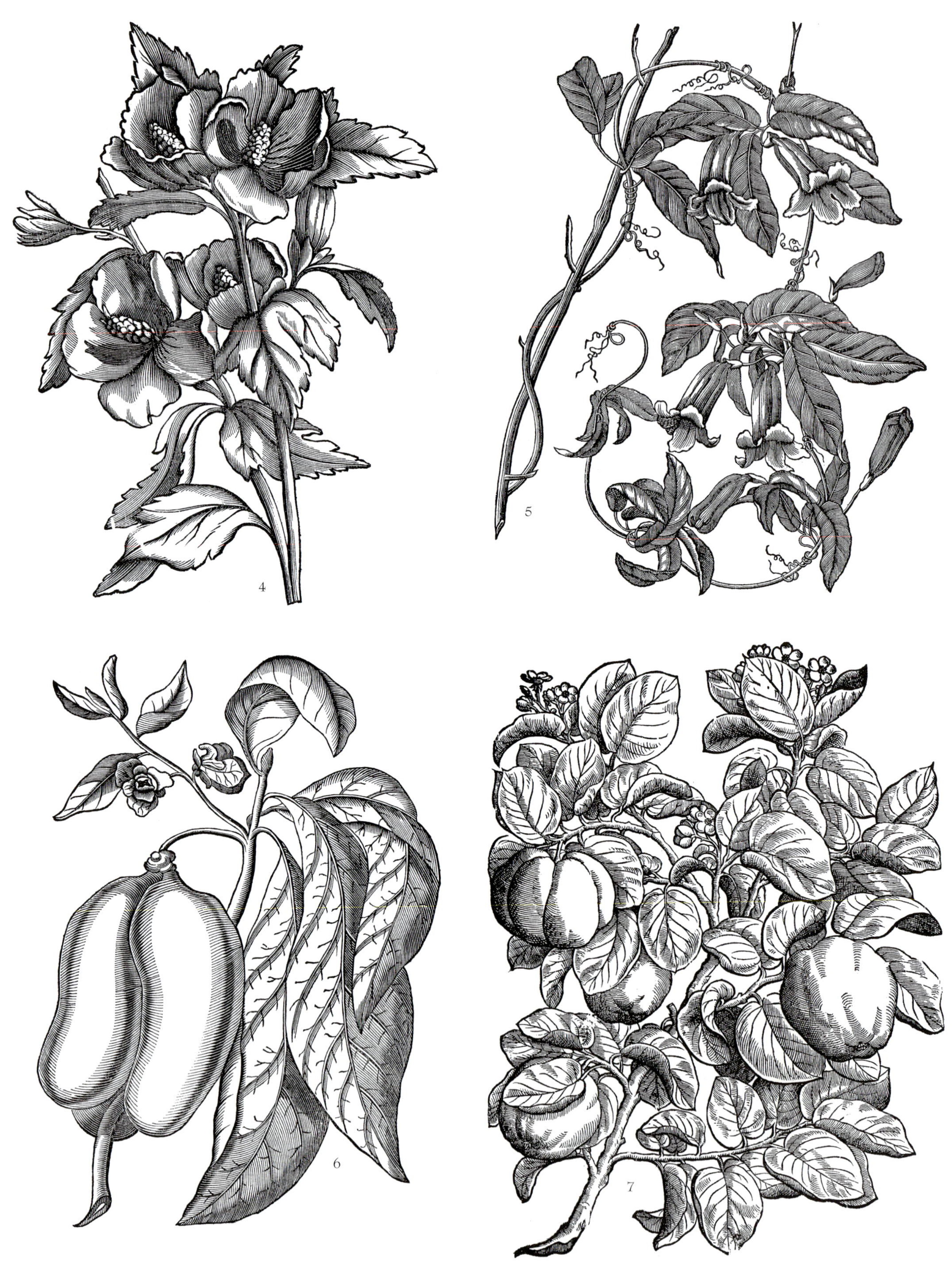
4
5
6
7

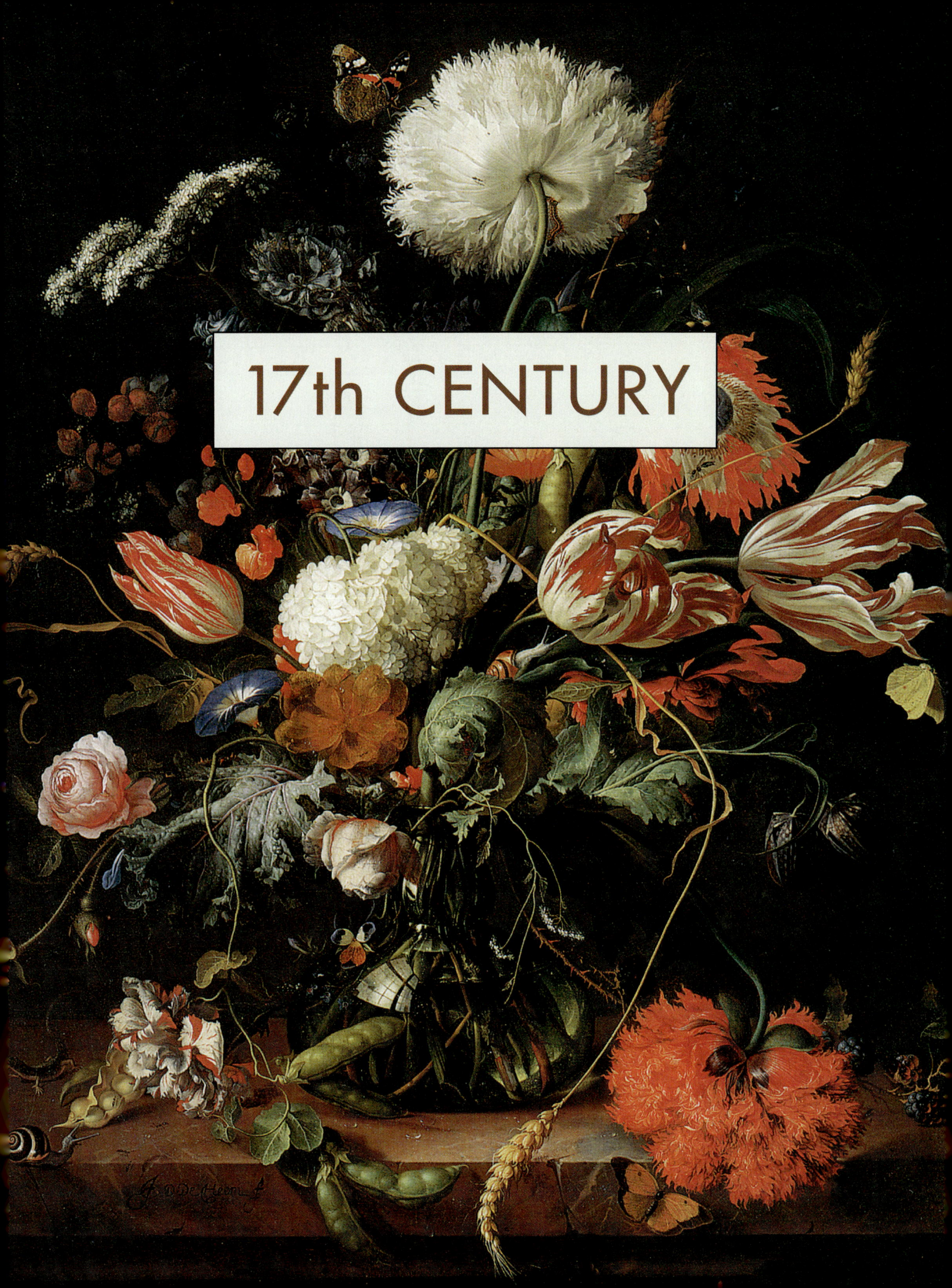
17th CENTURY

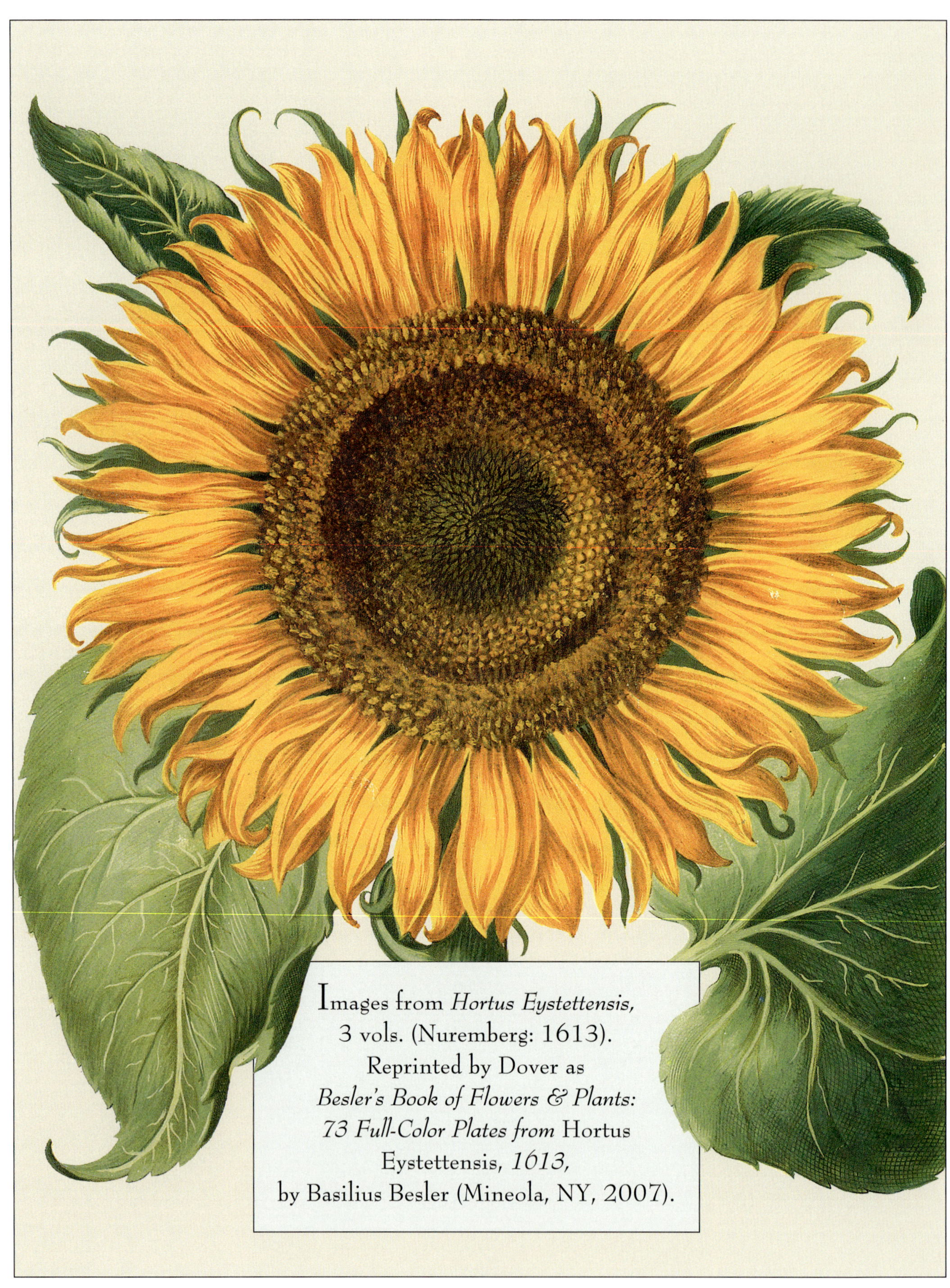

Images from *Hortus Eystettensis*,
3 vols. (Nuremberg: 1613).
Reprinted by Dover as
Besler's Book of Flowers & Plants: 73 Full-Color Plates from Hortus Eystettensis, *1613*,
by Basilius Besler (Mineola, NY, 2007).

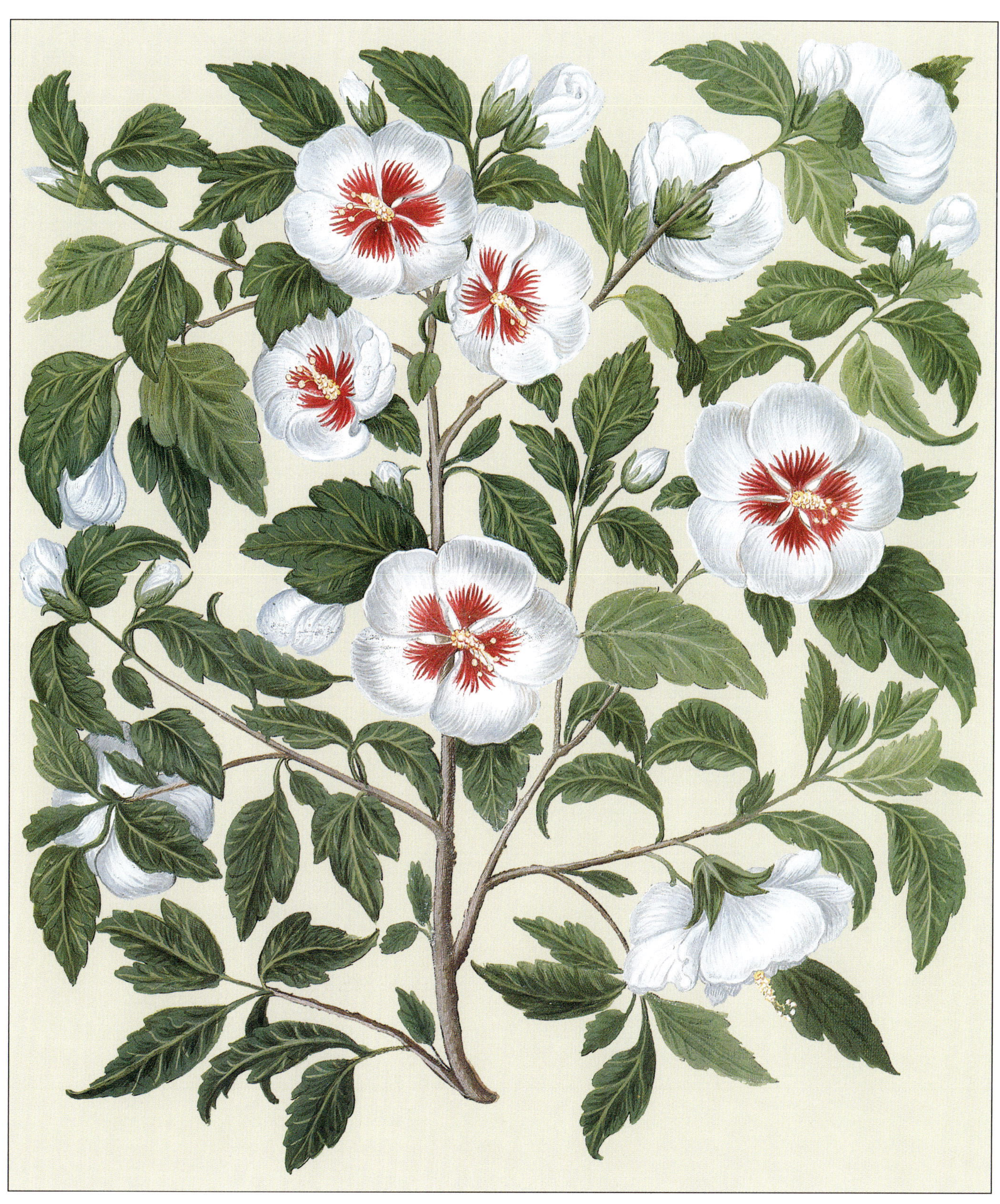

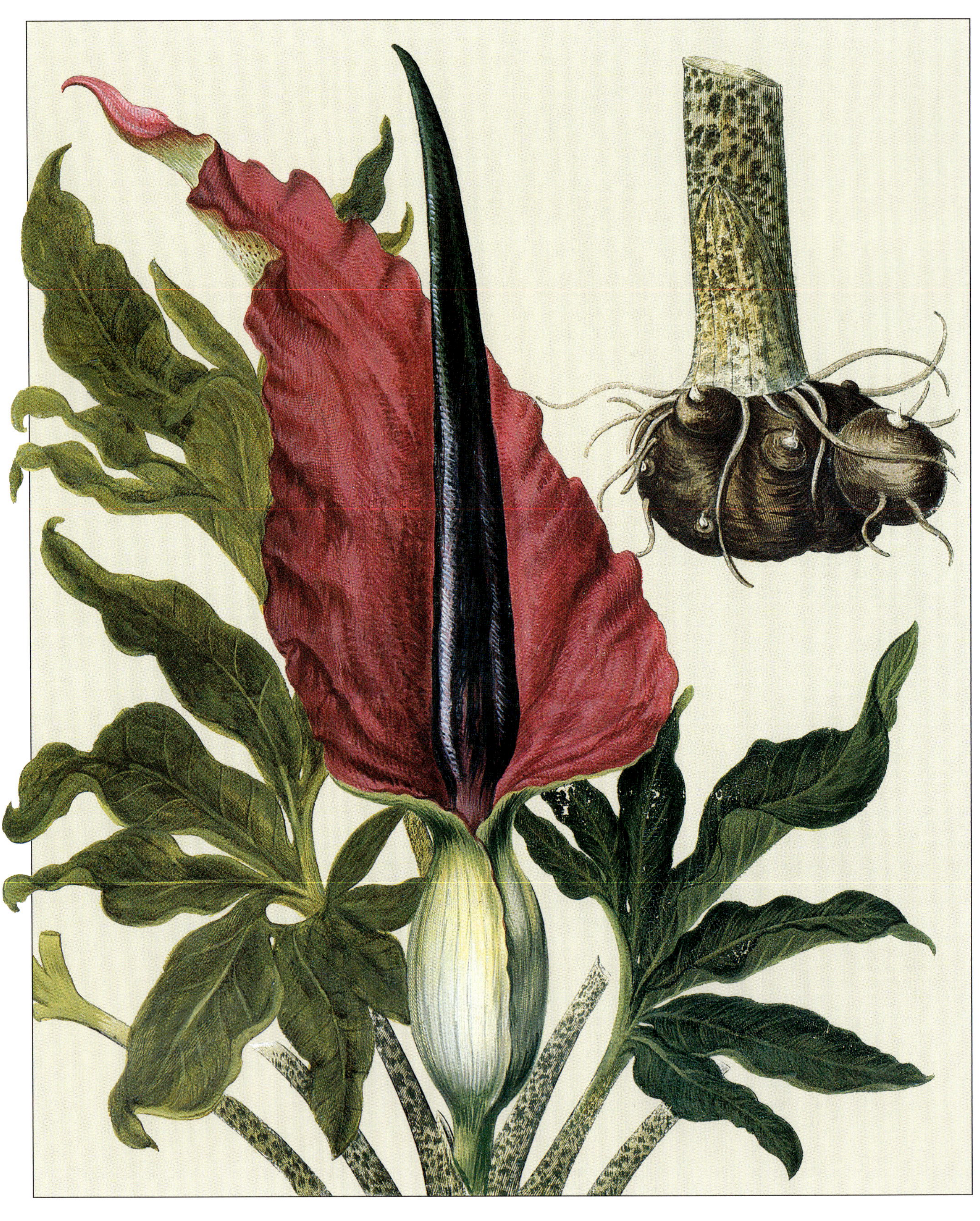

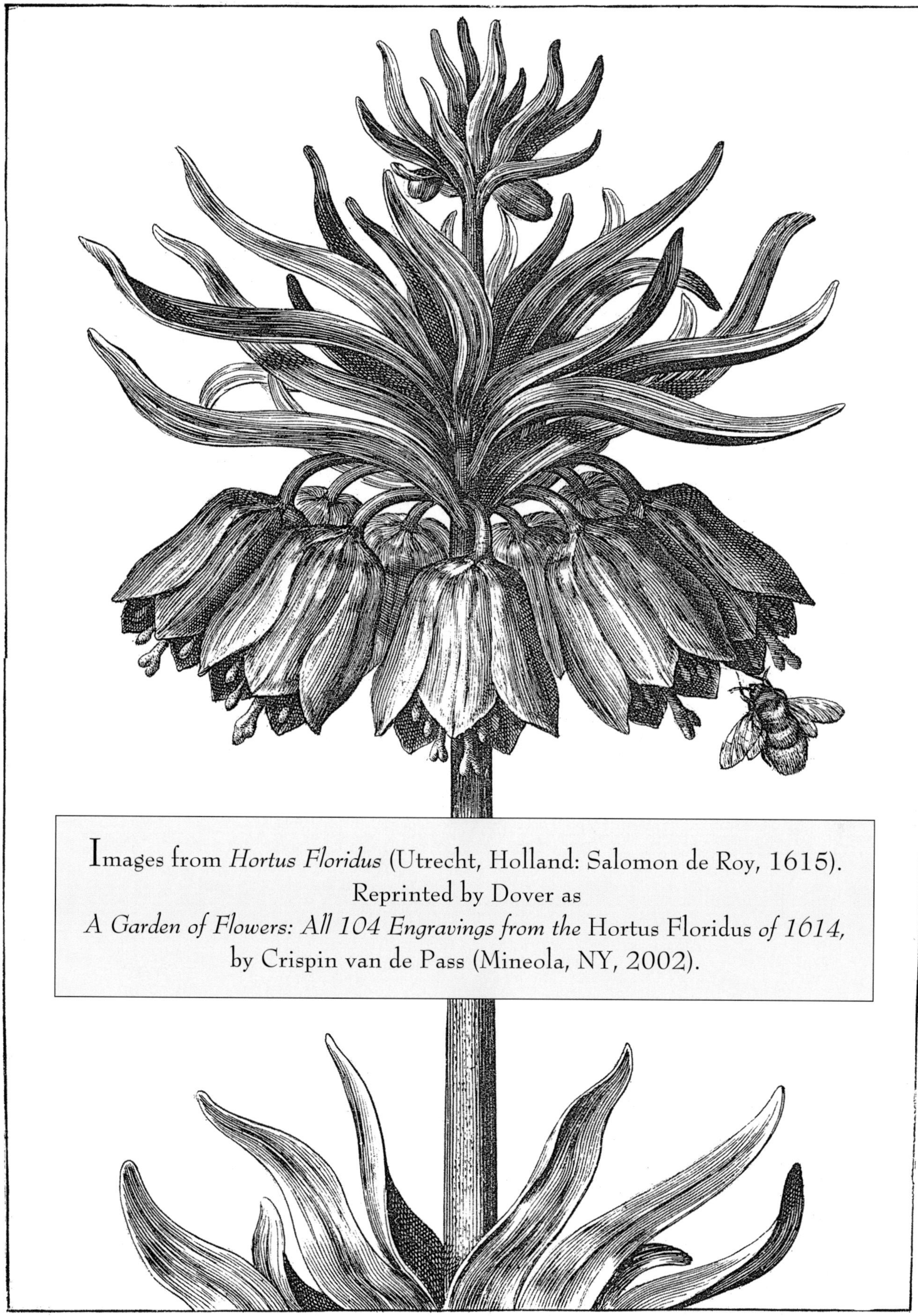

Images from *Hortus Floridus* (Utrecht, Holland: Salomon de Roy, 1615).
Reprinted by Dover as
A Garden of Flowers: All 104 Engravings from the Hortus Floridus *of 1614,*
by Crispin van de Pass (Mineola, NY, 2002).

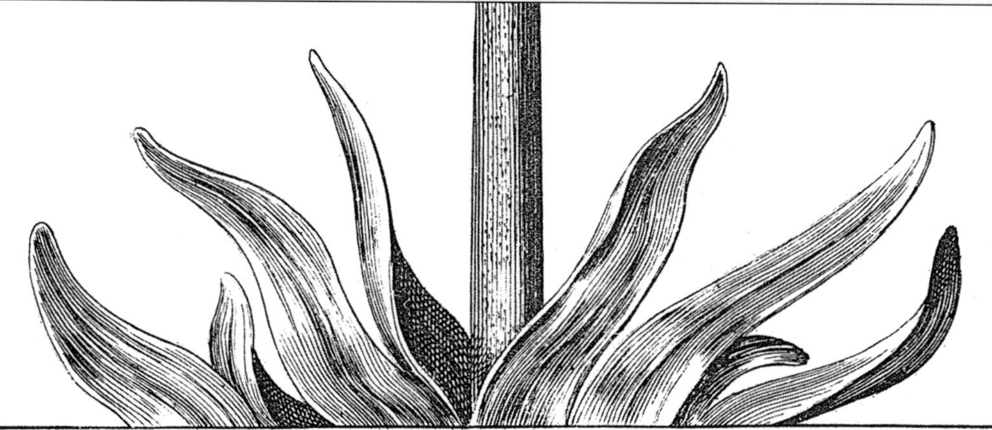

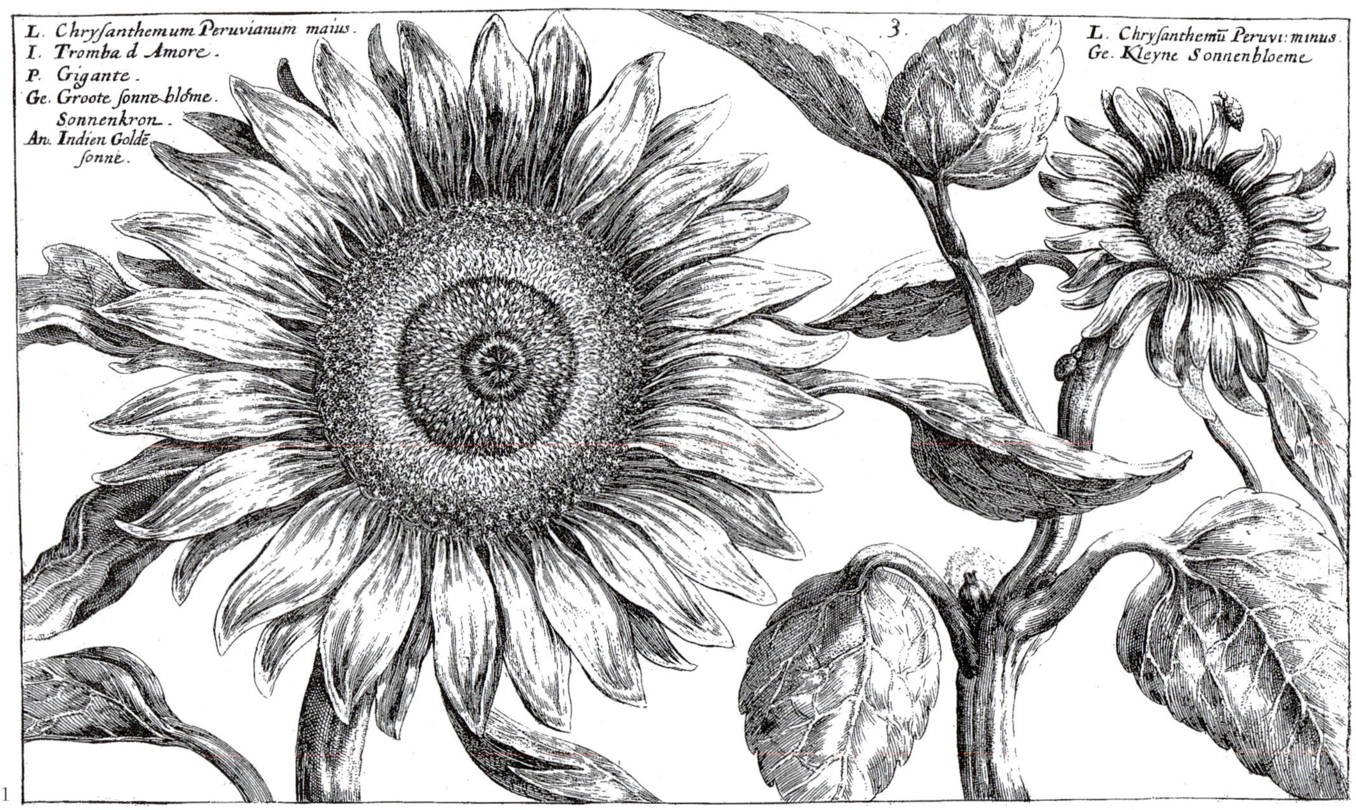

1

L. Malua roſca multiplex.
I. Malua magiore.
G. Roſe douter mer double.
Ge. Dubbel Winterroſen.

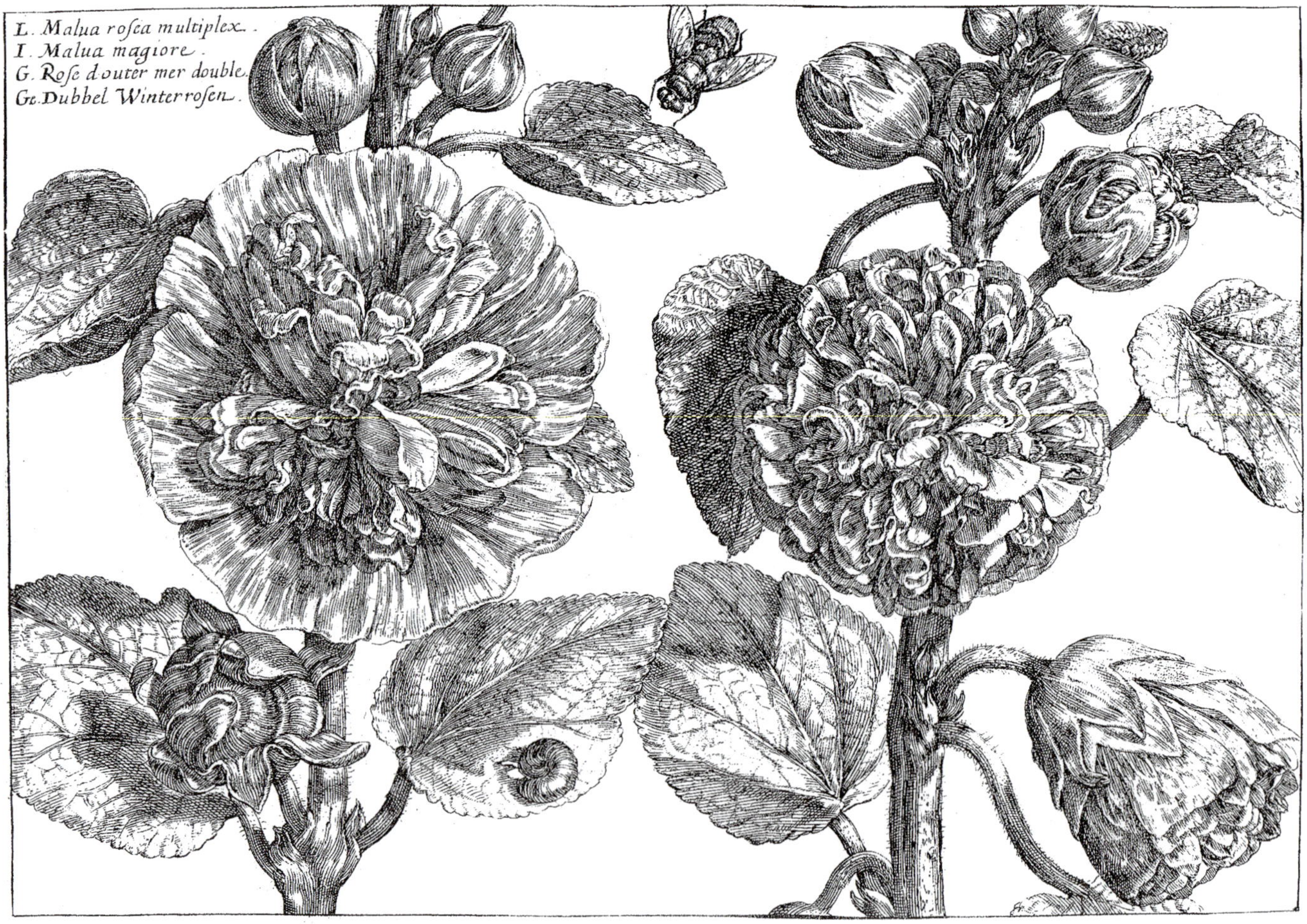

2

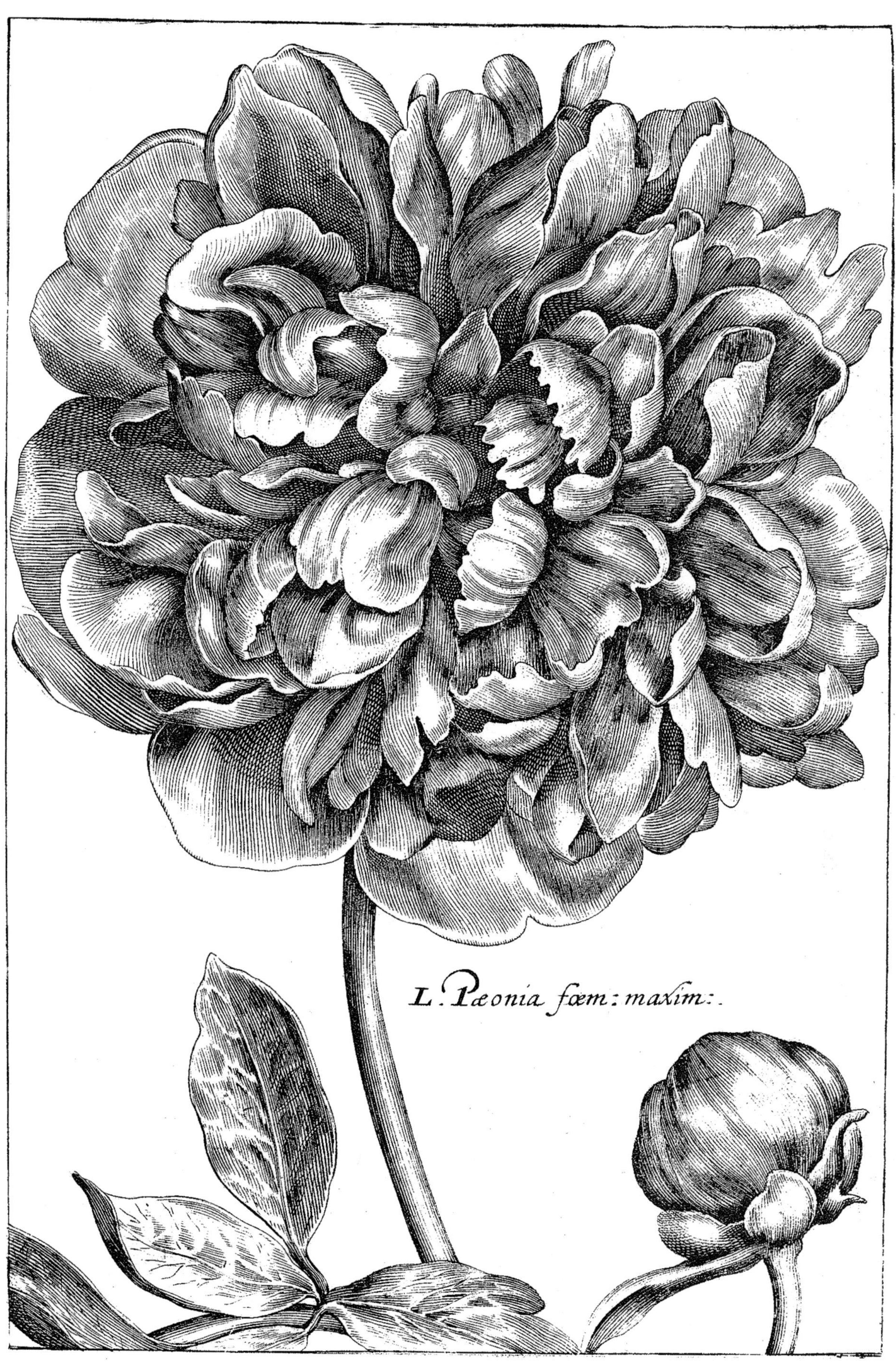
L. Pæonia fœm: maxim:.

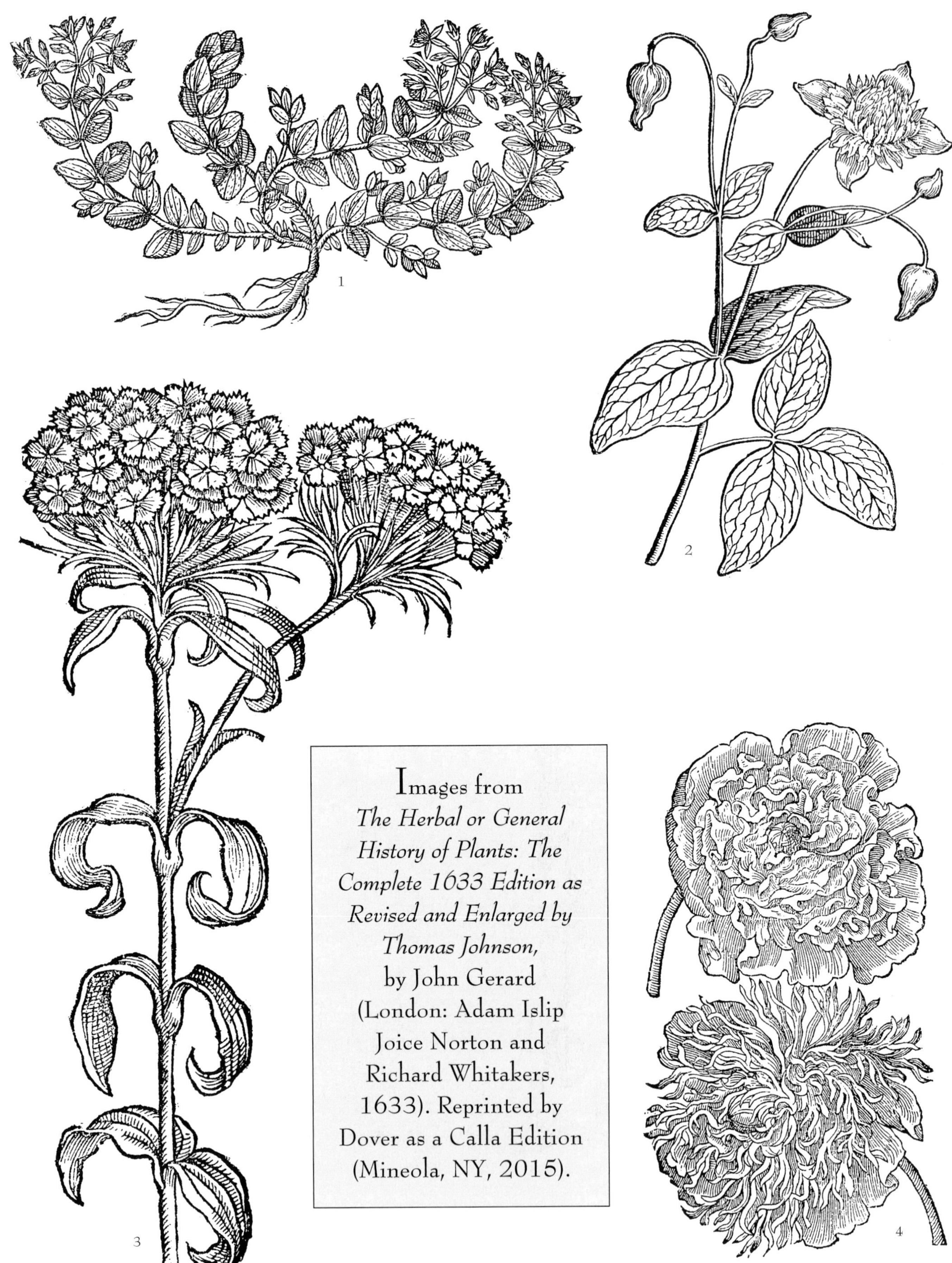

Images from
The Herbal or General History of Plants: The Complete 1633 Edition as Revised and Enlarged by Thomas Johnson,
by John Gerard
(London: Adam Islip Joice Norton and Richard Whitakers, 1633). Reprinted by Dover as a Calla Edition (Mineola, NY, 2015).

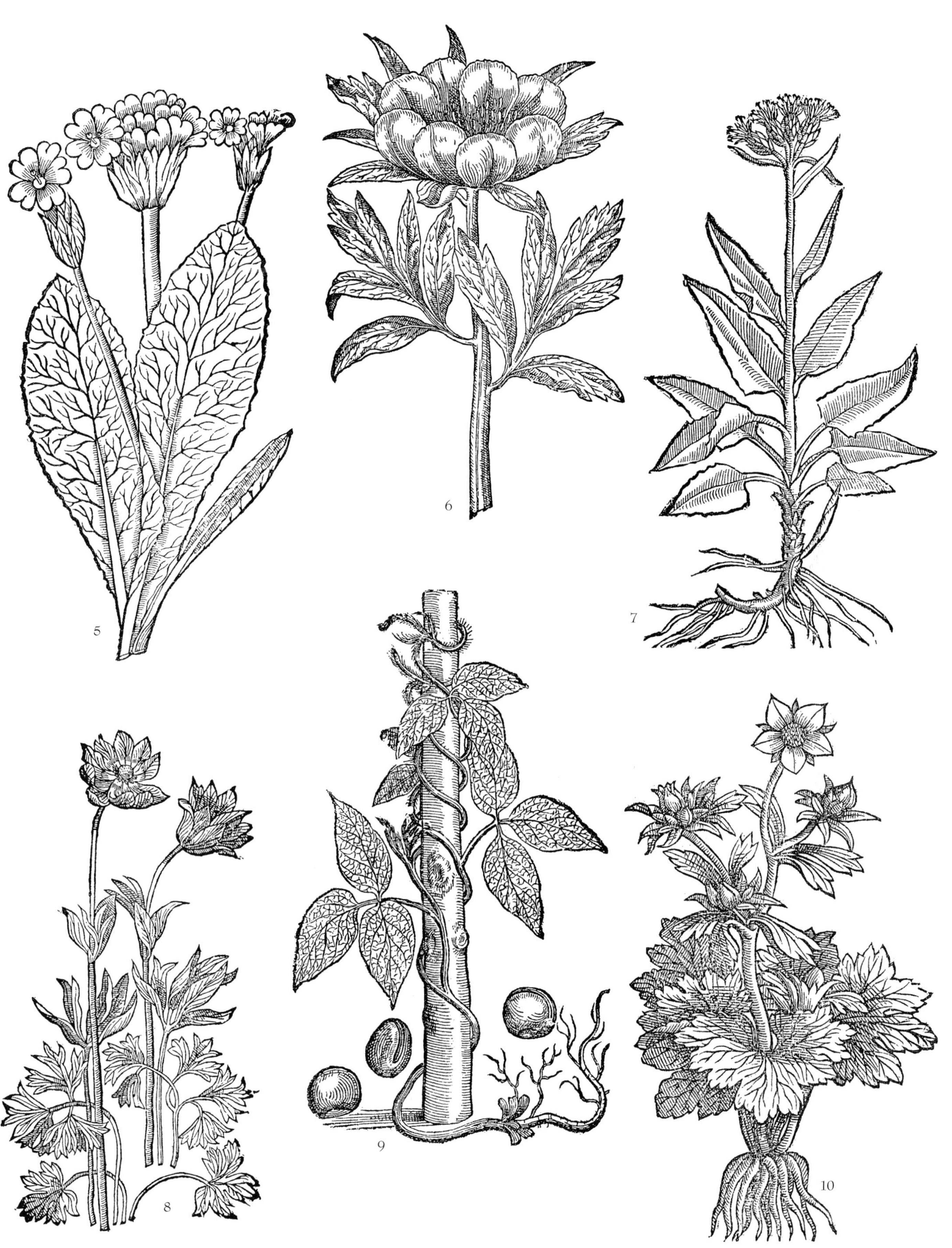
5
6
7
8
9
10

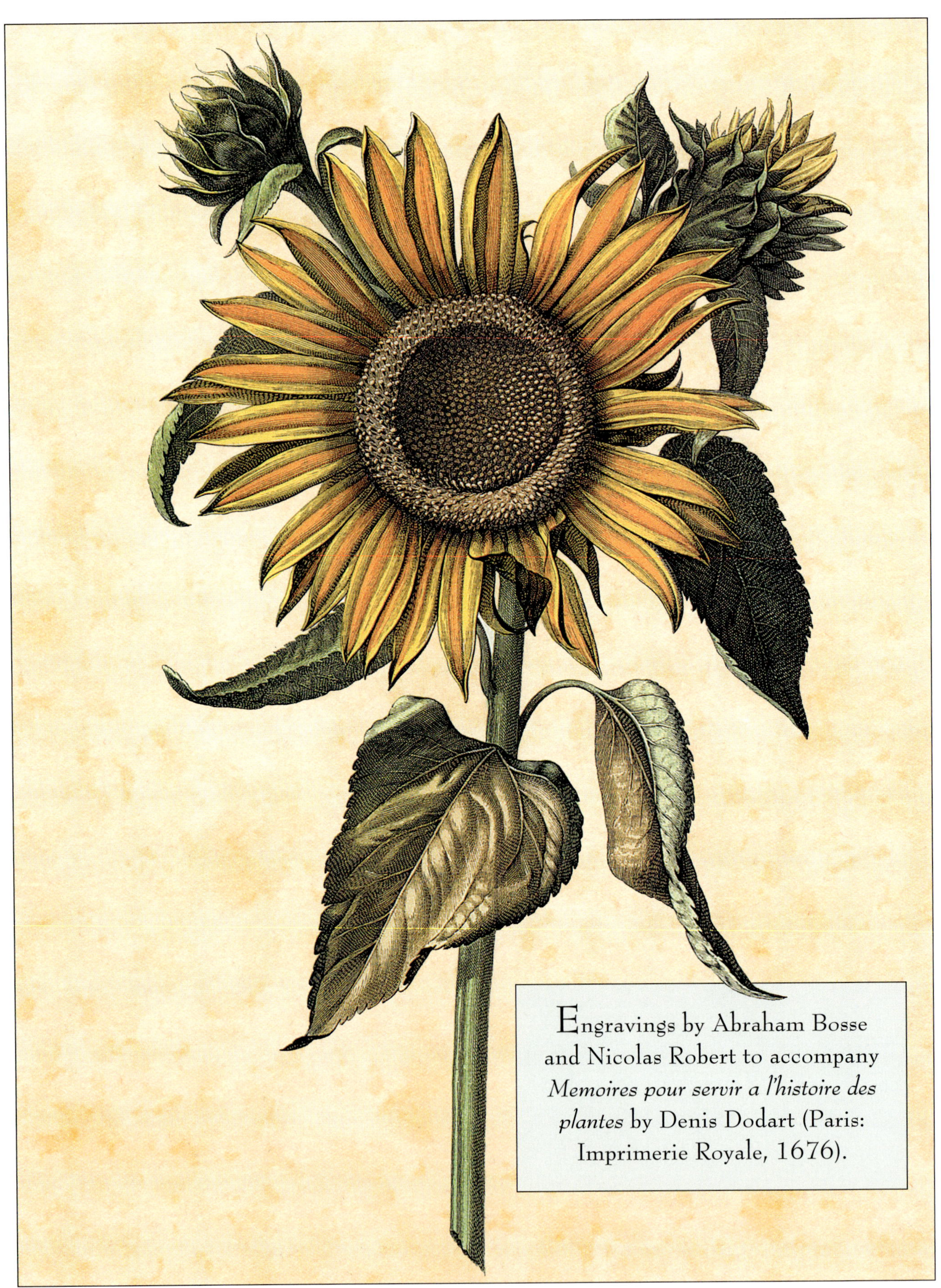

Engravings by Abraham Bosse and Nicolas Robert to accompany *Memoires pour servir a l'histoire des plantes* by Denis Dodart (Paris: Imprimerie Royale, 1676).

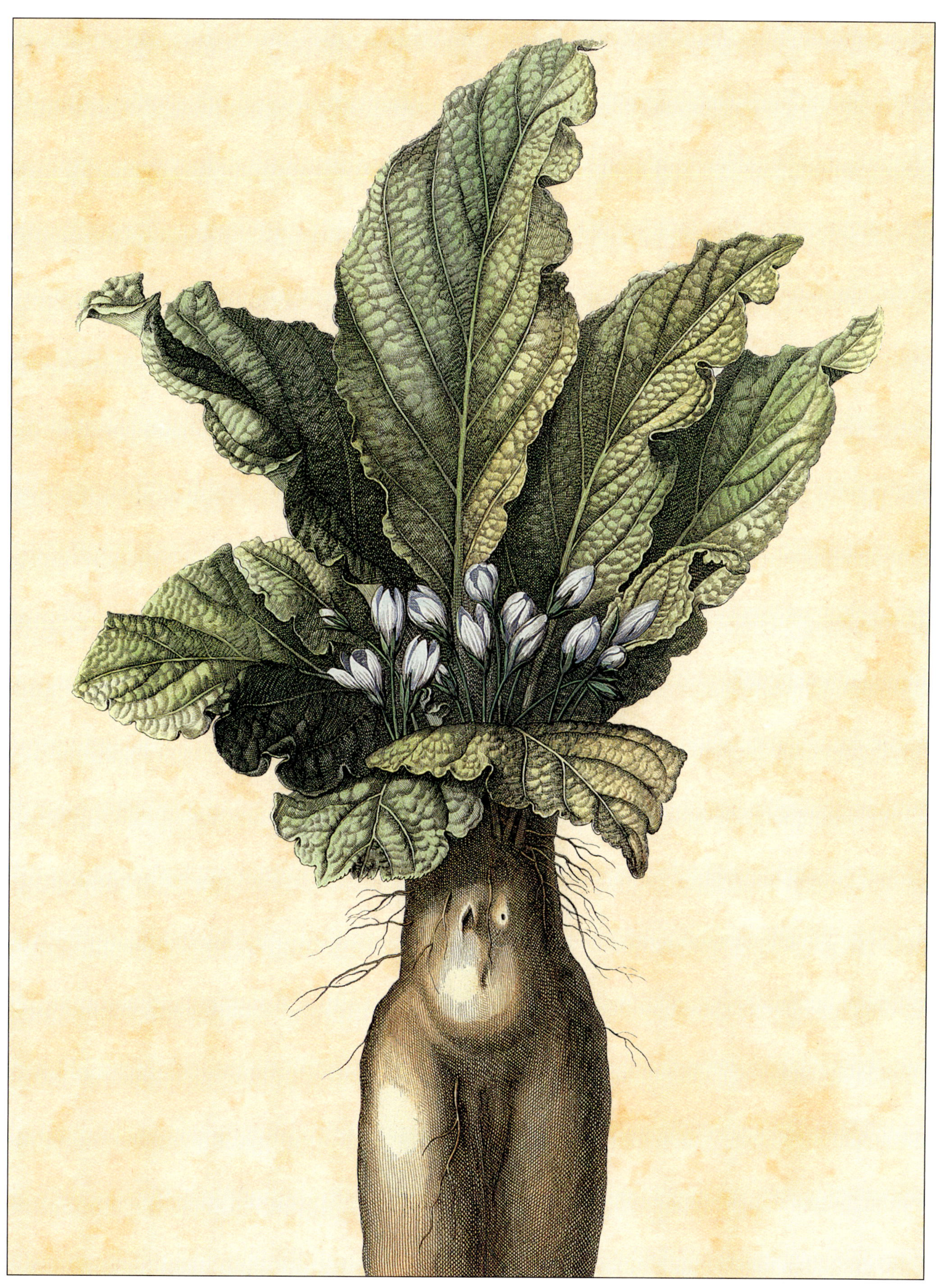

Images from
Naauwkeurige Beschryving der Aadgewassen (Leyden, Holland: Pieter vander Aa, 1696 and Utrecht, Holland: François Halma, 1696).
Reprinted by Dover as *Fantastic Floral Engravings: 118 Plates from the 1696* Accurate Description of Terrestrial Plants by Abraham Munting (New York, 1975).

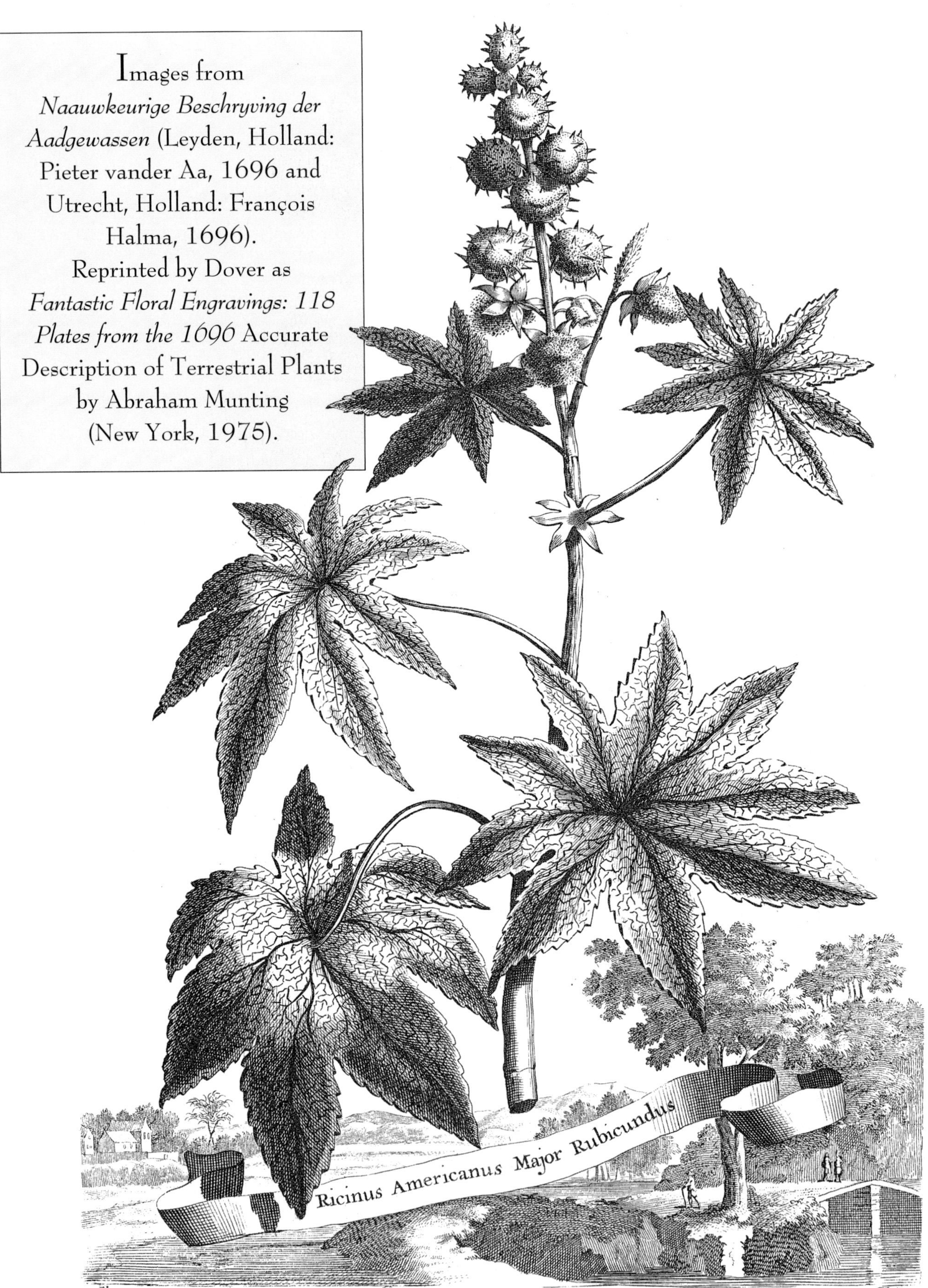

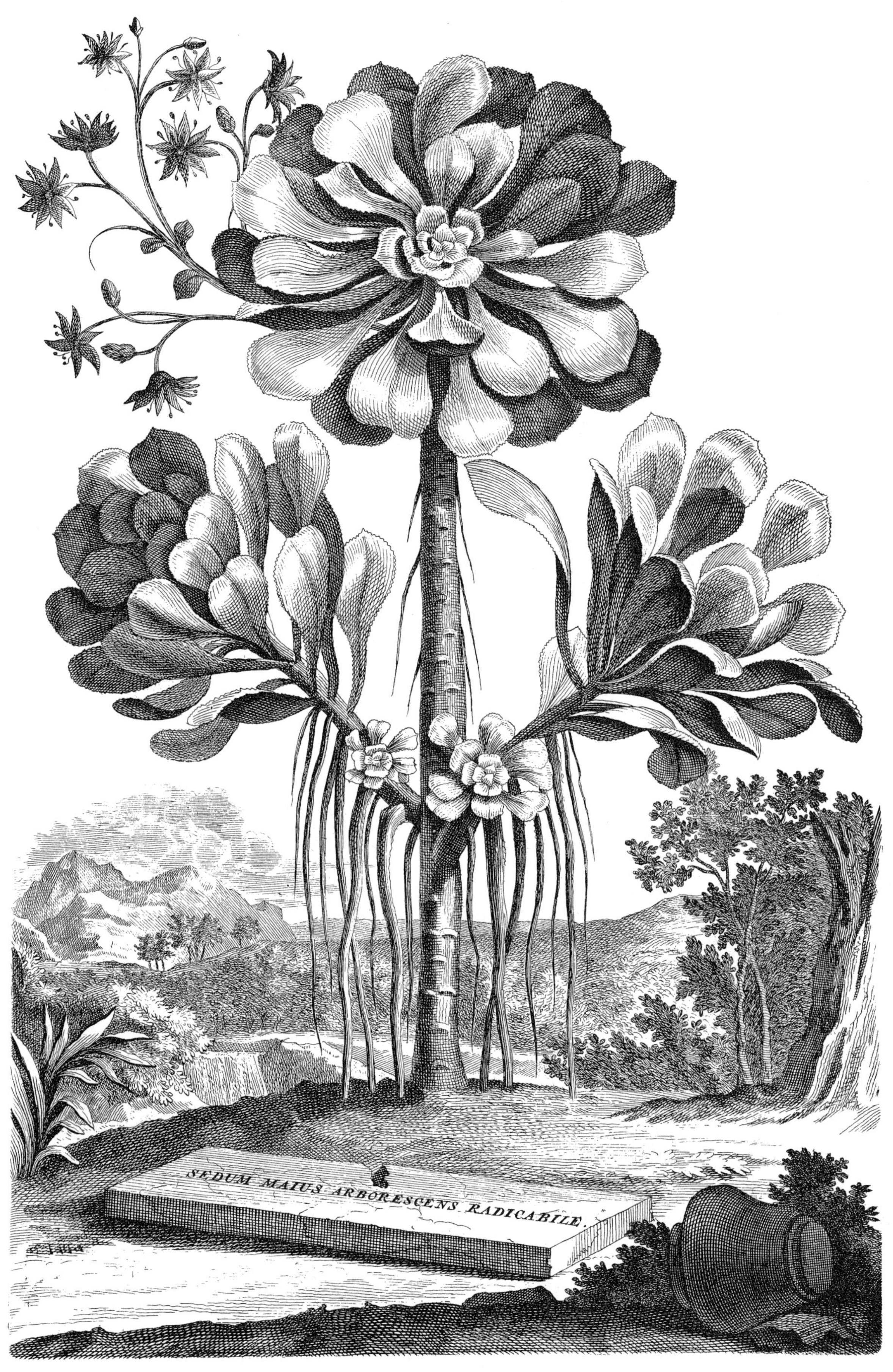
SEDUM MAIUS ARBORESCENS RADICABILE.

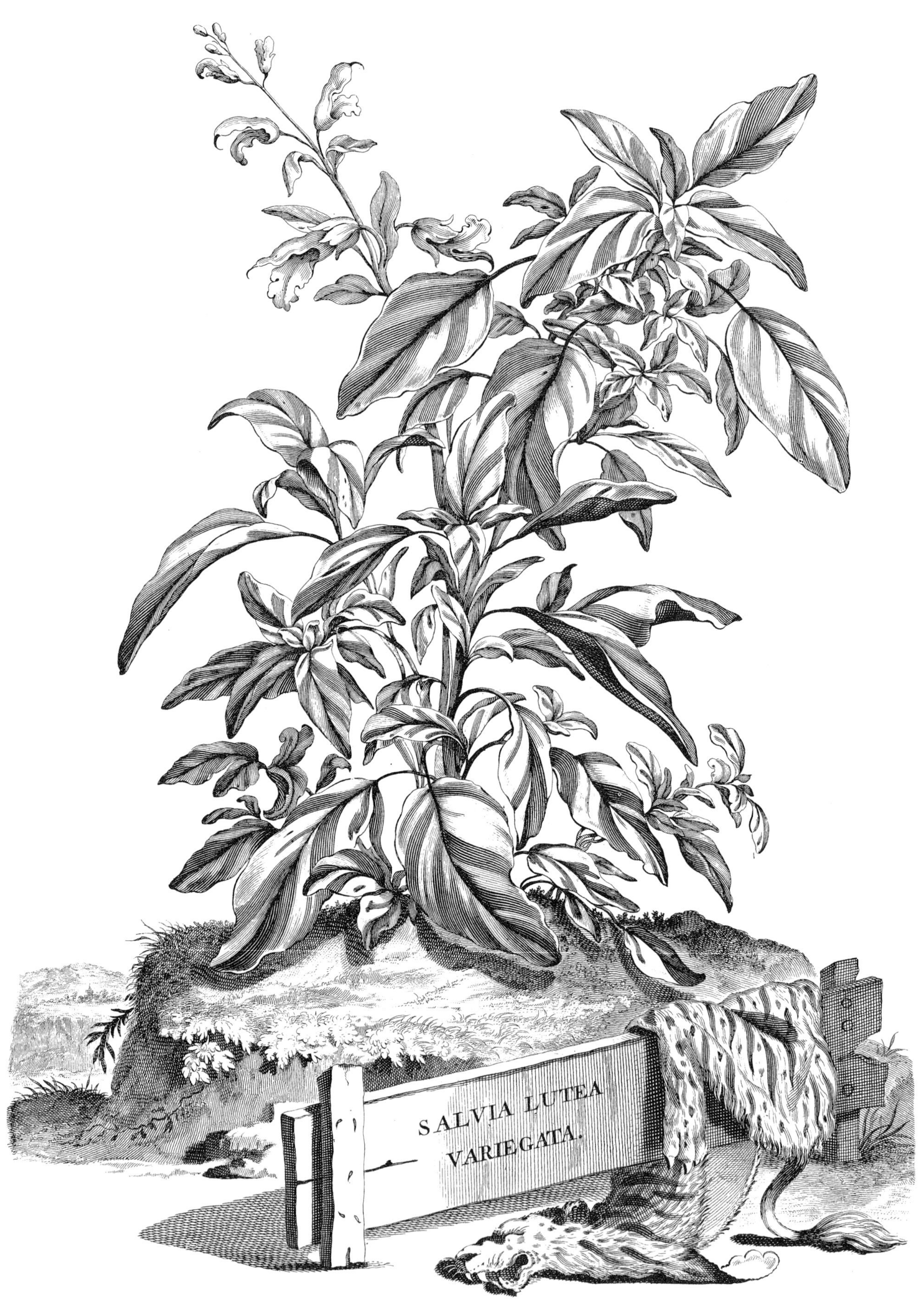
SALVIA LUTEA
VARIEGATA.

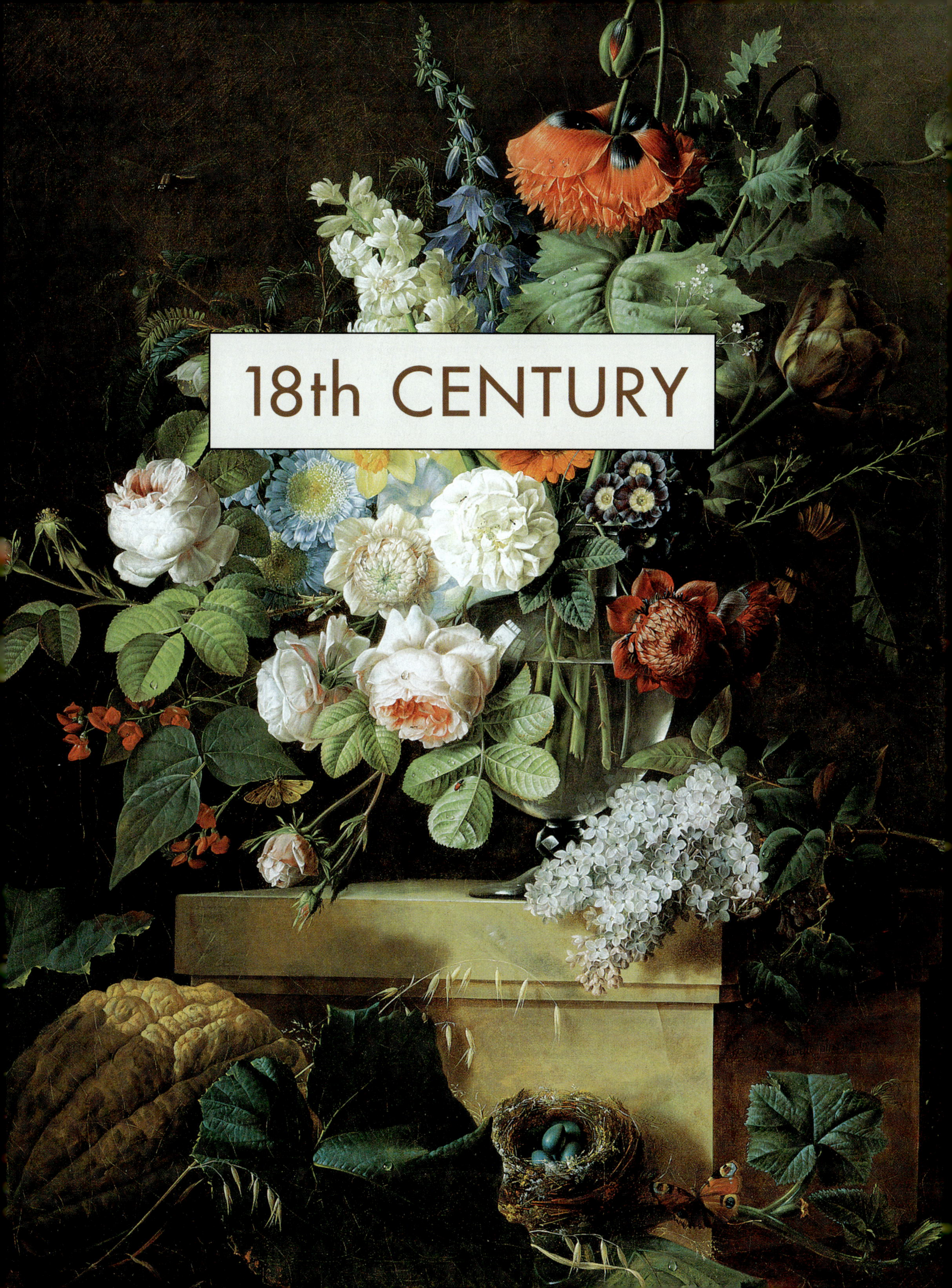

18th CENTURY

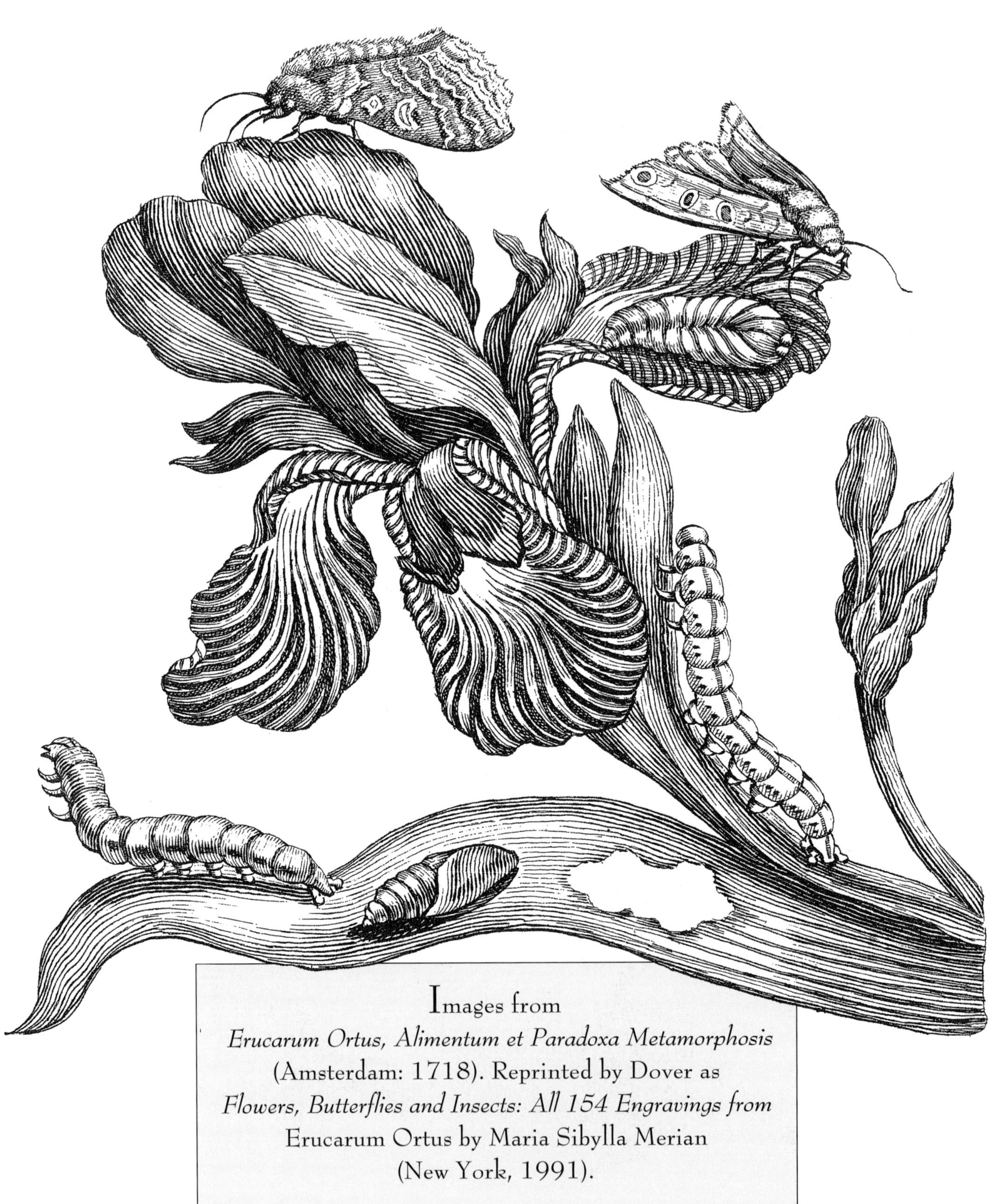

Images from
Erucarum Ortus, Alimentum et Paradoxa Metamorphosis
(Amsterdam: 1718). Reprinted by Dover as
Flowers, Butterflies and Insects: All 154 Engravings from
Erucarum Ortus by Maria Sibylla Merian
(New York, 1991).

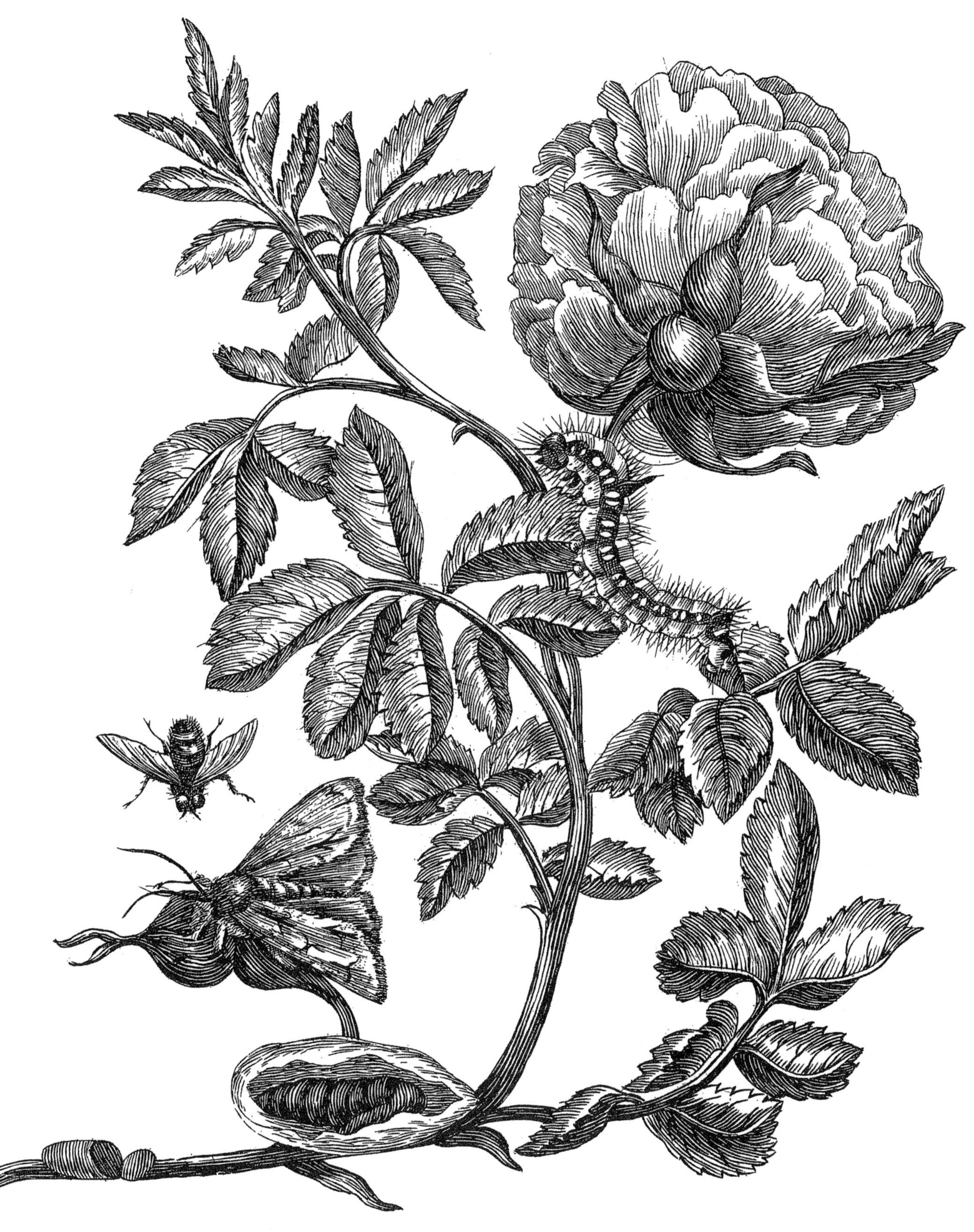

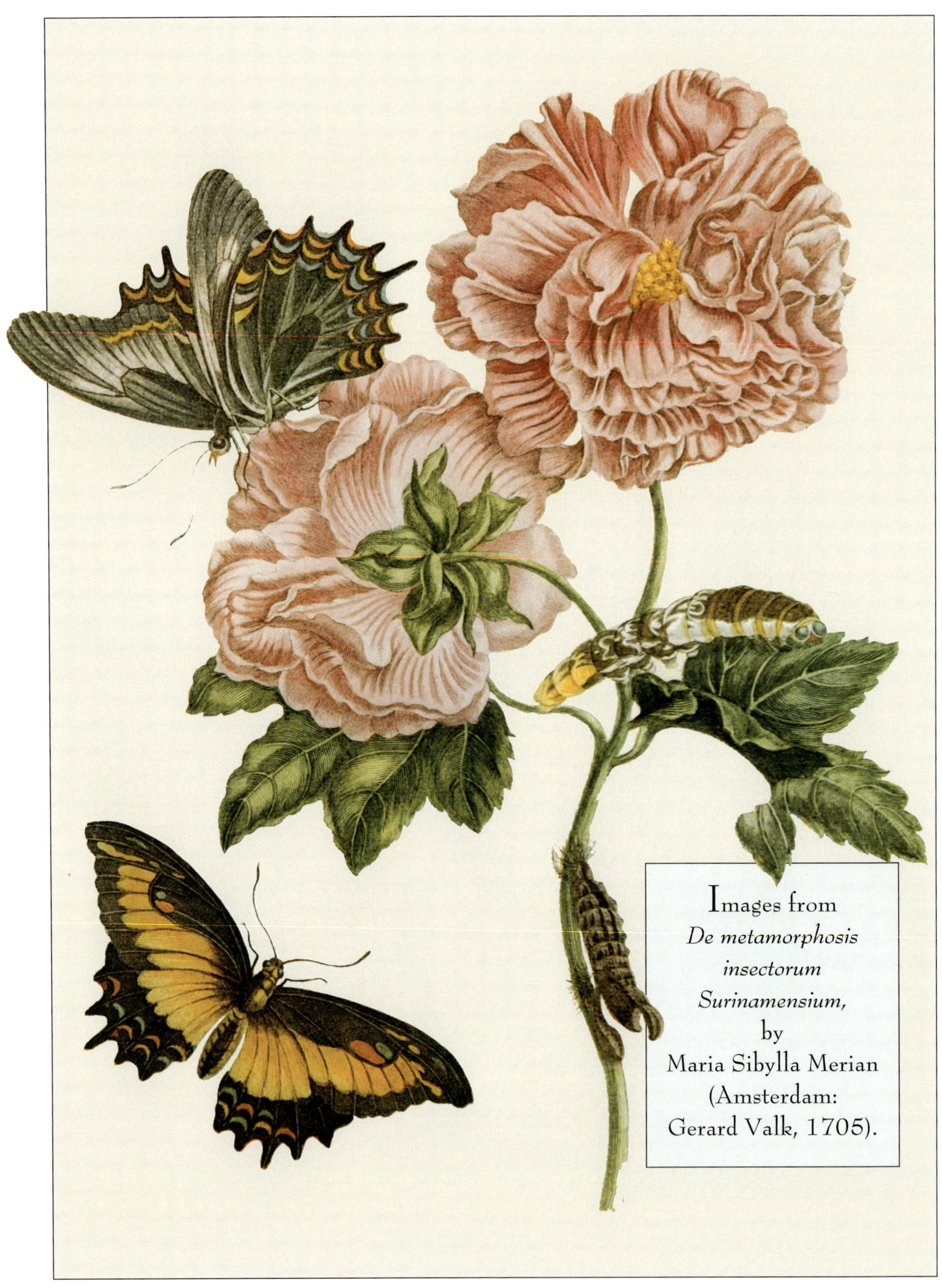

Images from *De metamorphosis insectorum Surinamensium,* by Maria Sibylla Merian (Amsterdam: Gerard Valk, 1705).

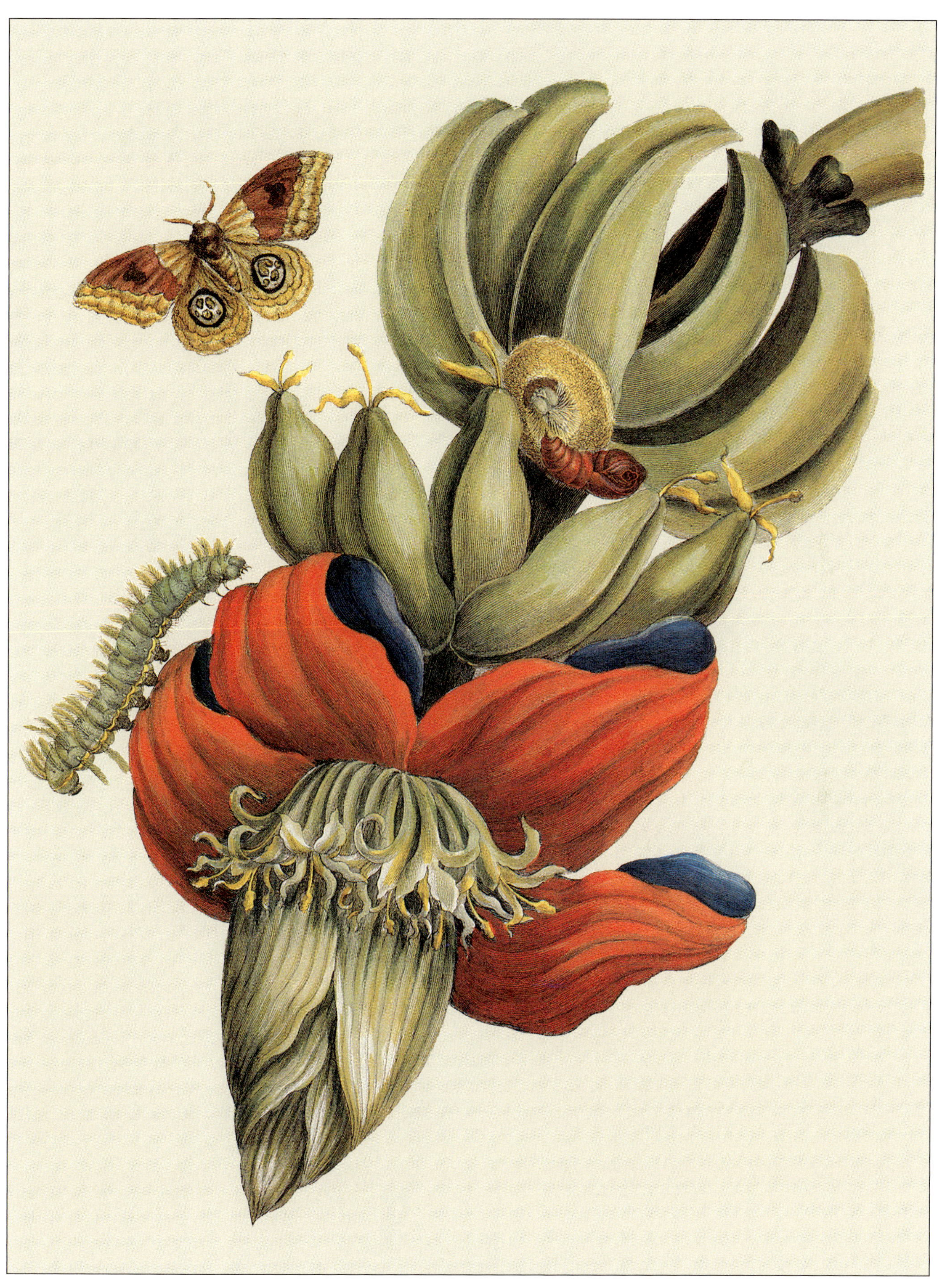

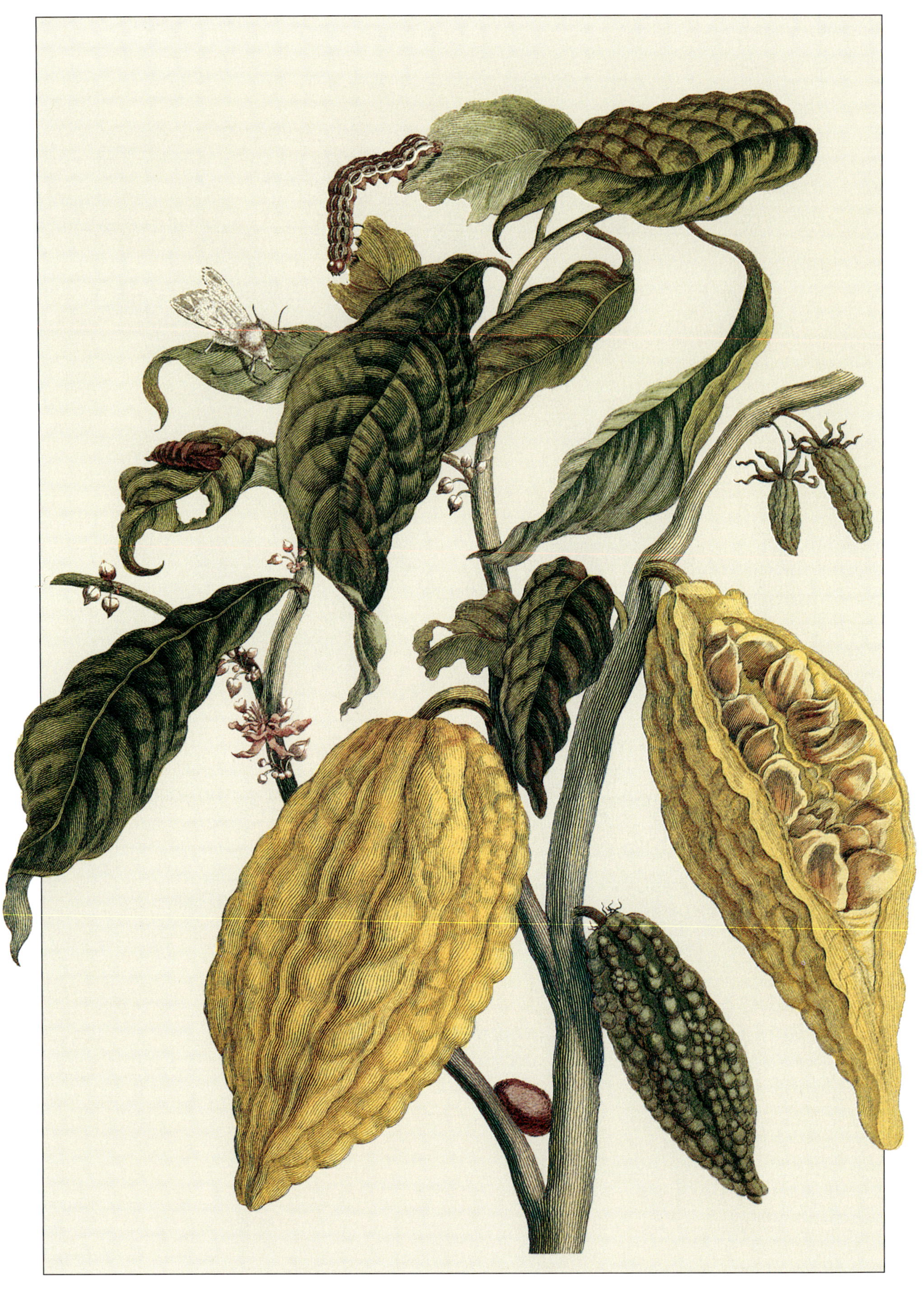

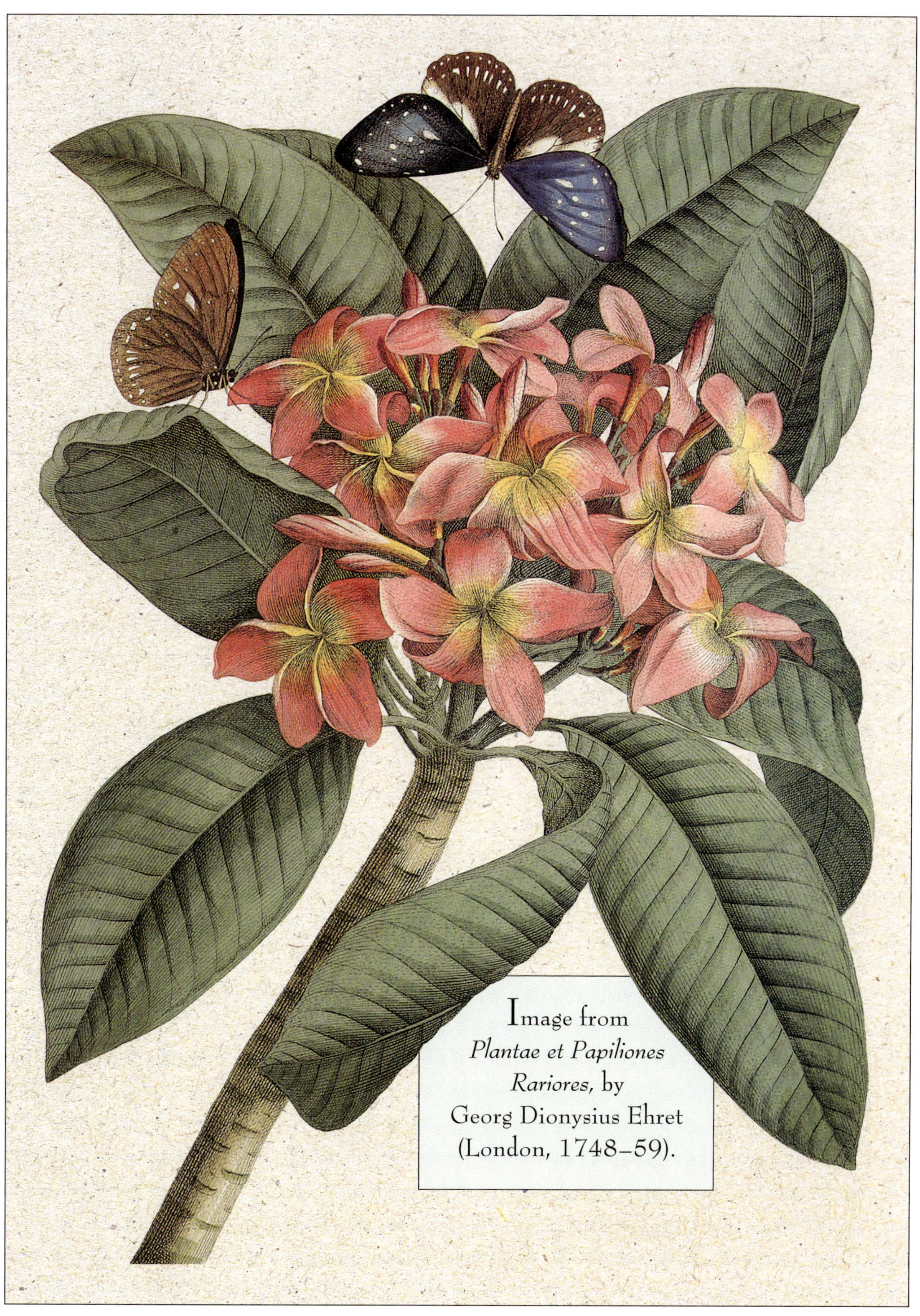

Image from *Plantae et Papiliones Rariores*, by Georg Dionysius Ehret (London, 1748–59).

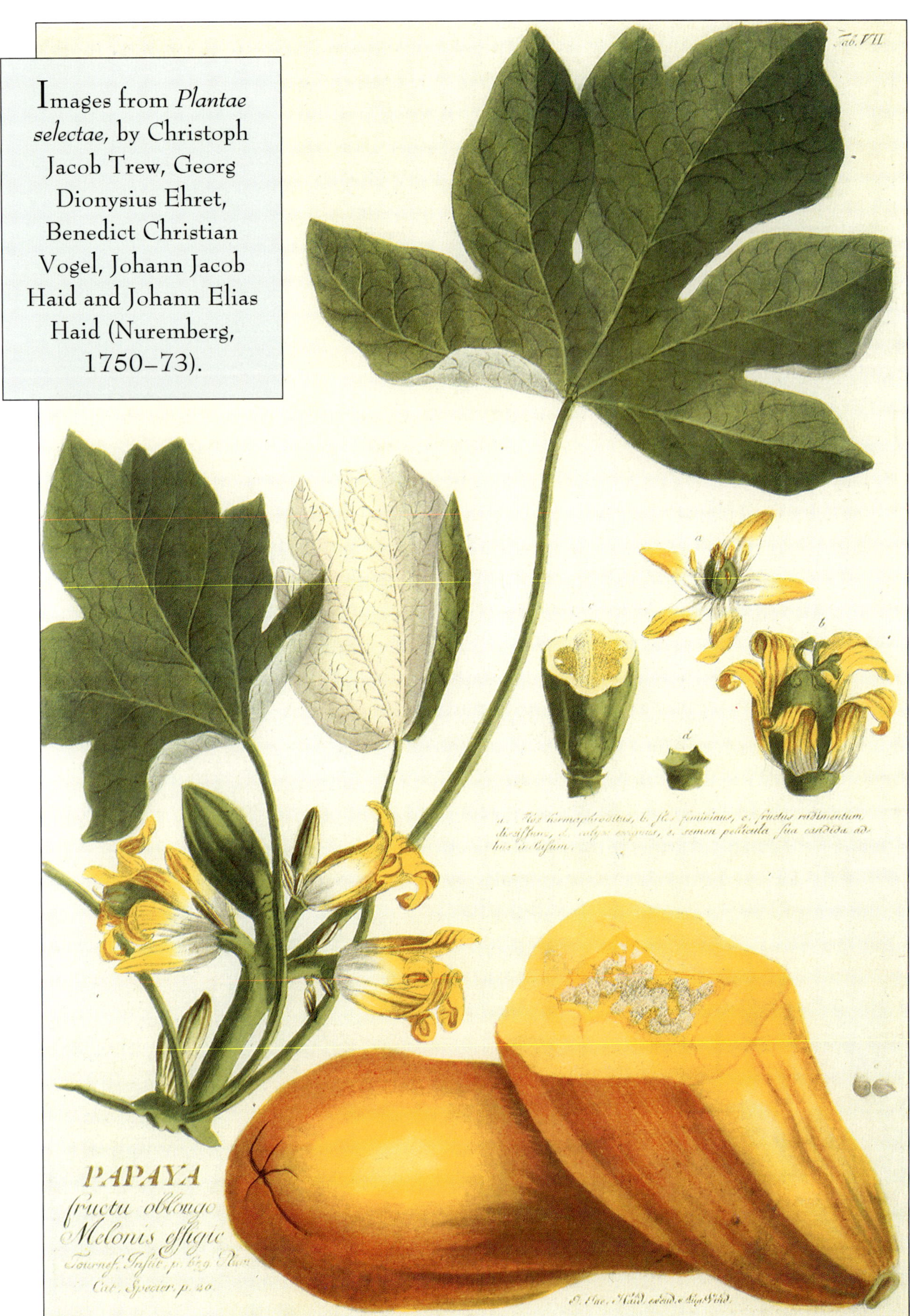

Images from *Plantae selectae,* by Christoph Jacob Trew, Georg Dionysius Ehret, Benedict Christian Vogel, Johann Jacob Haid and Johann Elias Haid (Nuremberg, 1750–73).

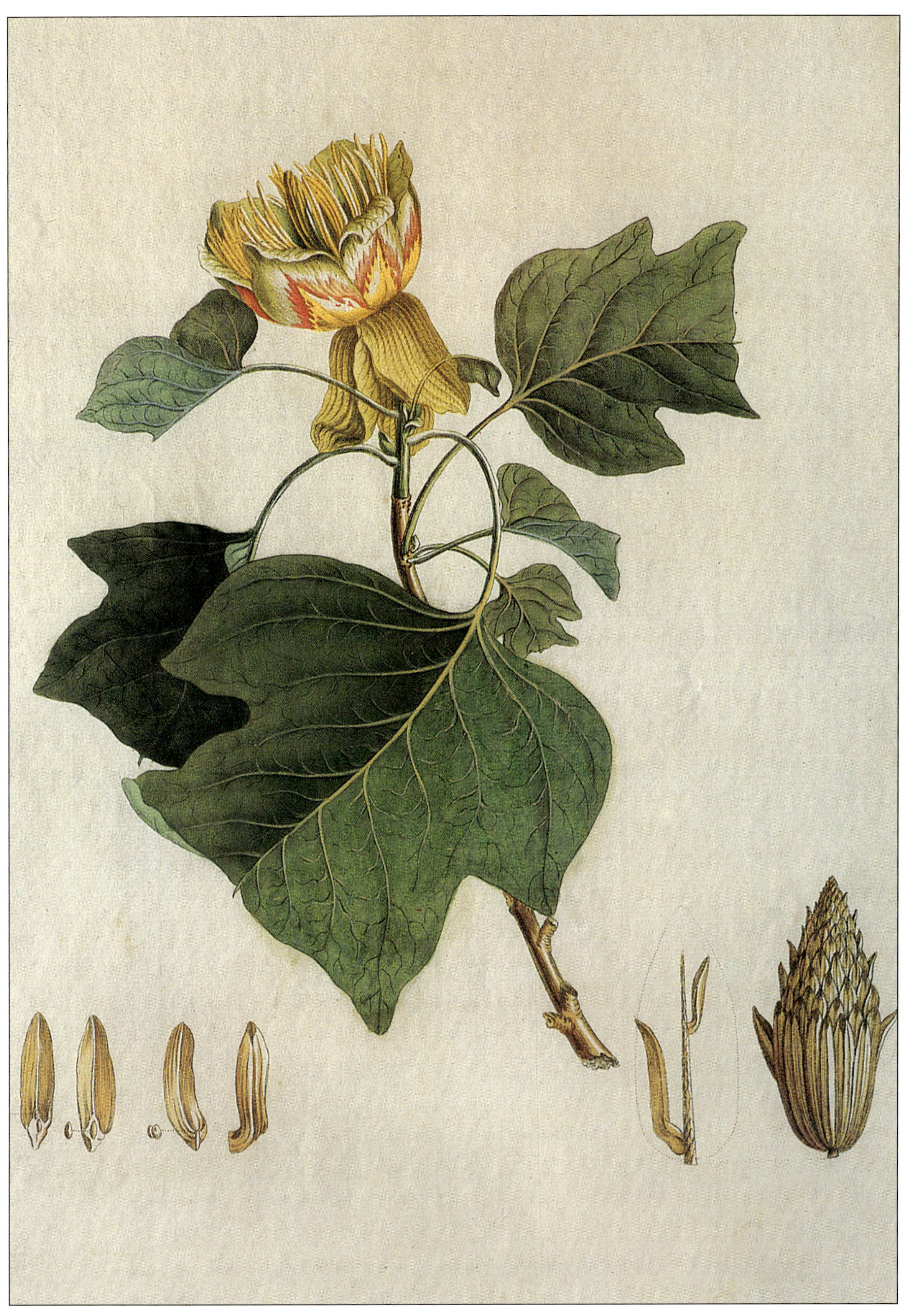

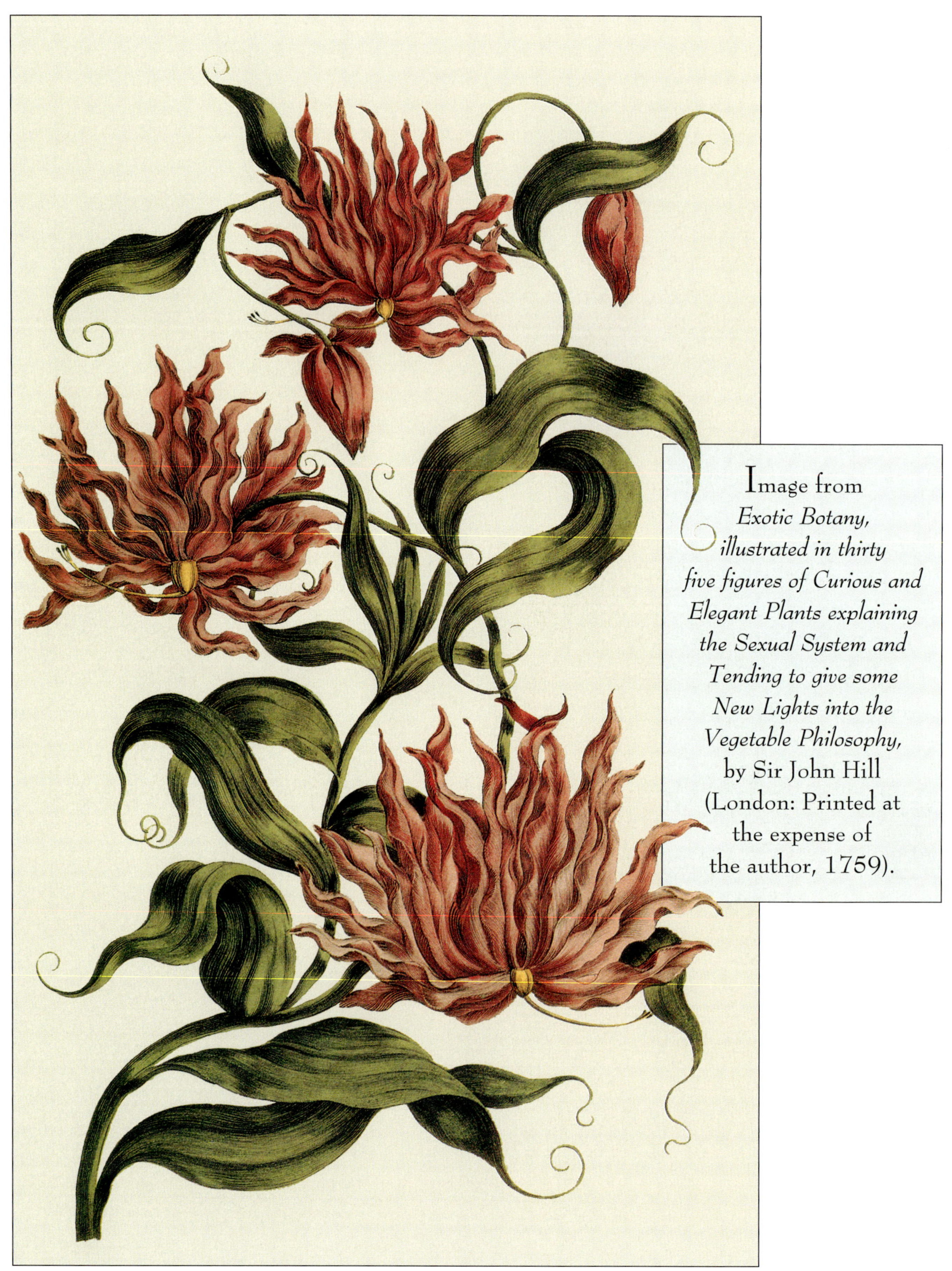

Image from *Exotic Botany, illustrated in thirty five figures of Curious and Elegant Plants explaining the Sexual System and Tending to give some New Lights into the Vegetable Philosophy,* by Sir John Hill (London: Printed at the expense of the author, 1759).

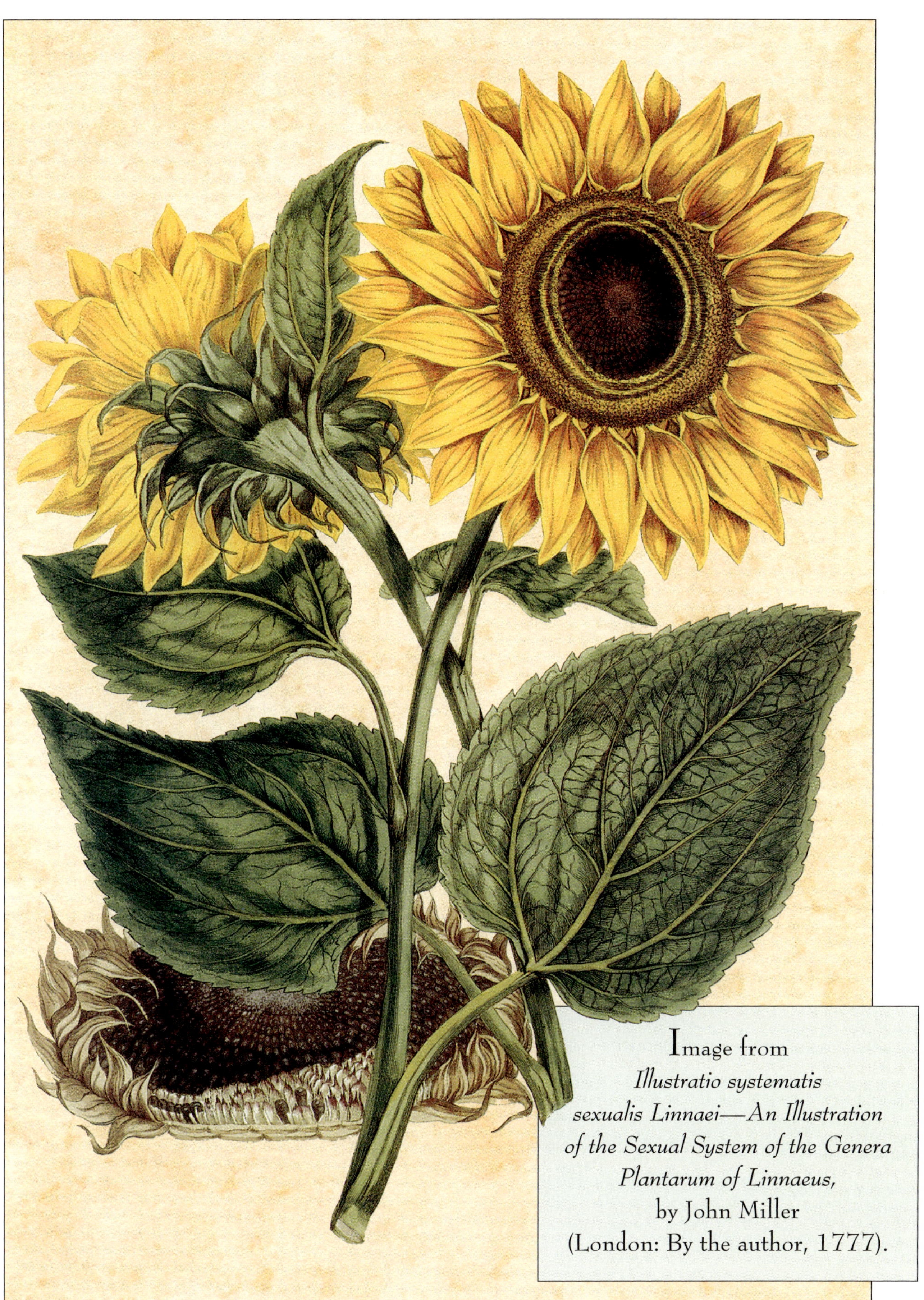

Image from
Illustratio systematis sexualis Linnaei—An Illustration of the Sexual System of the Genera Plantarum of Linnaeus,
by John Miller
(London: By the author, 1777).

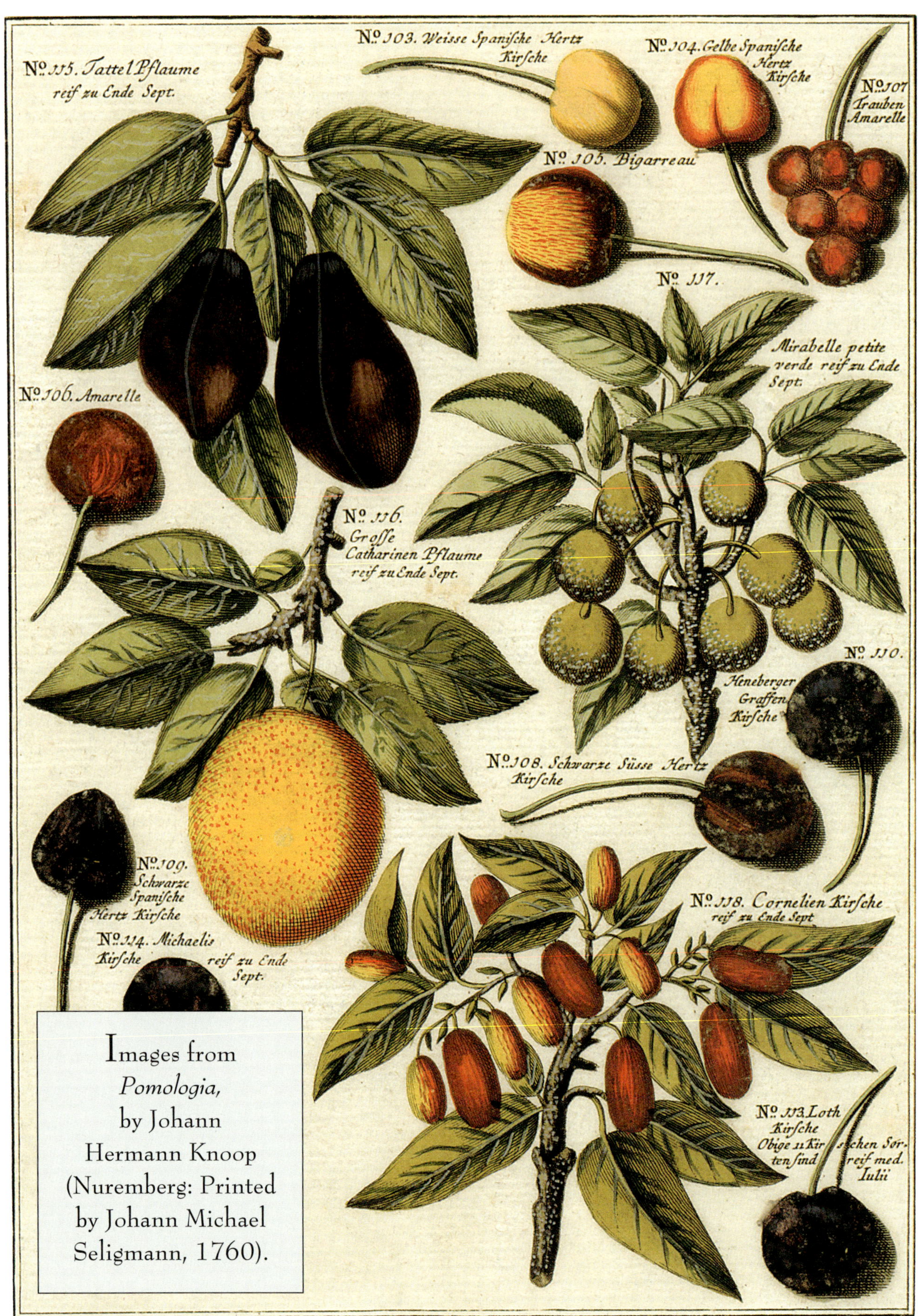

Images from *Pomologia*, by Johann Hermann Knoop (Nuremberg: Printed by Johann Michael Seligmann, 1760).

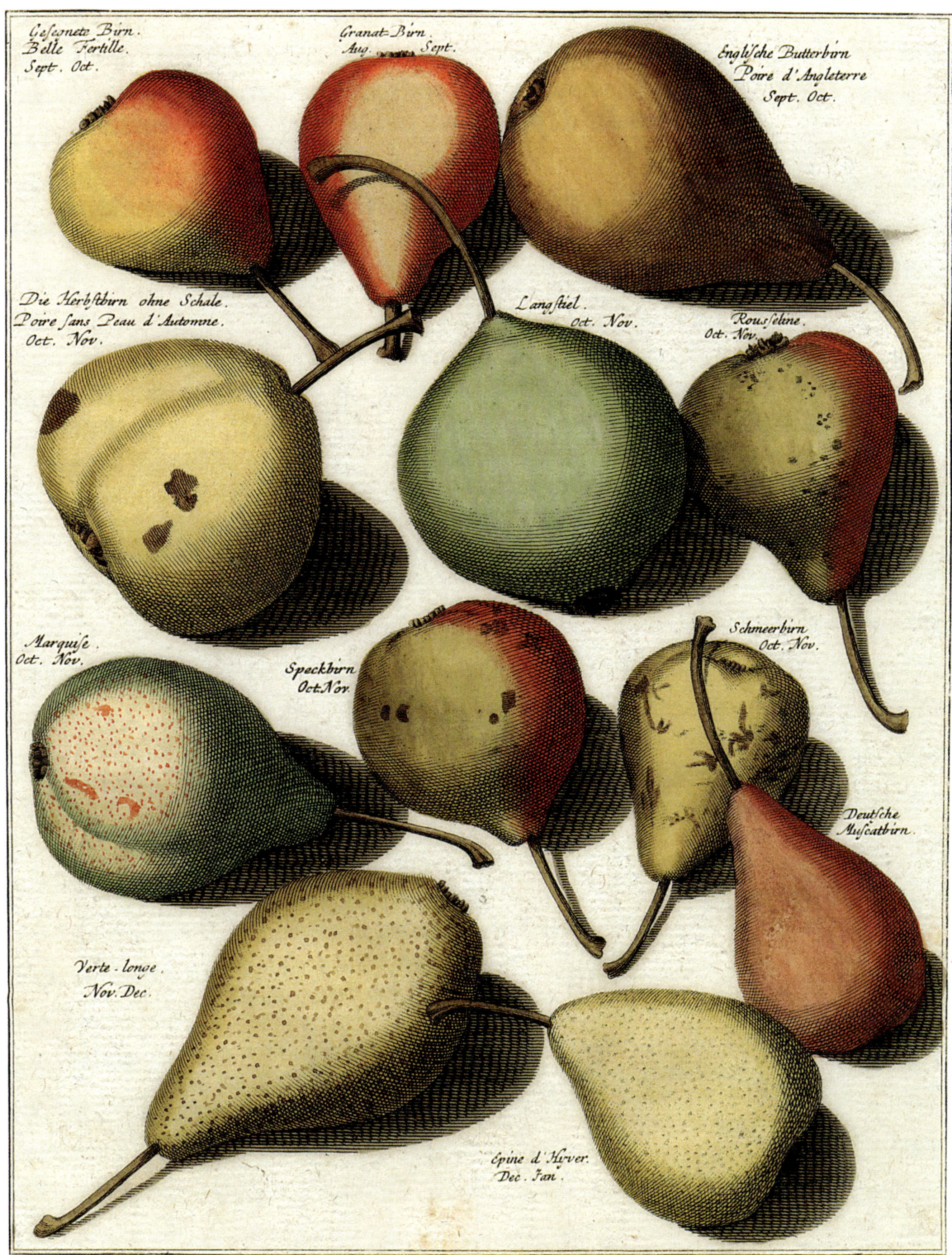
Geſegnete Birn.
Belle Fertille.
Sept. Oct.
Granat-Birn.
Aug. Sept.
Engliſche Butterbirn
Poire d'Angleterre
Sept. Oct.
Die Herbſtbirn ohne Schale.
Poire ſans Peau d'Automne.
Oct. Nov.
Langſtiel.
Oct. Nov.
Rouſſeline.
Oct. Nov.
Marquiſe.
Oct. Nov.
Speckbirn
Oct. Nov.
Schmeerbirn
Oct. Nov.
Deutſche
Muſcatbirn.
Verte-longe.
Nov. Dec.
Epine d'Hyver.
Dec. Jan.

Images selected from among the approximately 2,000 watercolors of flowers and fruits produced by Pierre-Joseph Redouté beginning in the 1780s and published in numerous illustrated books and as individual prints. Published by Dover in *Redouté's Flowers and Fruits CD-ROM and Book* (Mineola, NY, 2004).

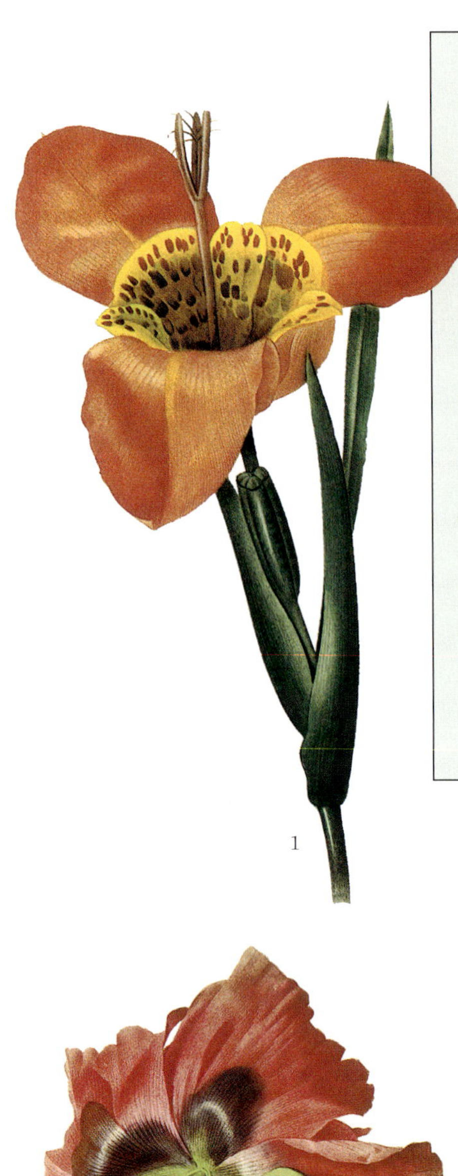

1

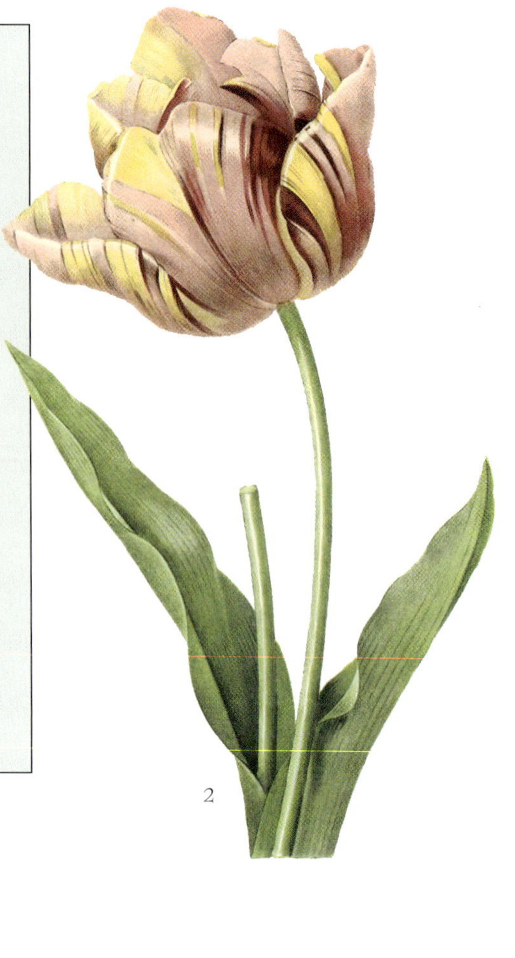

2

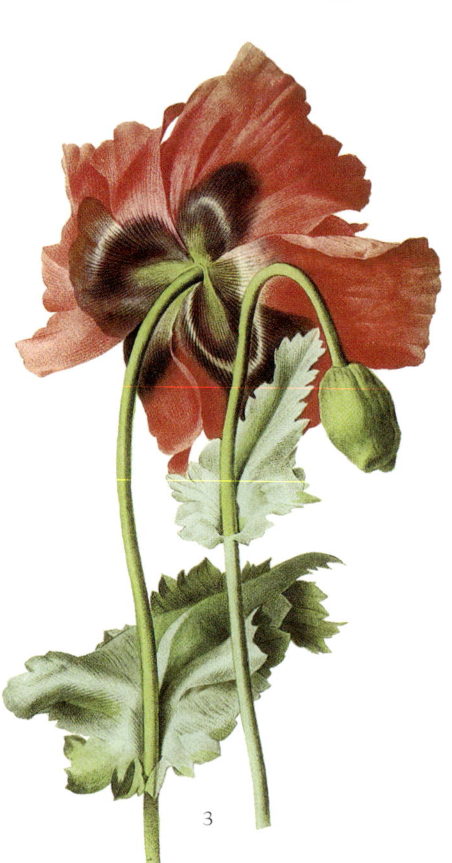

3

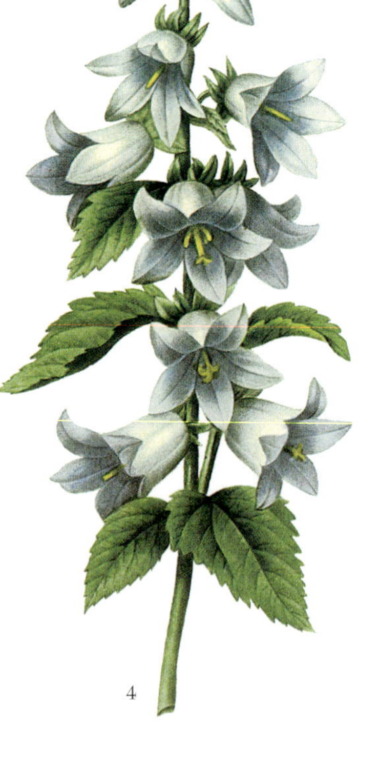

4

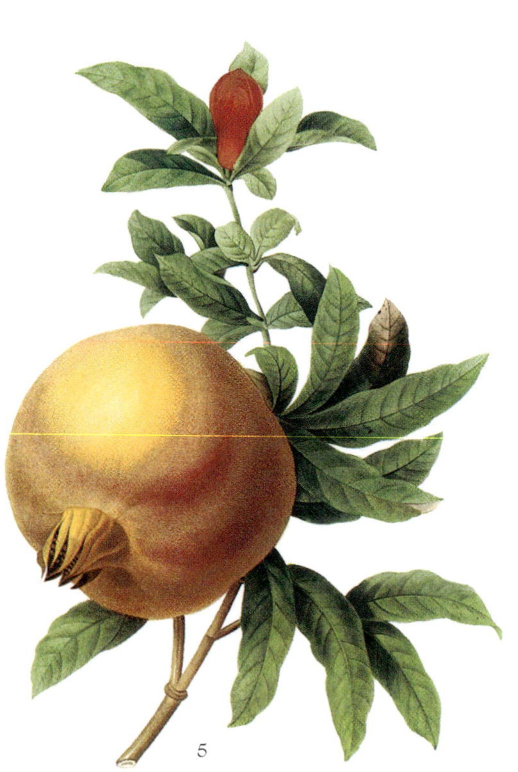

5

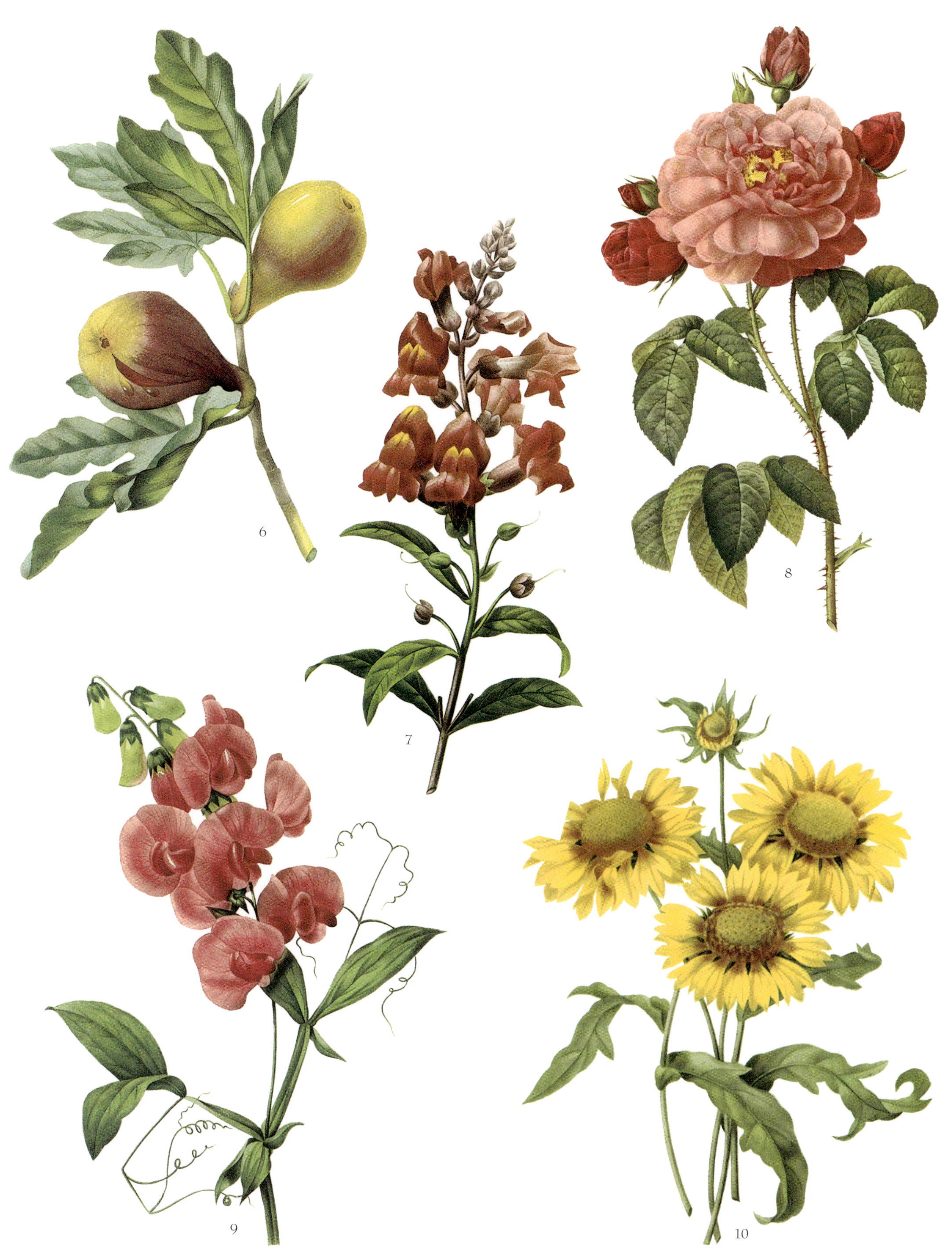
6
7
8
9
10

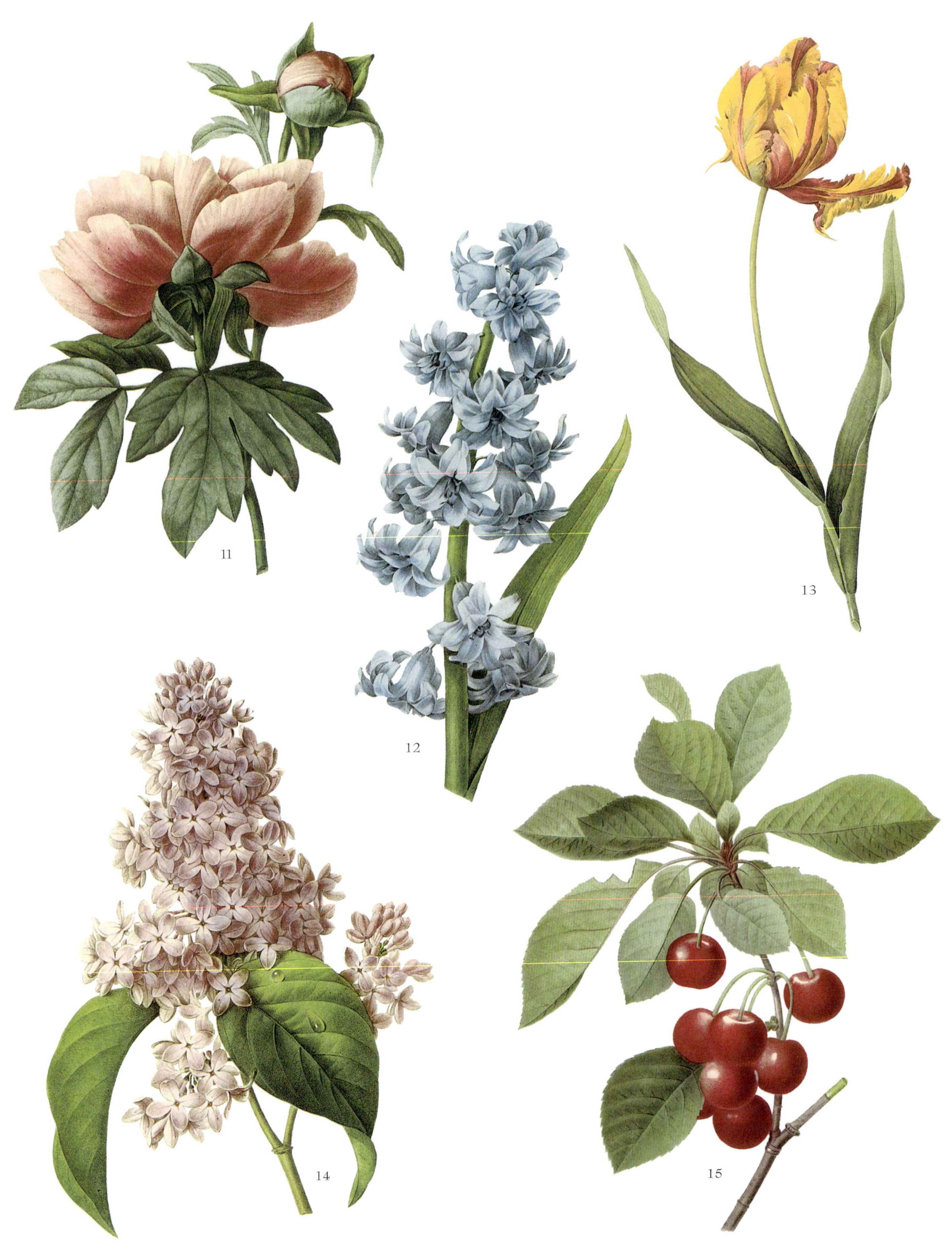
11
12
13
14
15

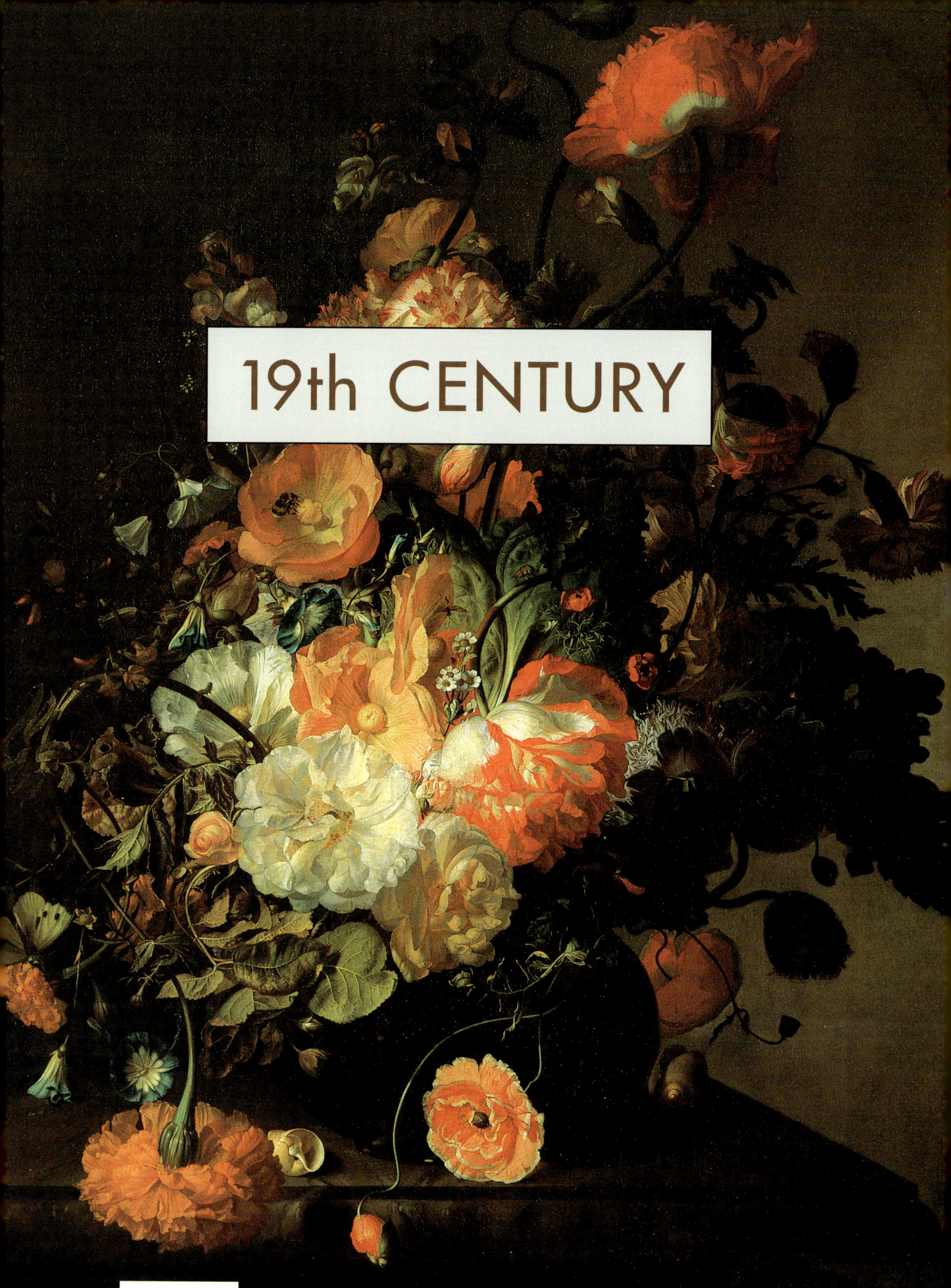

19th CENTURY

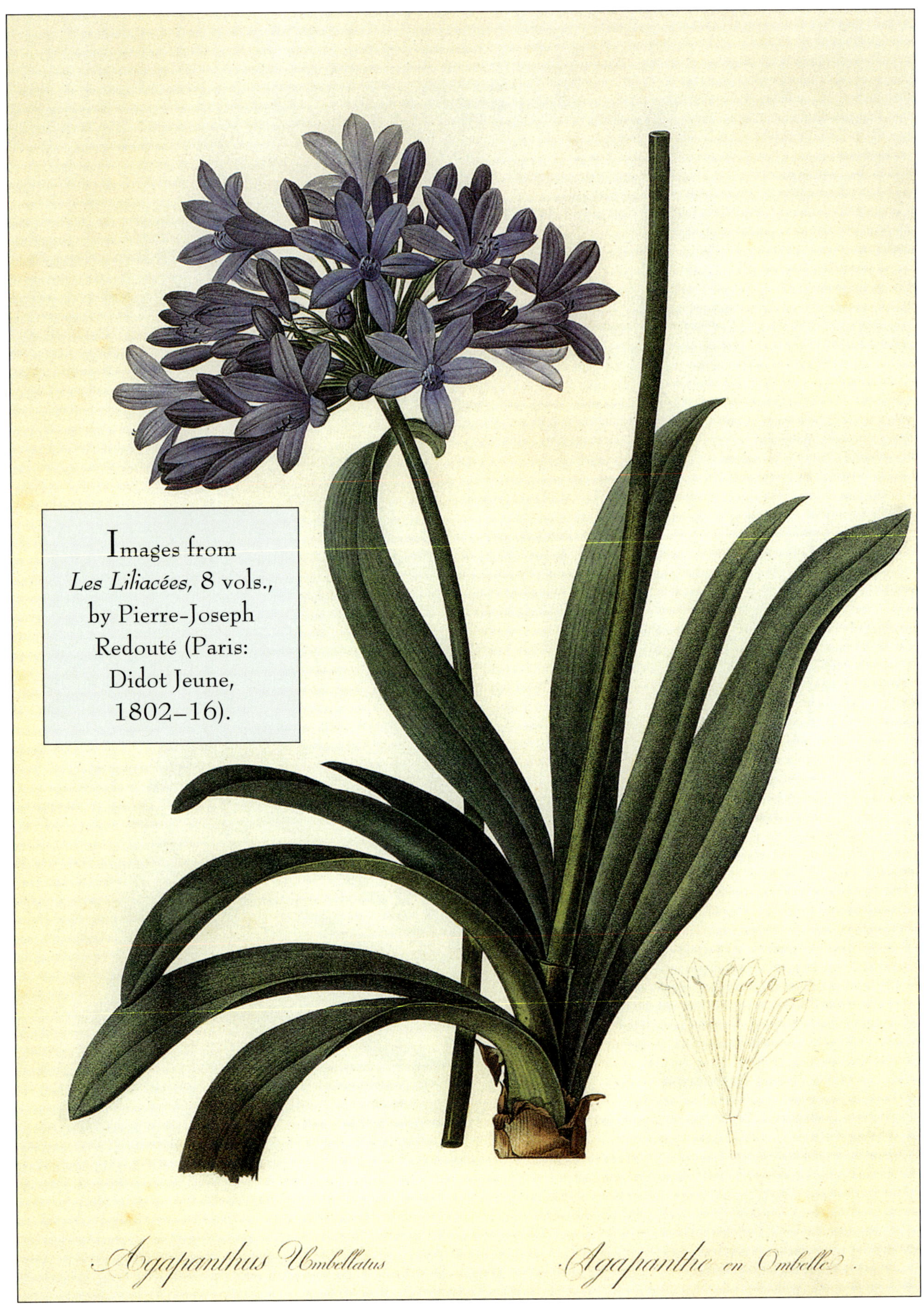

Images from *Les Liliacées,* 8 vols., by Pierre-Joseph Redouté (Paris: Didot Jeune, 1802–16).

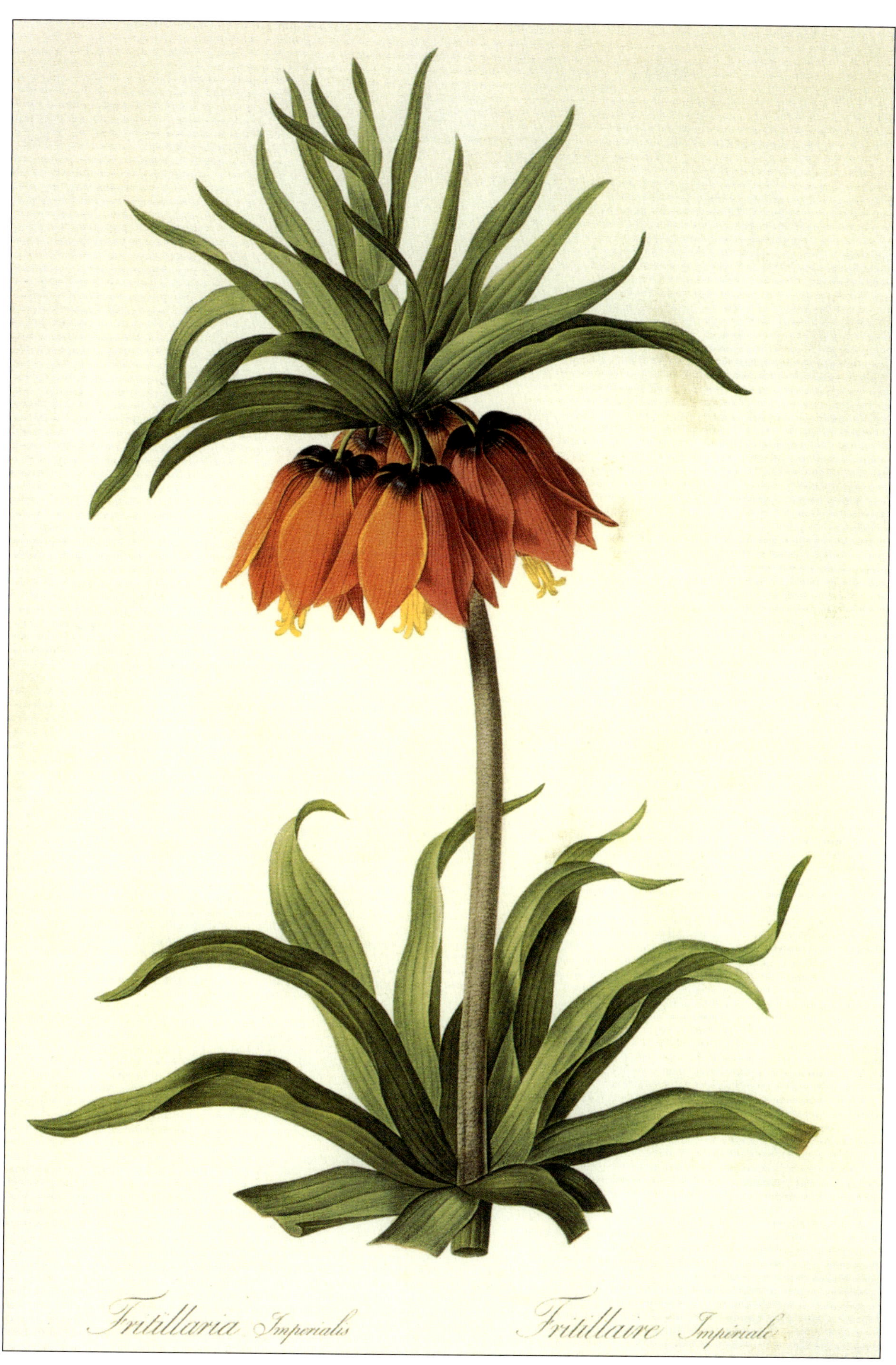
Fritillaria Imperialis
Fritillaire Impériale

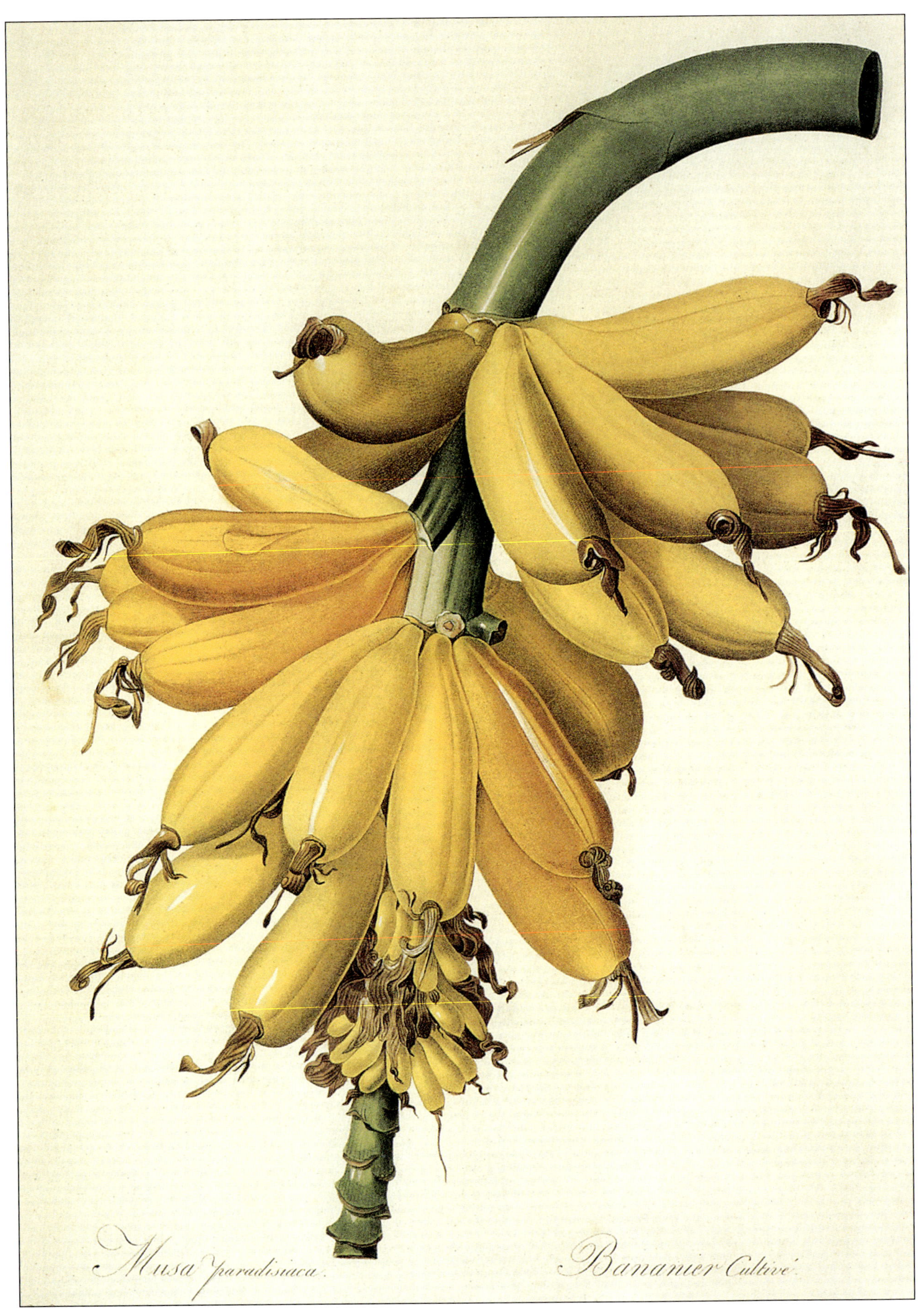
Musa paradisiaca.
Bananier Cultivé

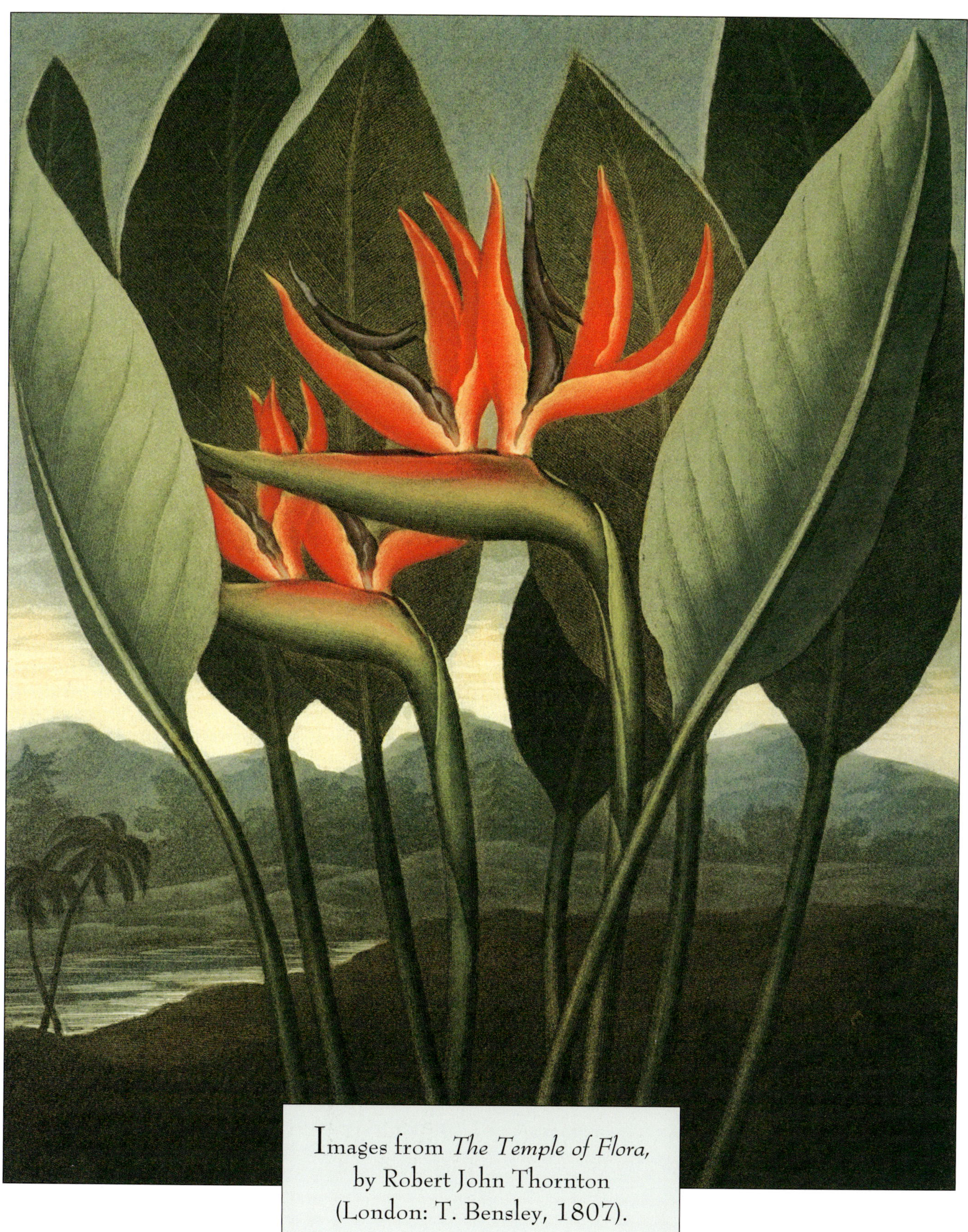

Images from *The Temple of Flora*, by Robert John Thornton (London: T. Bensley, 1807).

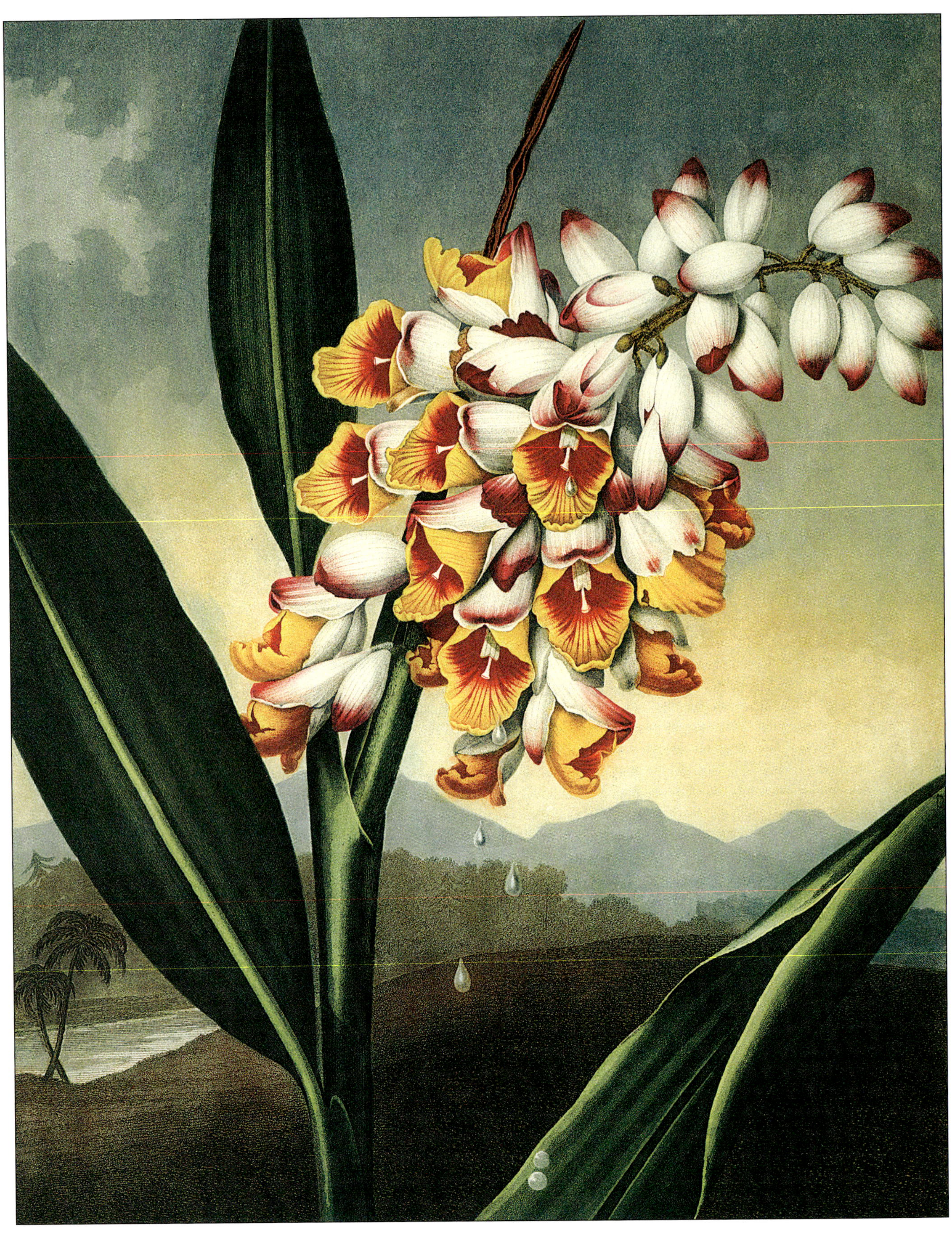

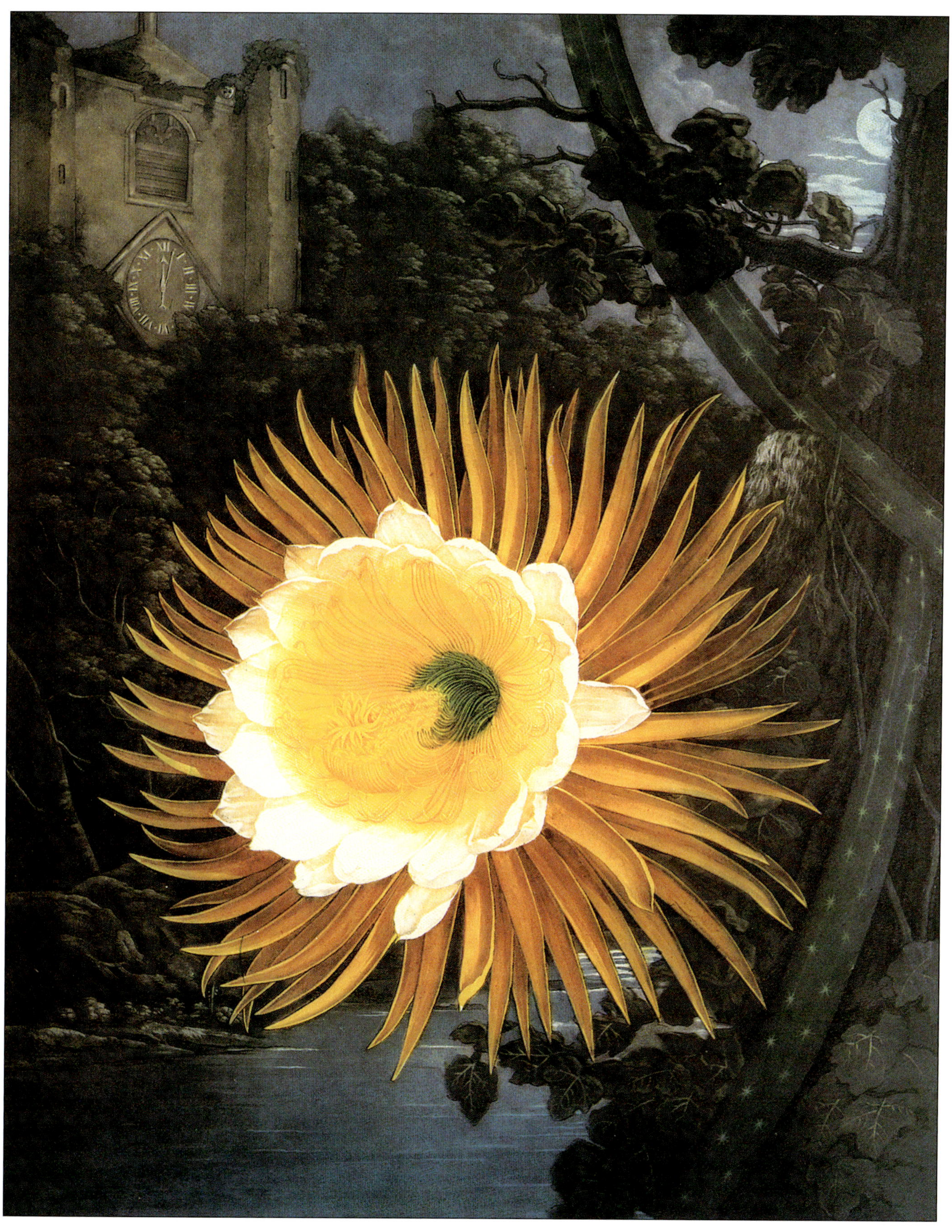

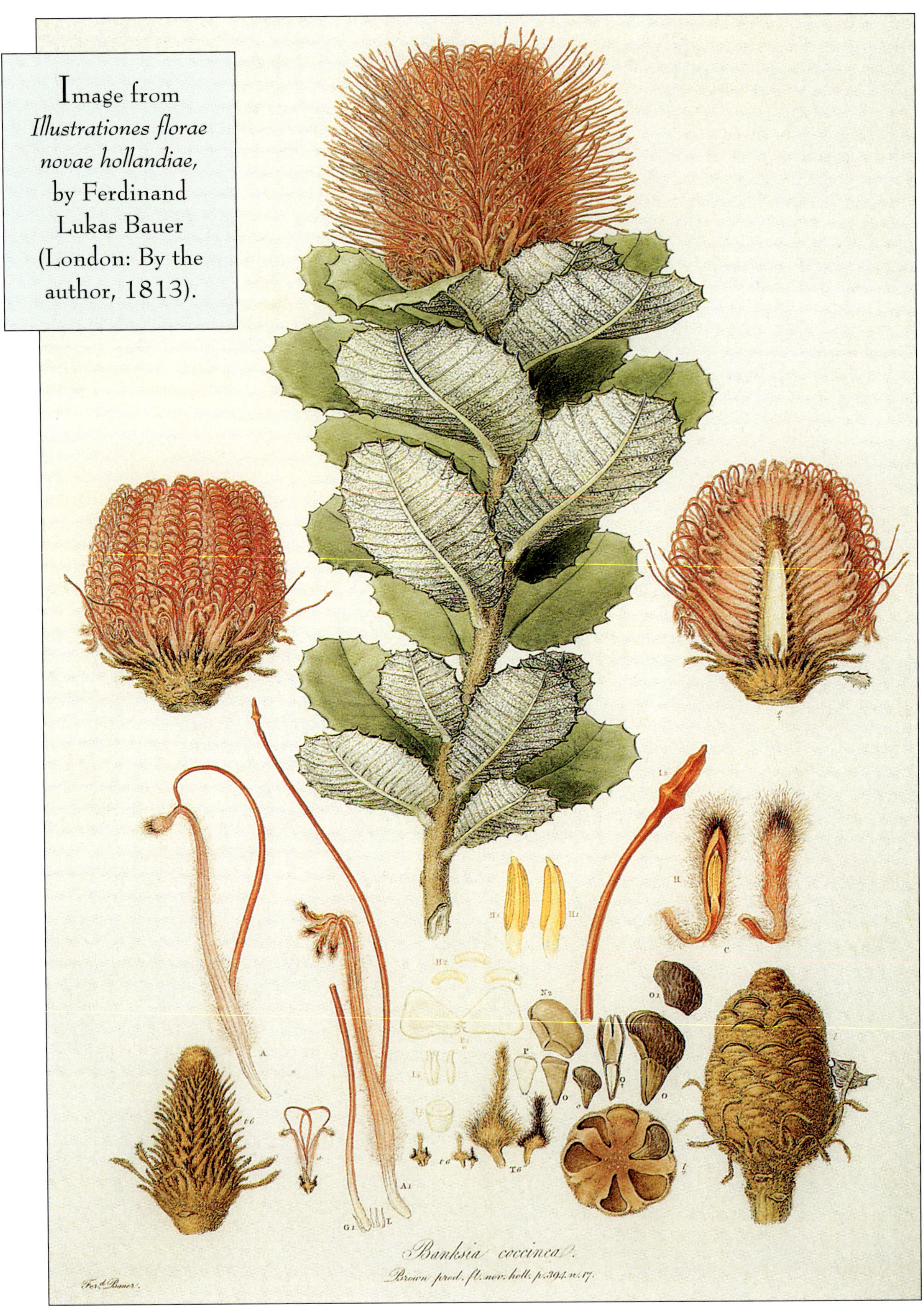

Image from *Illustrationes florae novae hollandiae,* by Ferdinand Lukas Bauer (London: By the author, 1813).

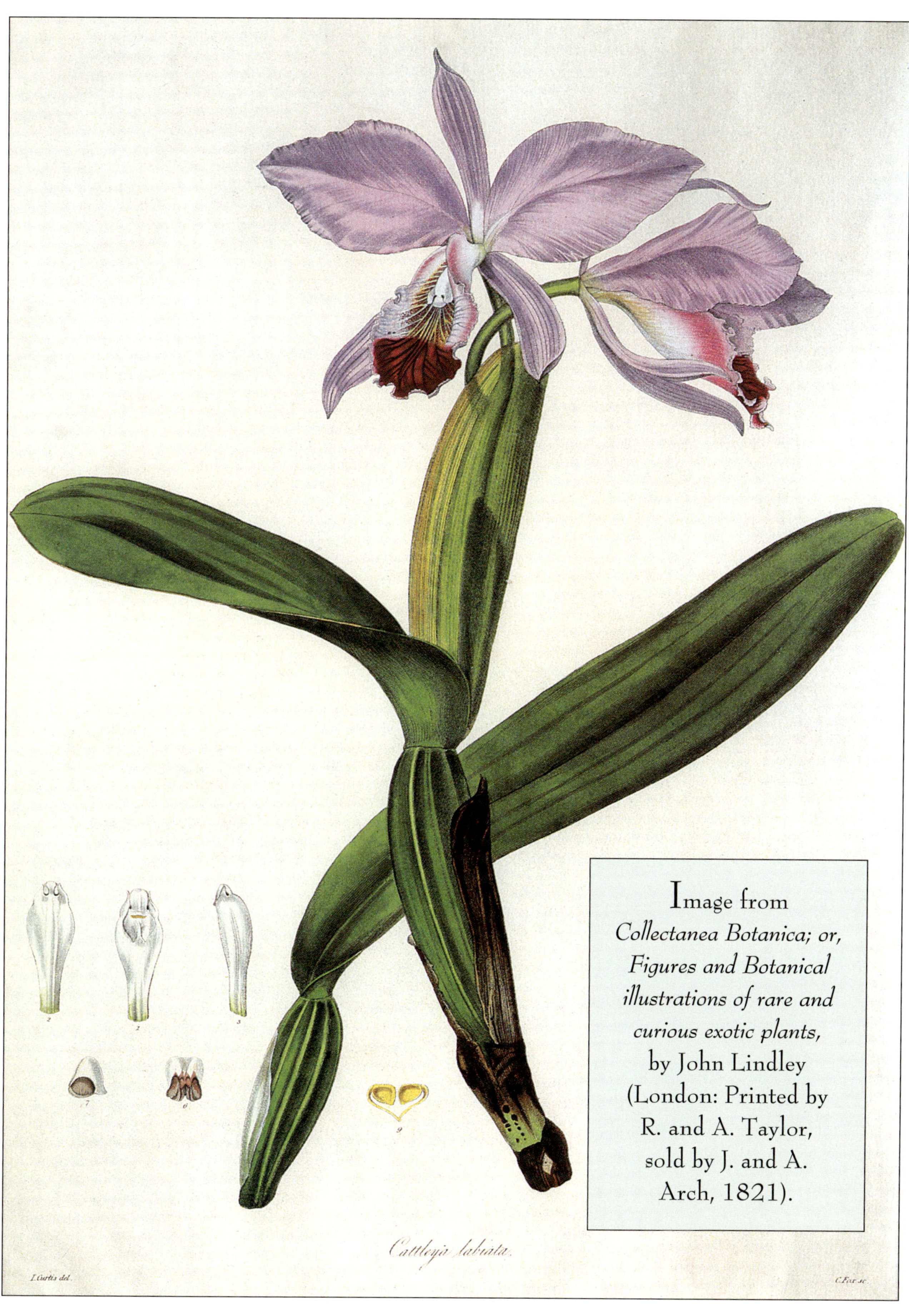

Image from *Collectanea Botanica; or, Figures and Botanical illustrations of rare and curious exotic plants,* by John Lindley (London: Printed by R. and A. Taylor, sold by J. and A. Arch, 1821).

Images from *Les Roses*, by Pierre-Joseph Redouté (Paris: Firmin Didot, 1817–24). Published by Dover as *Redouté Rose Prints: A Portfolio of 6 Self-Matted Full-Color Prints* (New York, 1990).

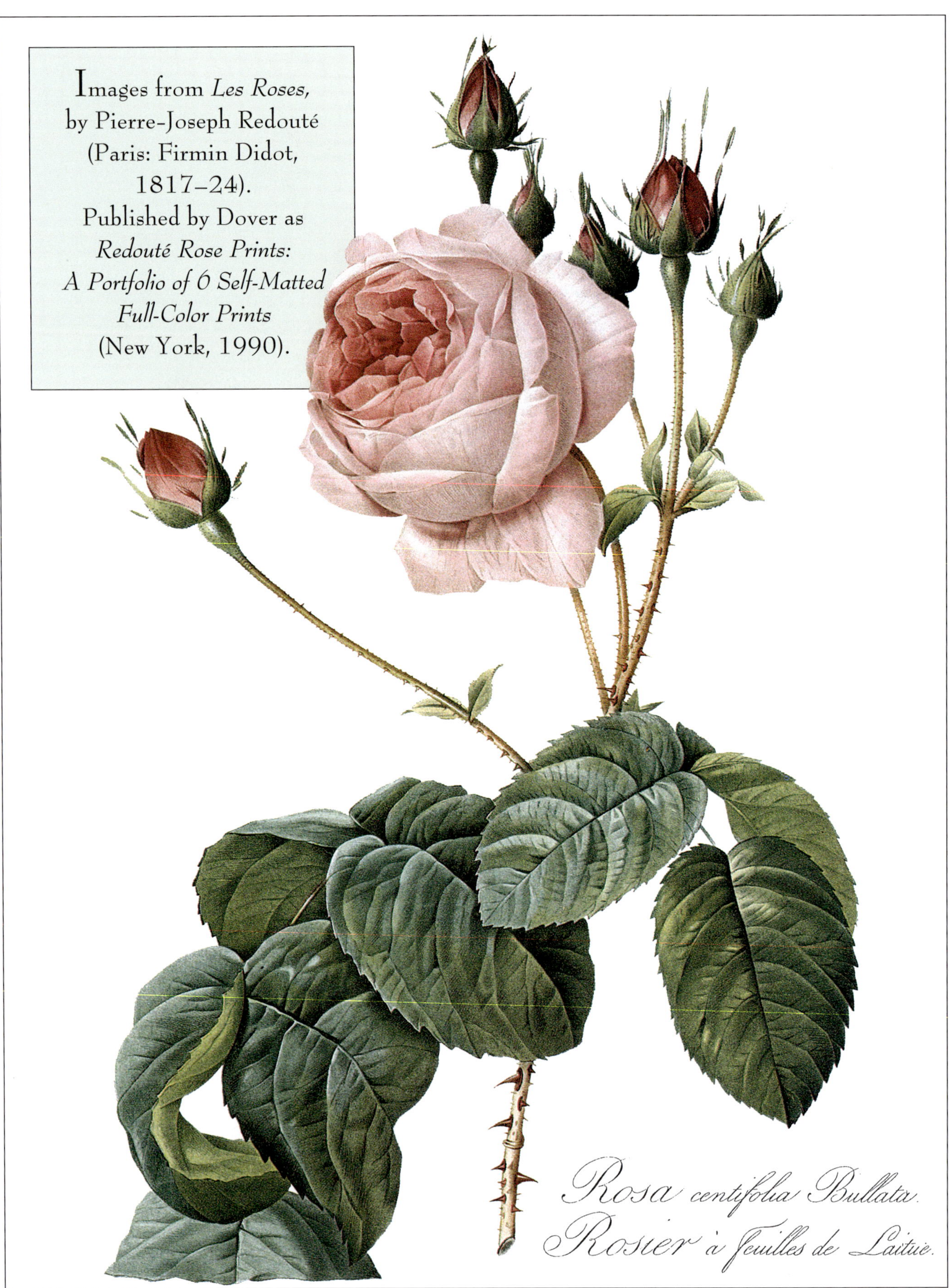

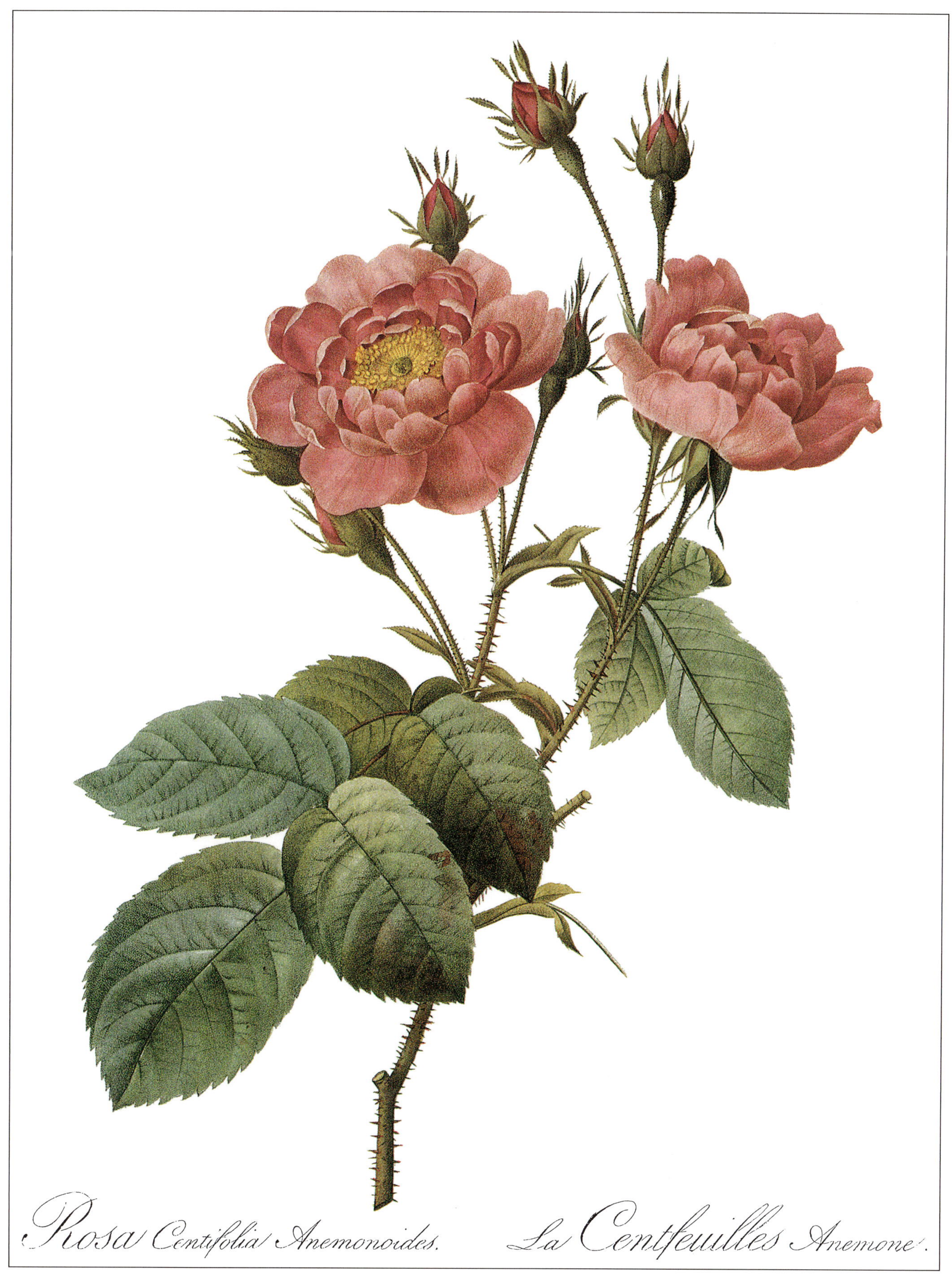
Rosa Centifolia Anemonoides.
La Centfeuilles Anemone.

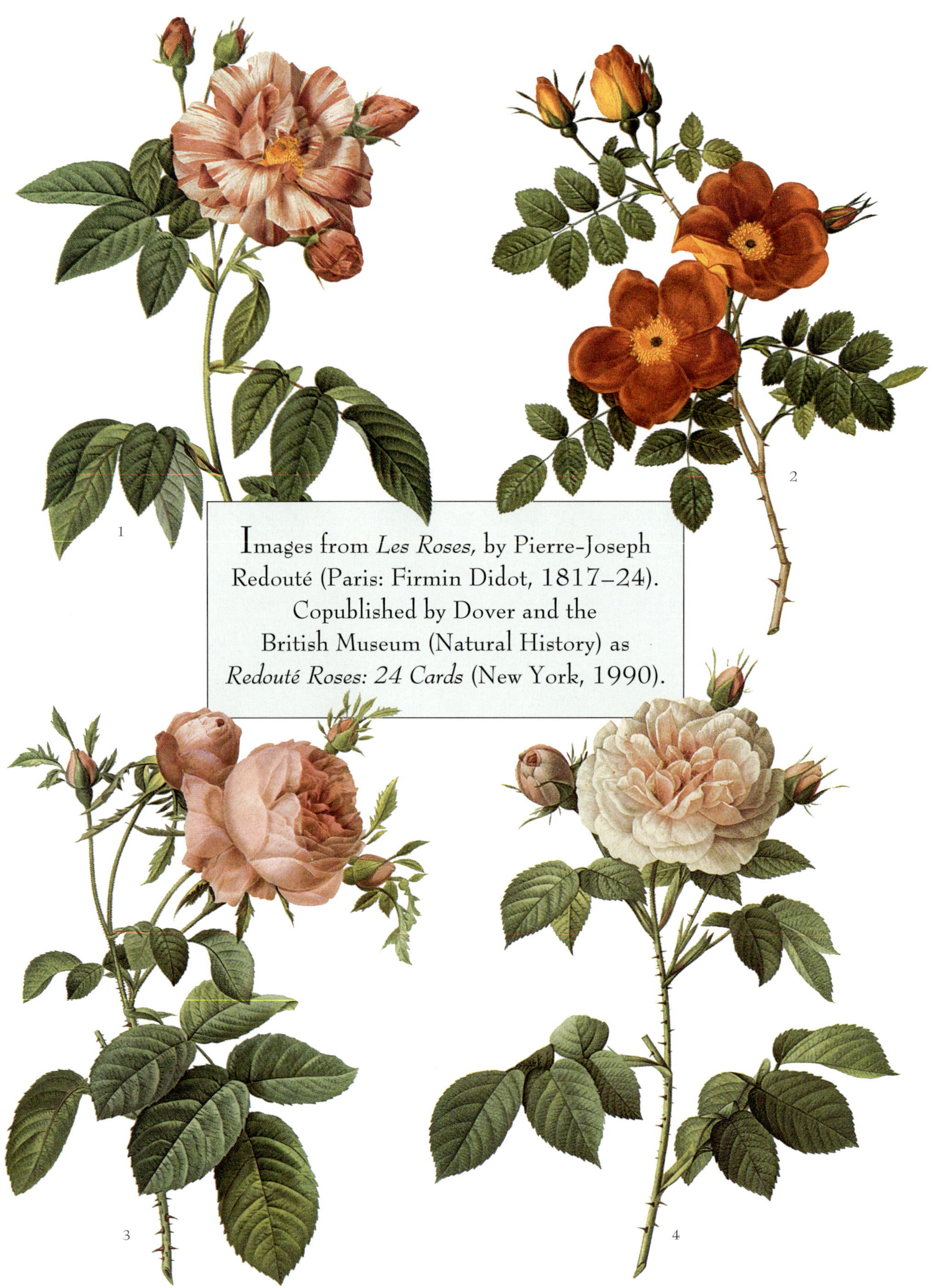

Images from *Les Roses,* by Pierre-Joseph Redouté (Paris: Firmin Didot, 1817–24). Copublished by Dover and the British Museum (Natural History) as *Redouté Roses: 24 Cards* (New York, 1990).

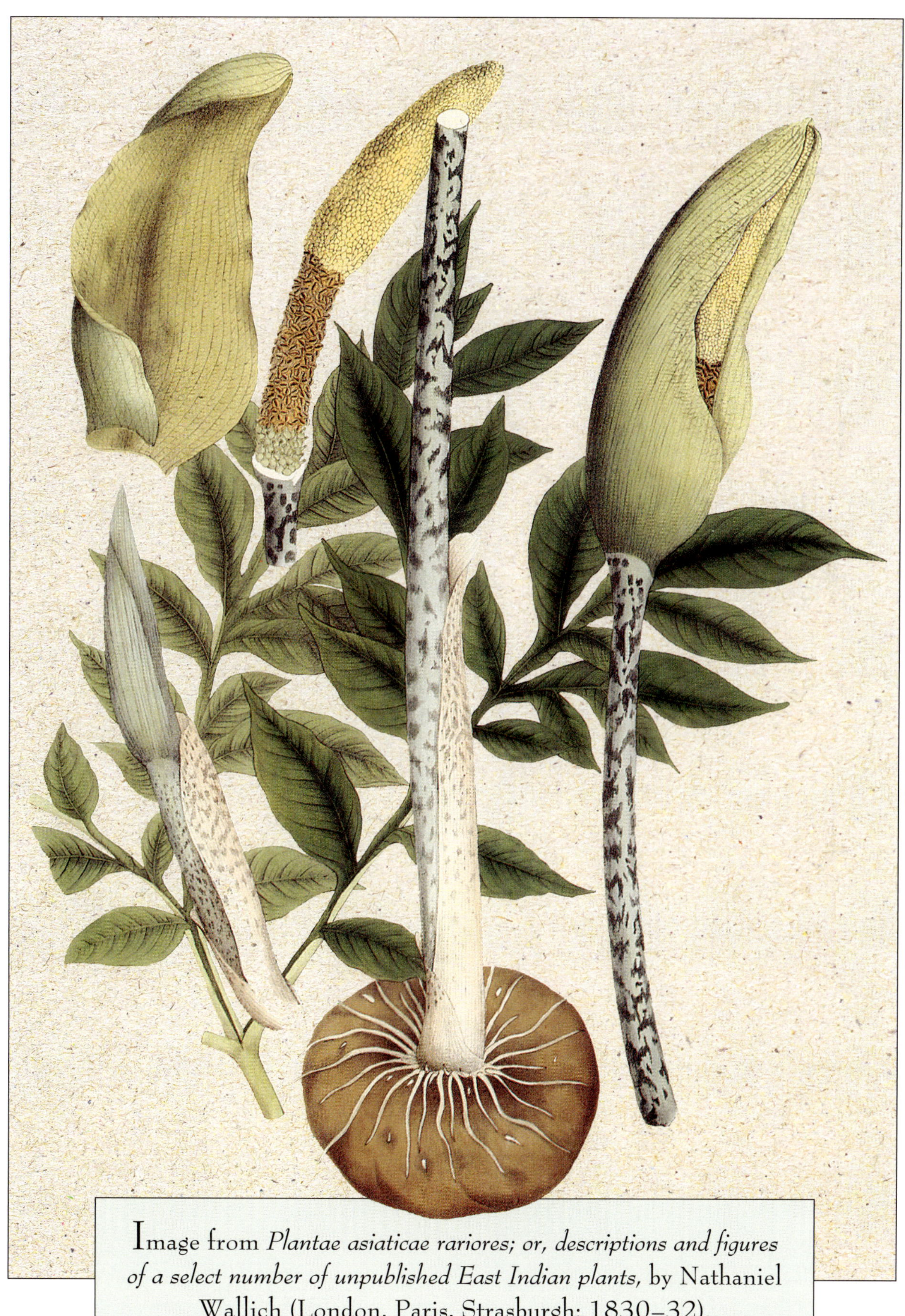

Image from *Plantae asiaticae rariores; or, descriptions and figures of a select number of unpublished East Indian plants,* by Nathaniel Wallich (London, Paris, Strasburgh: 1830–32).

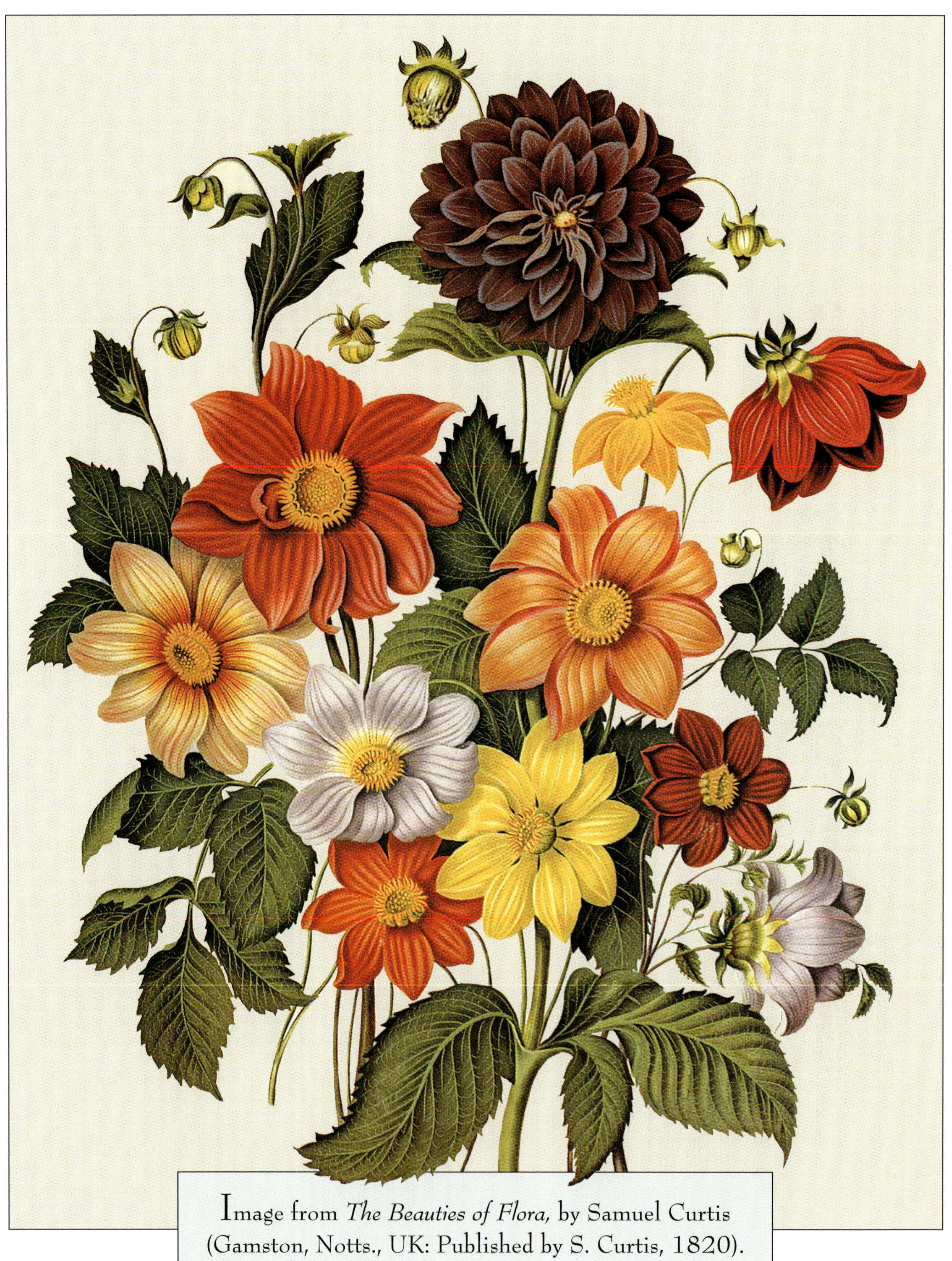

Image from *The Beauties of Flora,* by Samuel Curtis (Gamston, Notts., UK: Published by S. Curtis, 1820).

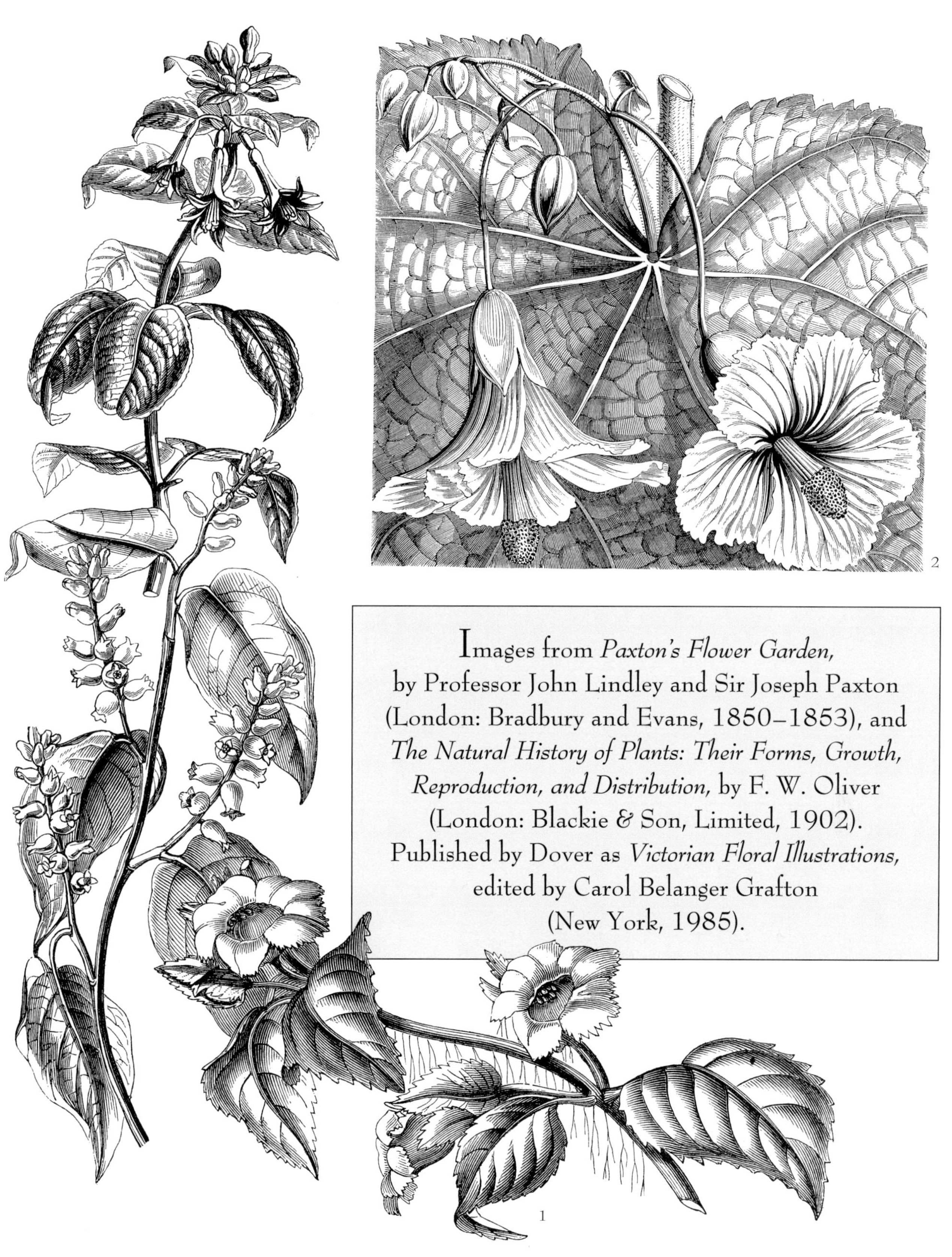

Images from *Paxton's Flower Garden,*
by Professor John Lindley and Sir Joseph Paxton
(London: Bradbury and Evans, 1850–1853), and
The Natural History of Plants: Their Forms, Growth, Reproduction, and Distribution, by F. W. Oliver
(London: Blackie & Son, Limited, 1902).
Published by Dover as *Victorian Floral Illustrations,*
edited by Carol Belanger Grafton
(New York, 1985).

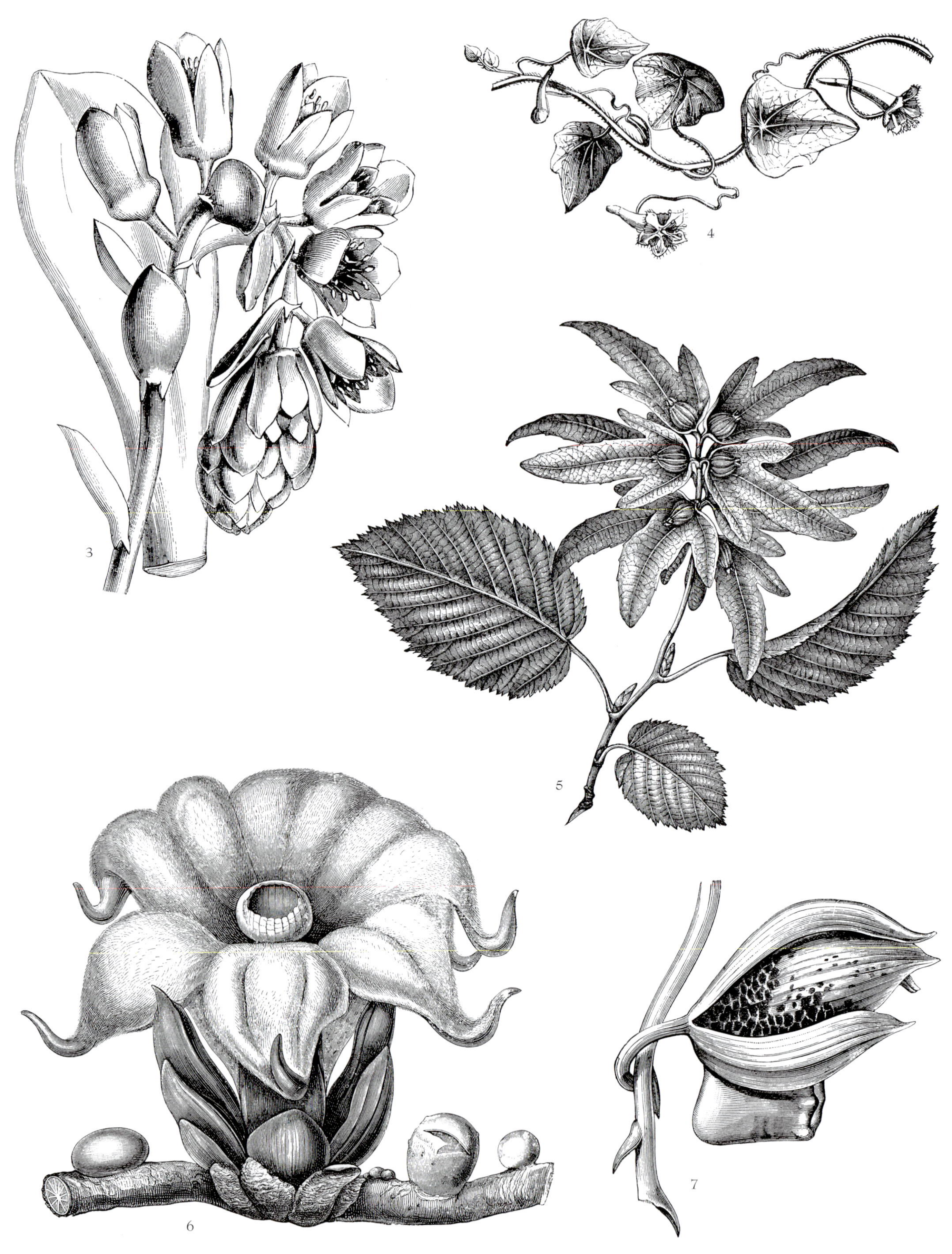
3
4
5
6
7

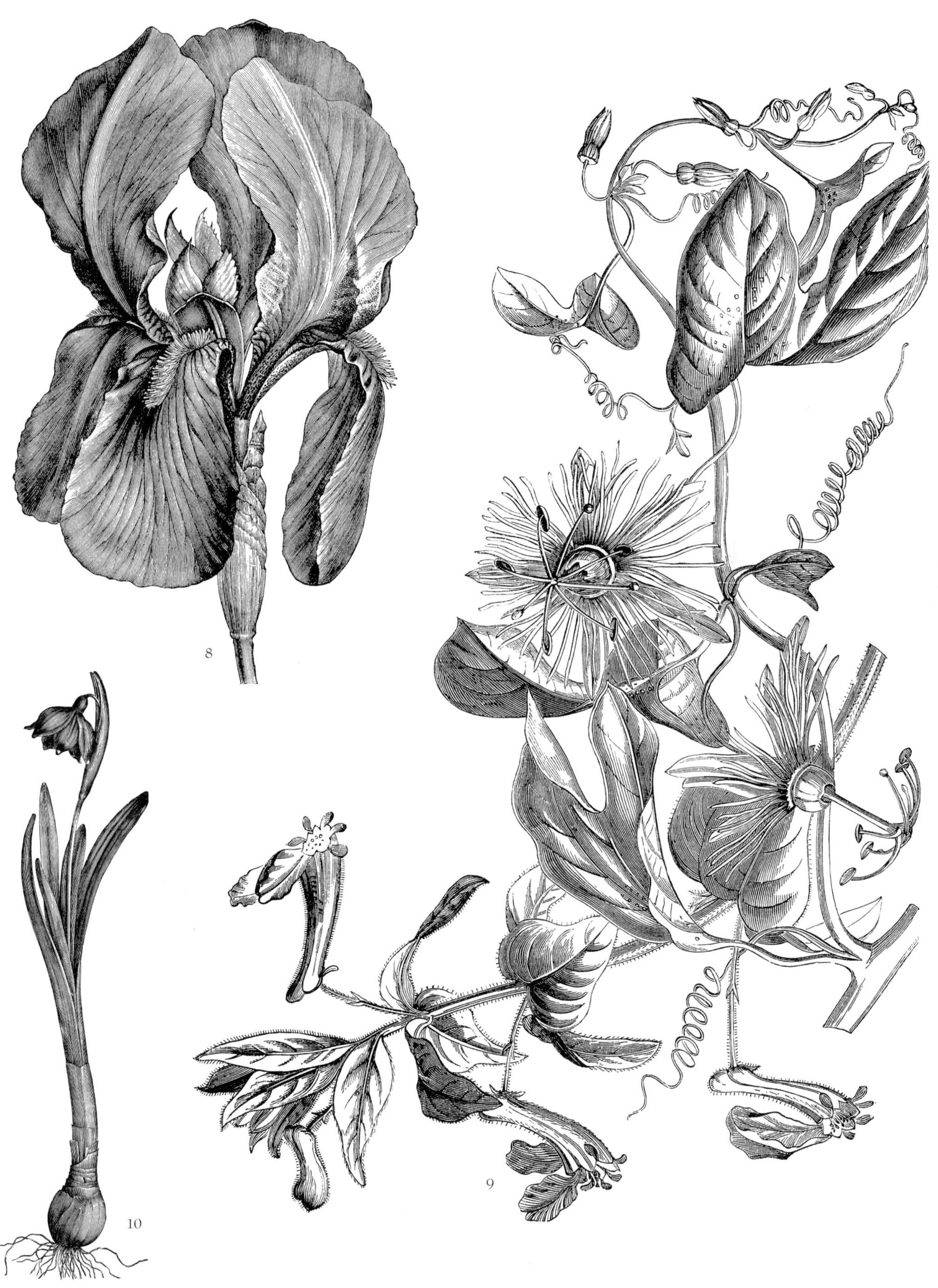
8
9
10

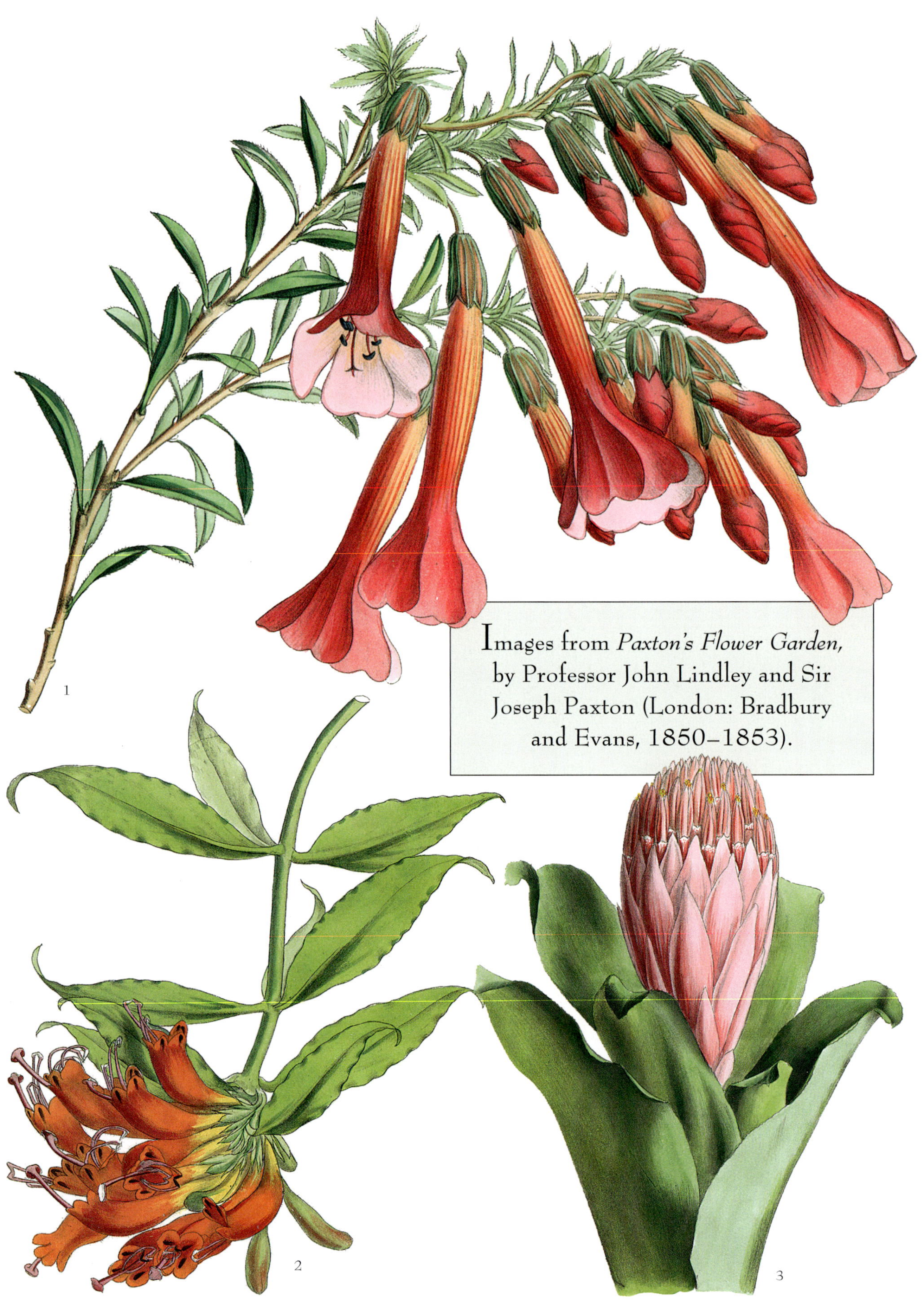

Images from *Paxton's Flower Garden*, by Professor John Lindley and Sir Joseph Paxton (London: Bradbury and Evans, 1850–1853).

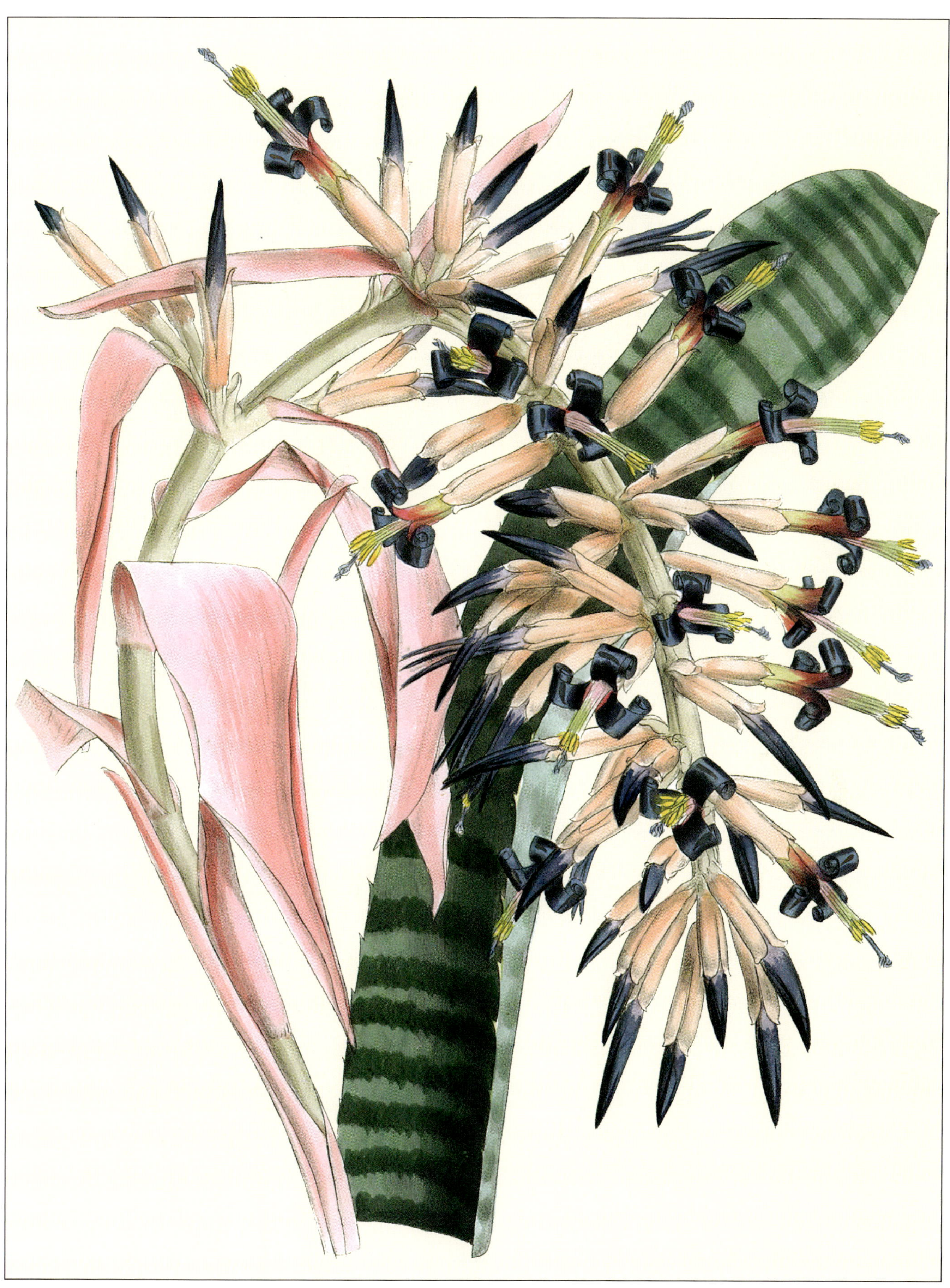

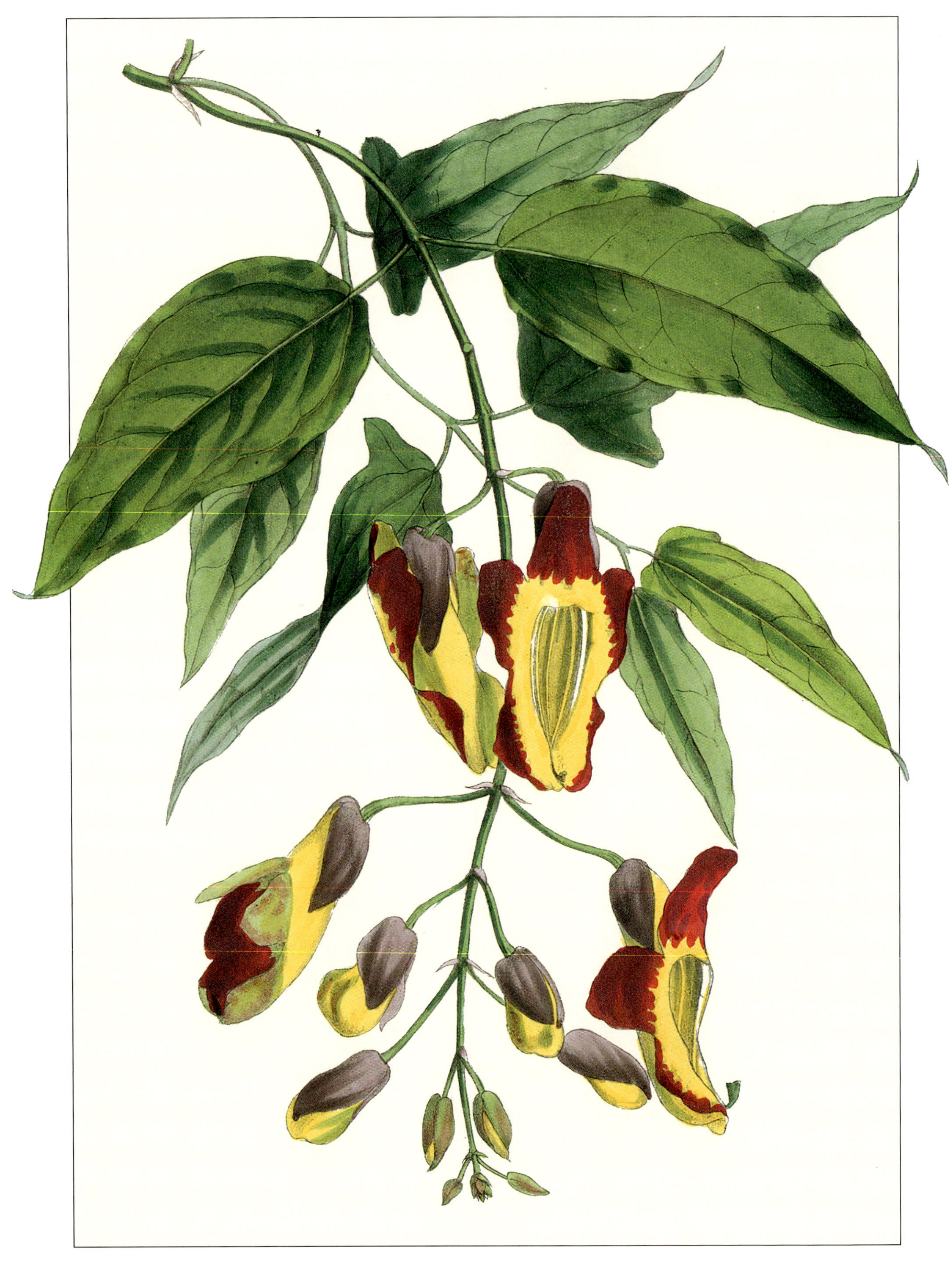

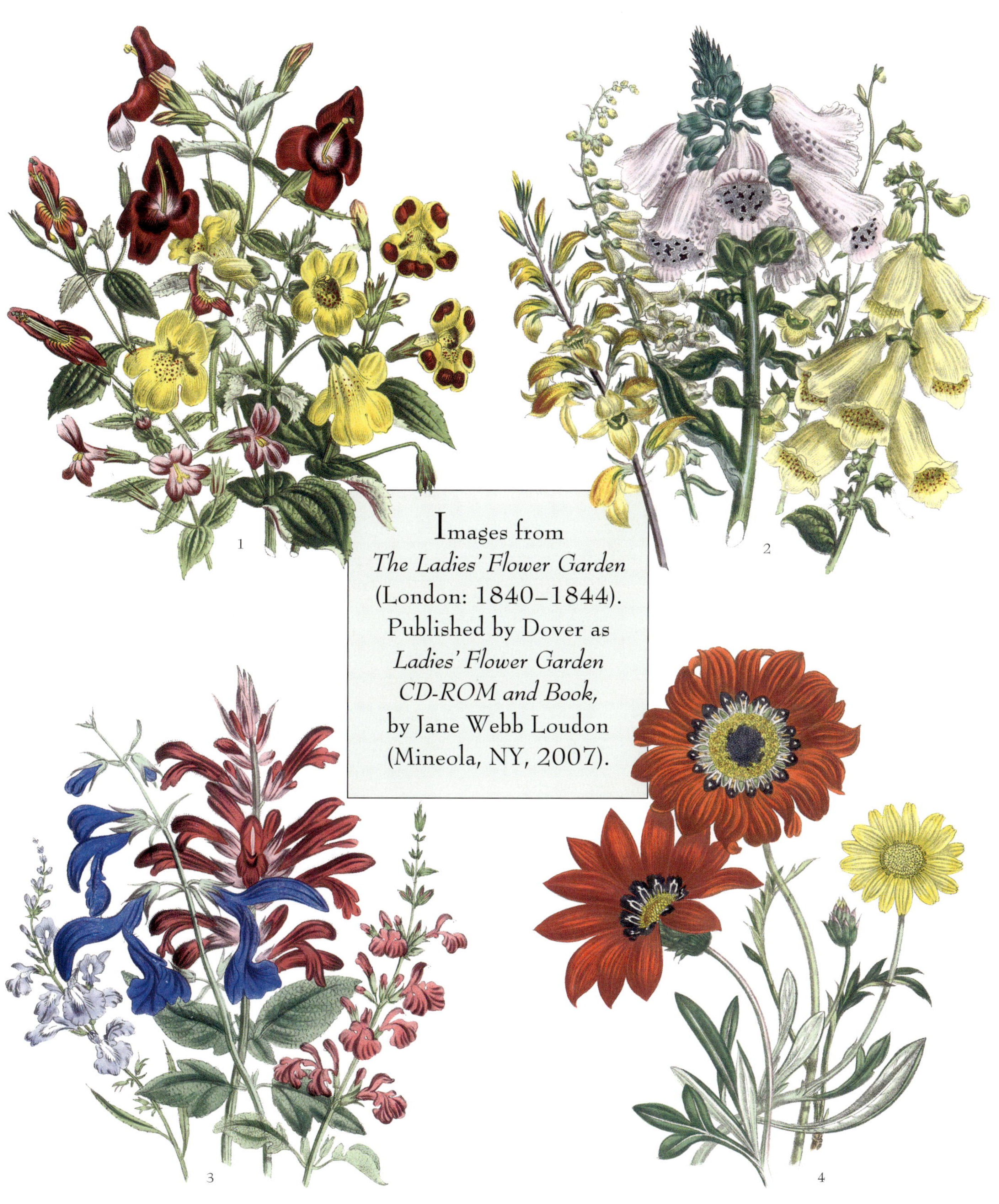

Images from
The Ladies' Flower Garden
(London: 1840–1844).
Published by Dover as
Ladies' Flower Garden
CD-ROM and Book,
by Jane Webb Loudon
(Mineola, NY, 2007).

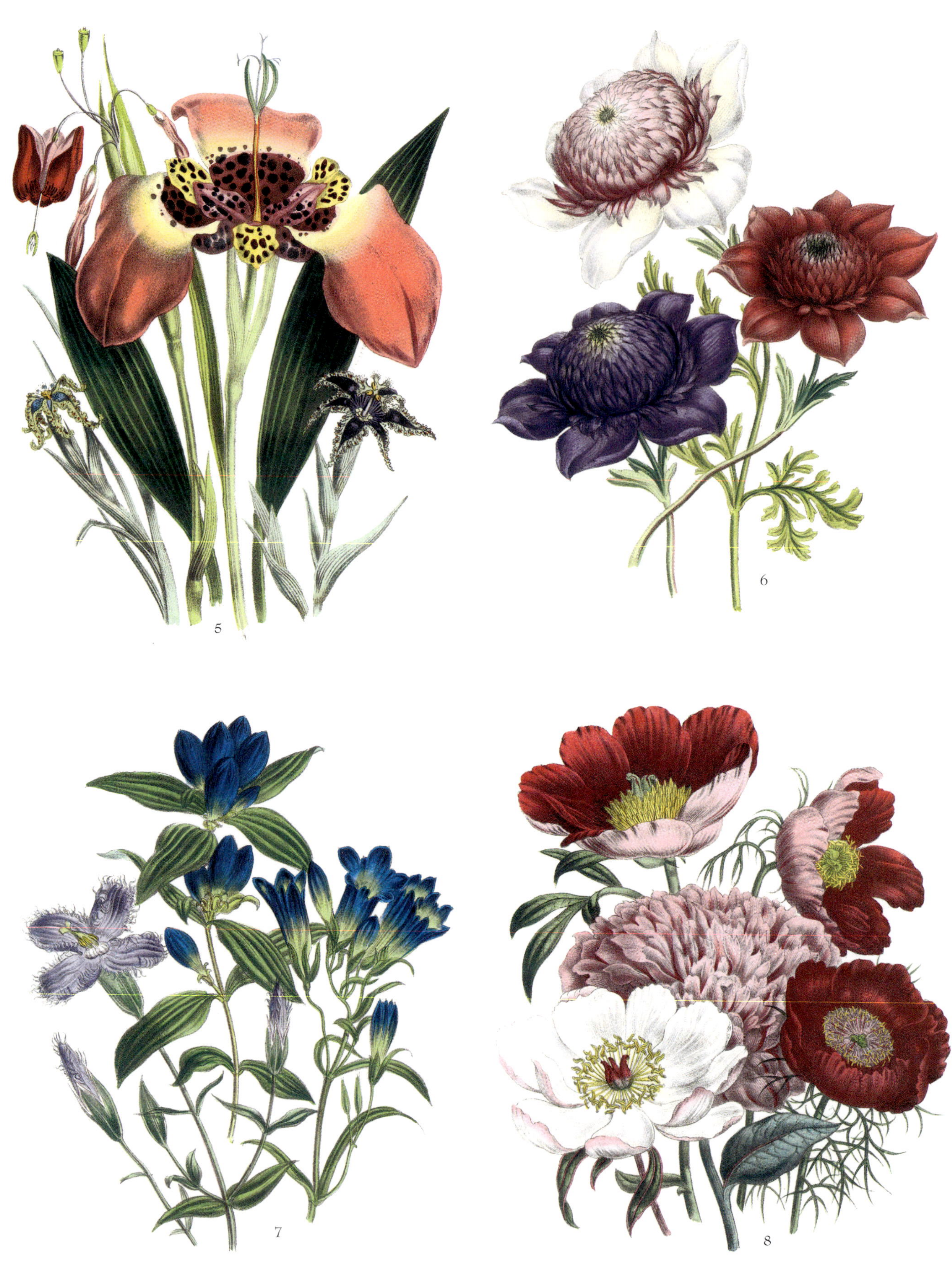
5
6
7
8

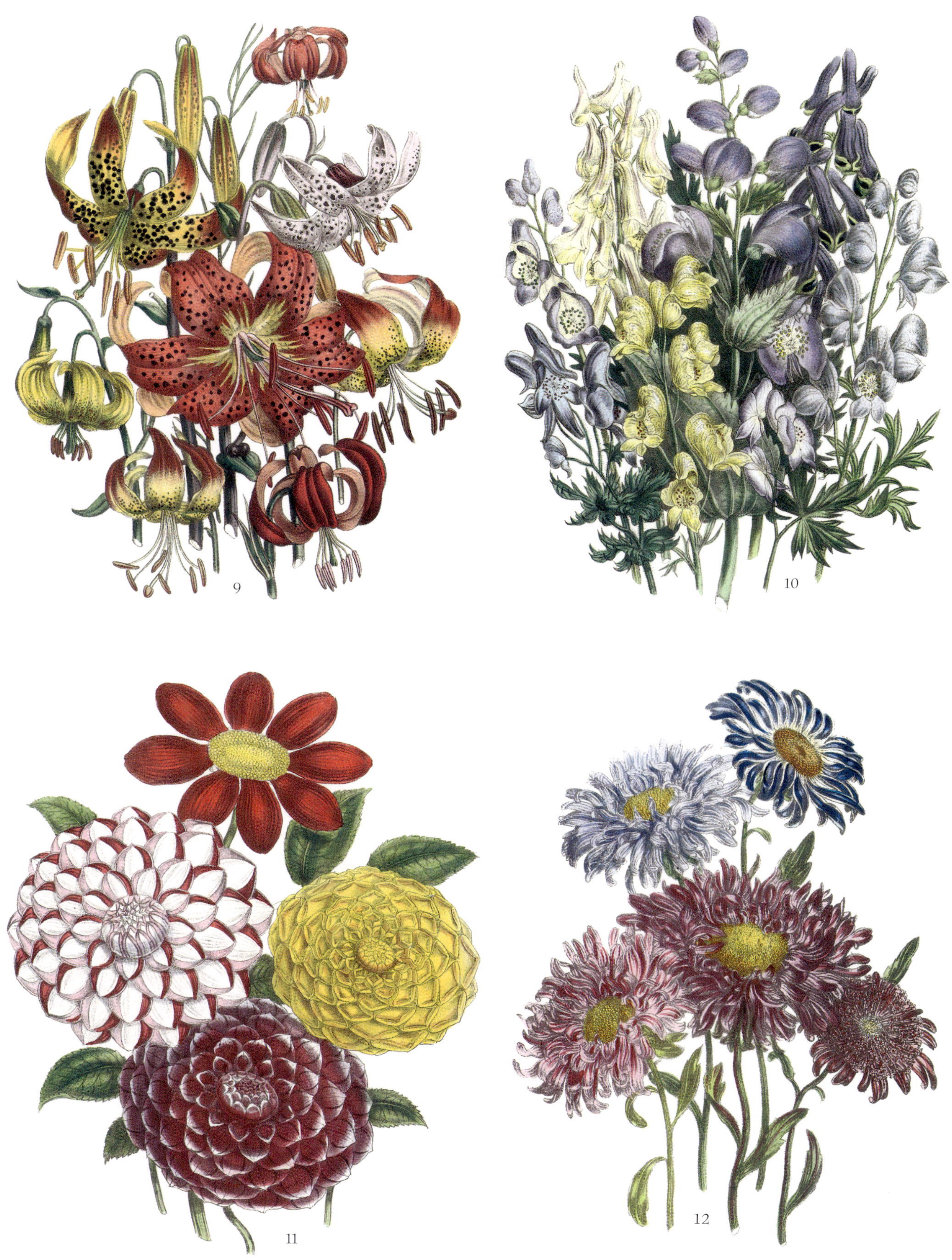
9
10
11
12

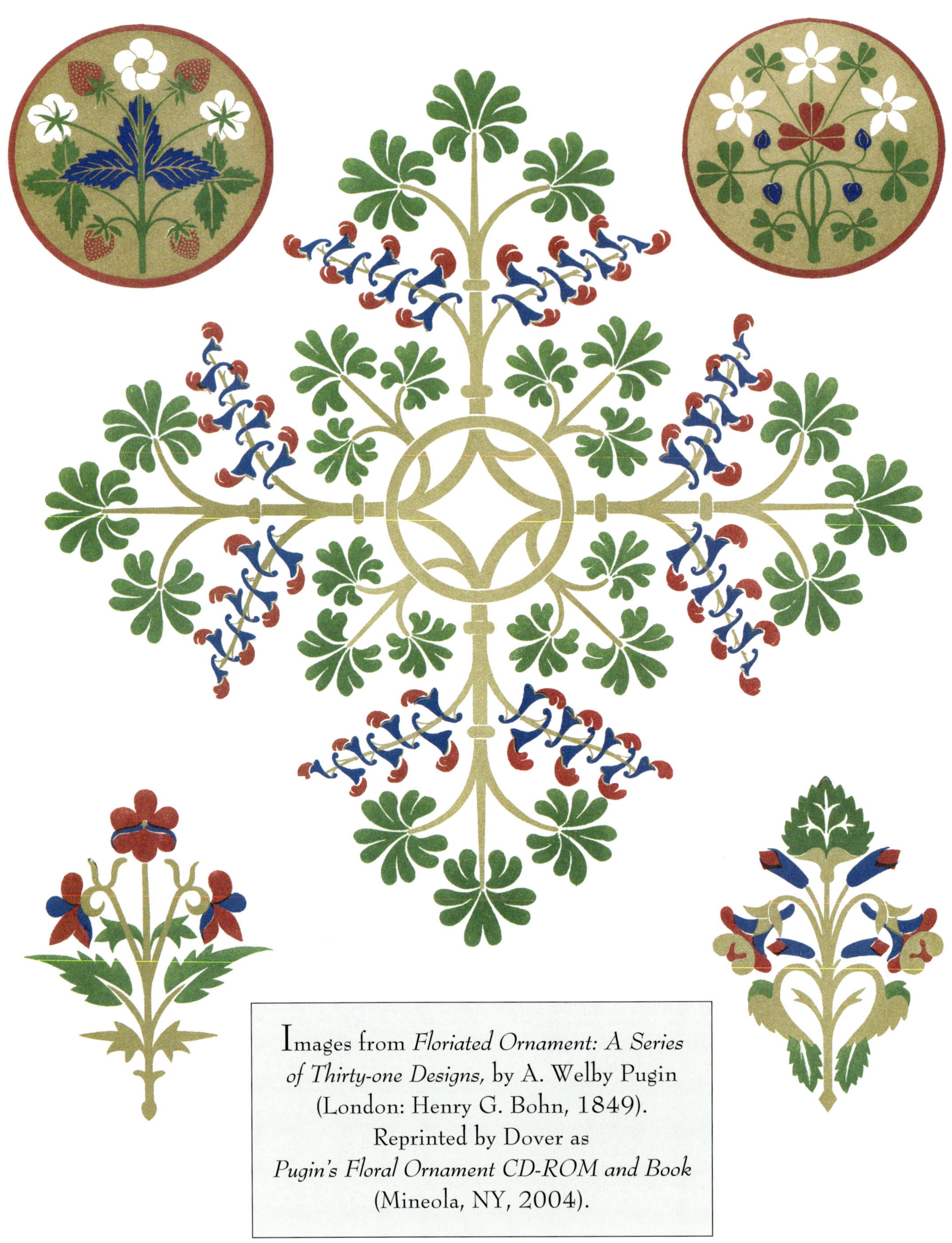

Images from *Floriated Ornament: A Series of Thirty-one Designs,* by A. Welby Pugin (London: Henry G. Bohn, 1849). Reprinted by Dover as *Pugin's Floral Ornament CD-ROM and Book* (Mineola, NY, 2004).

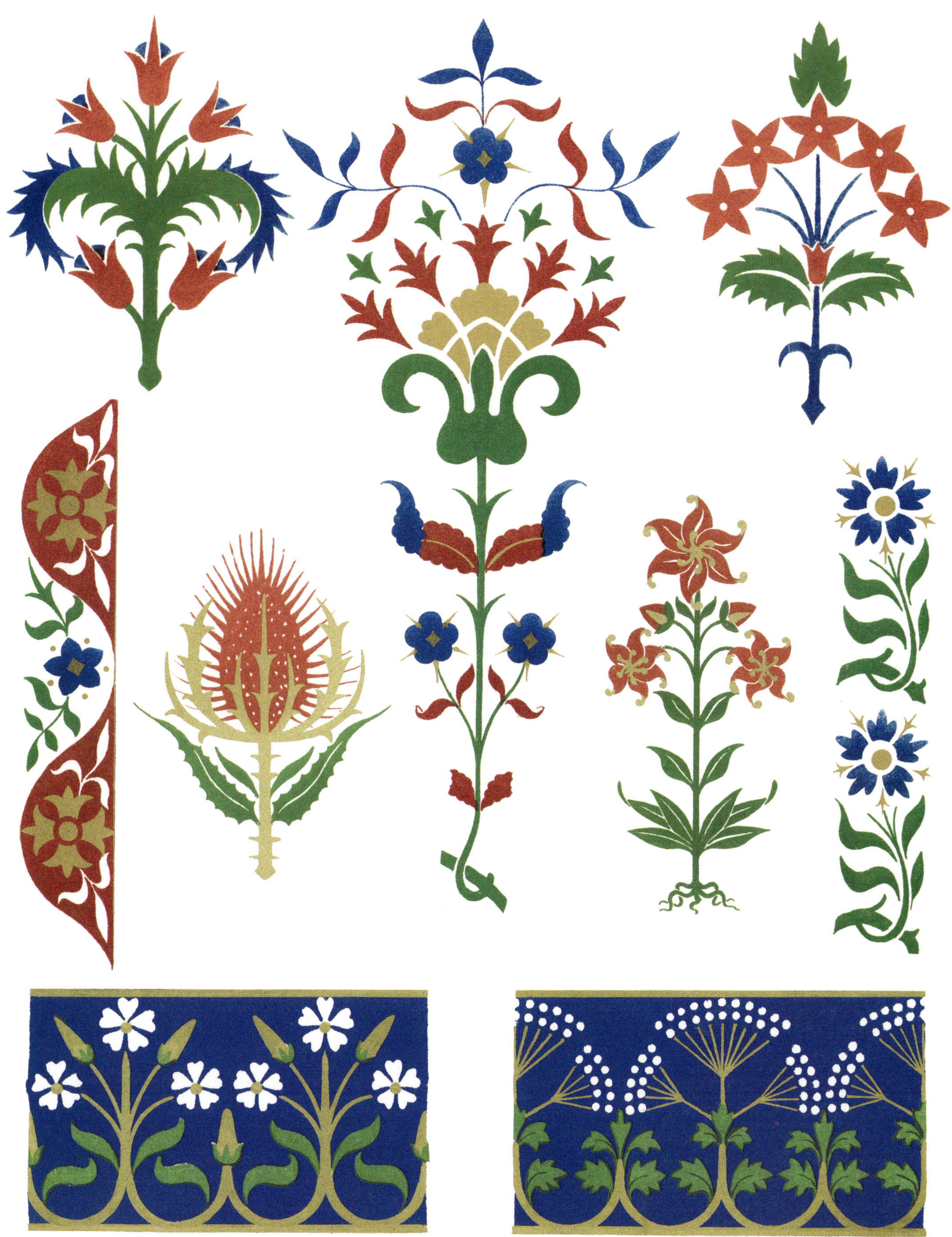

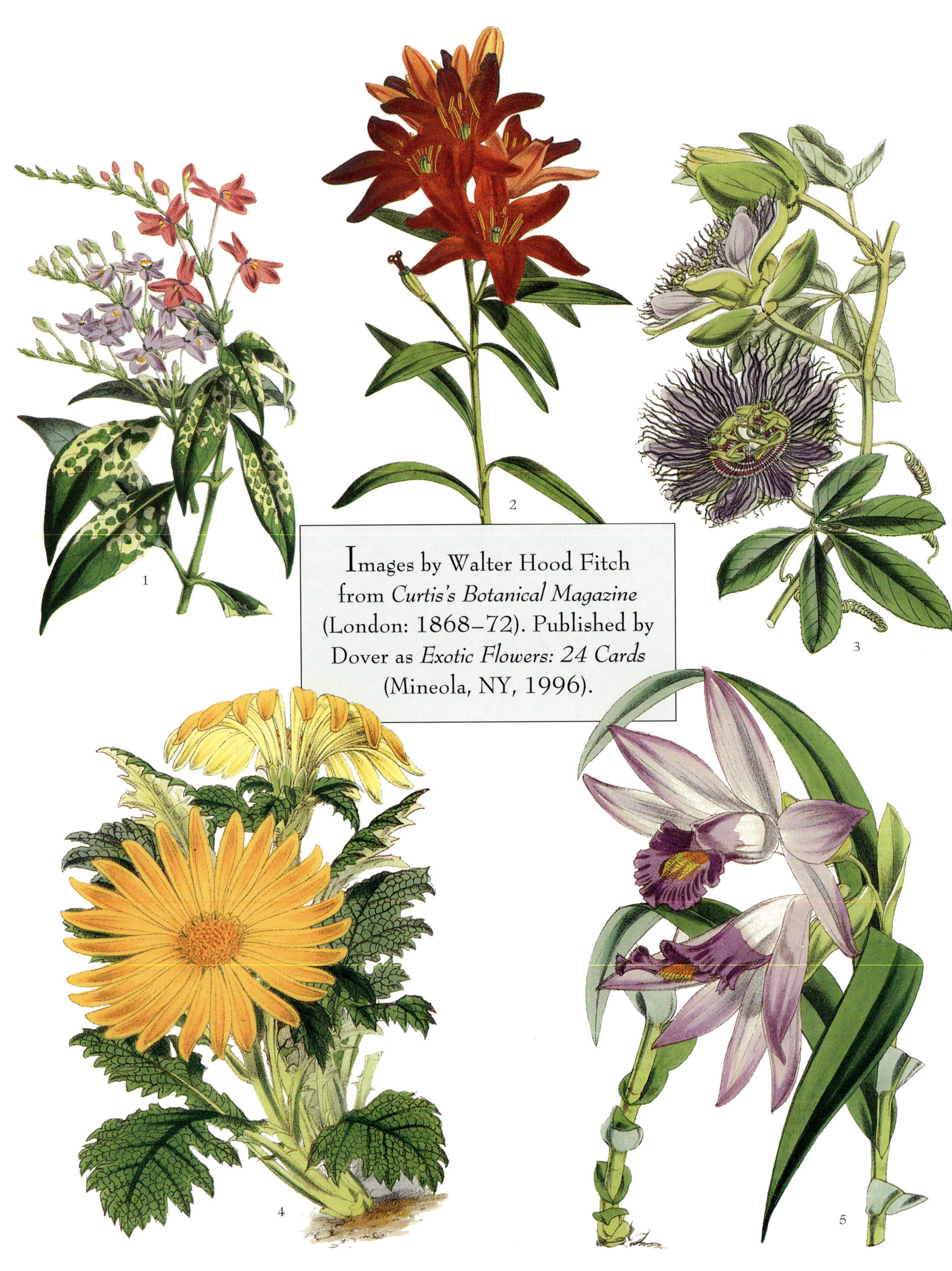

Images by Walter Hood Fitch from *Curtis's Botanical Magazine* (London: 1868–72). Published by Dover as *Exotic Flowers: 24 Cards* (Mineola, NY, 1996).

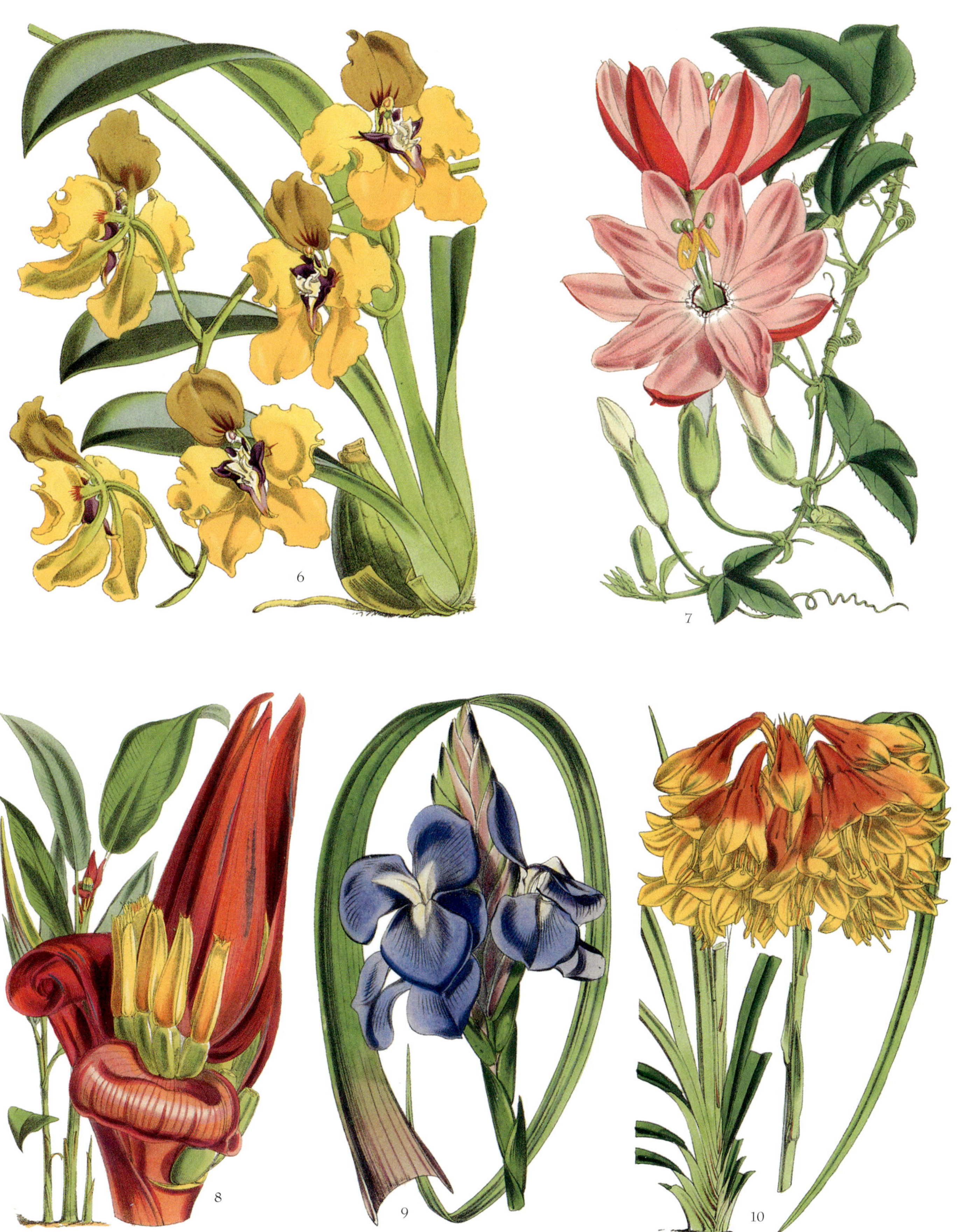
6
7
8
9
10

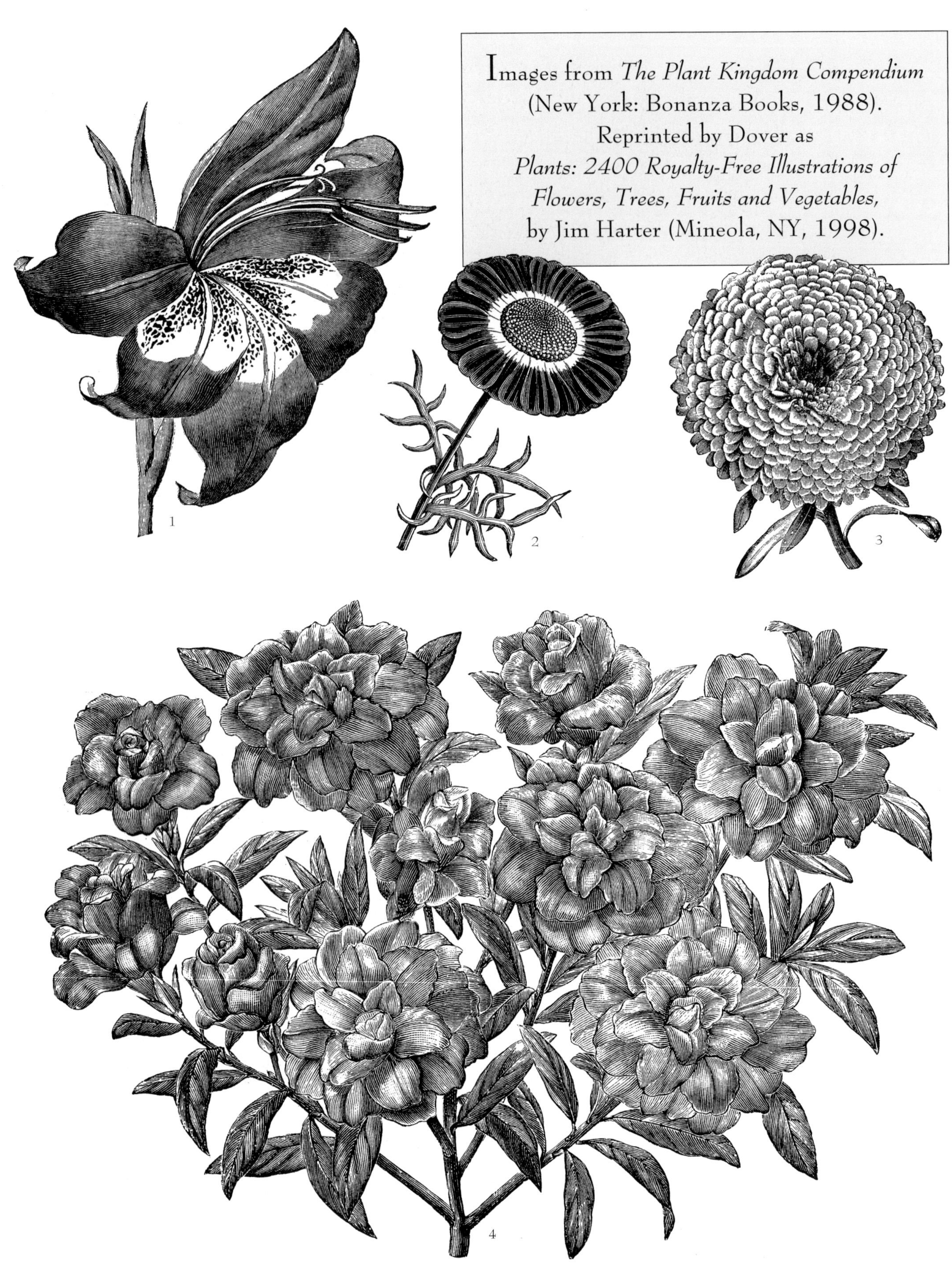

Images from *The Plant Kingdom Compendium* (New York: Bonanza Books, 1988). Reprinted by Dover as *Plants: 2400 Royalty-Free Illustrations of Flowers, Trees, Fruits and Vegetables*, by Jim Harter (Mineola, NY, 1998).

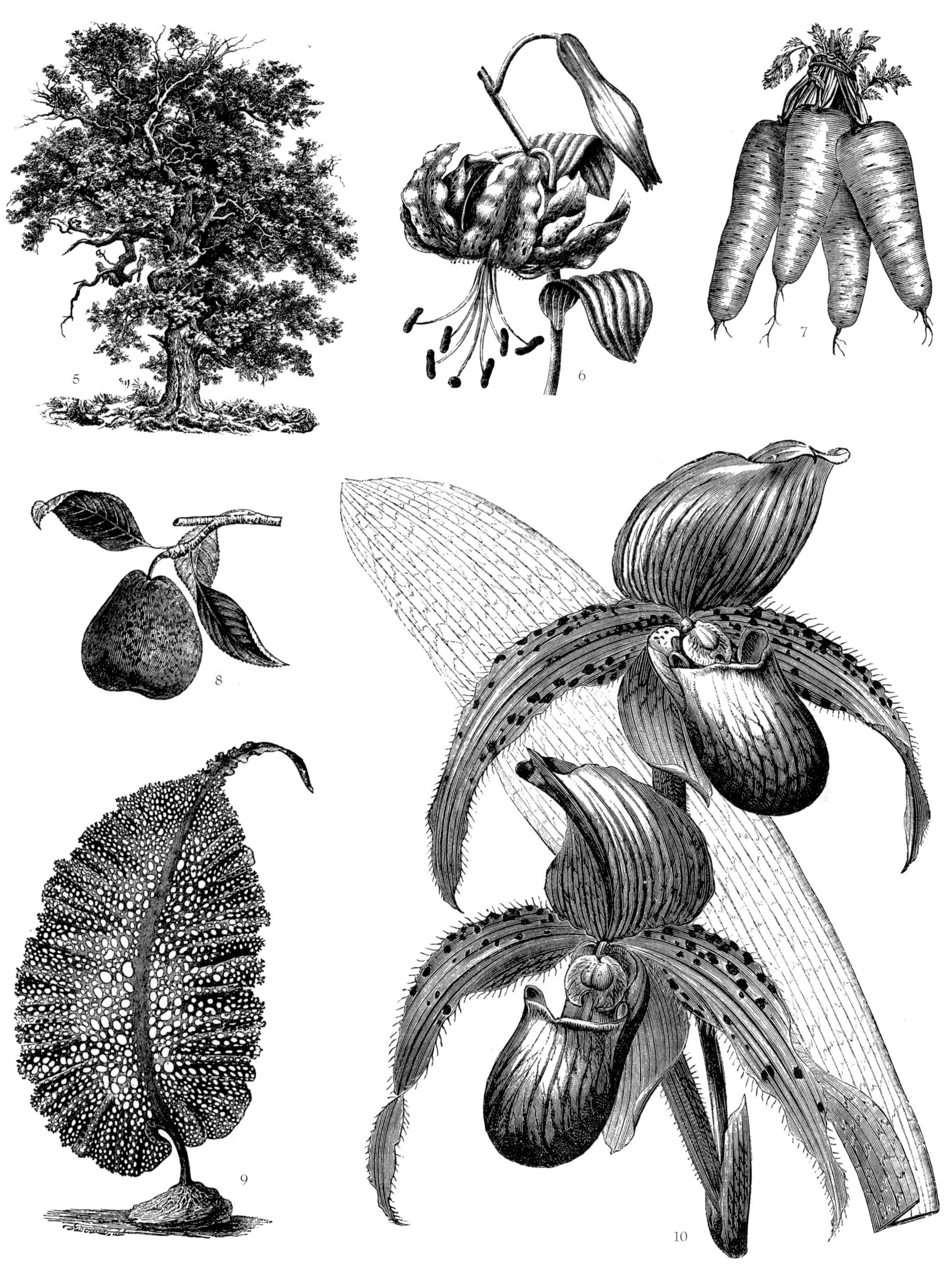
5
6
7
8
9
10

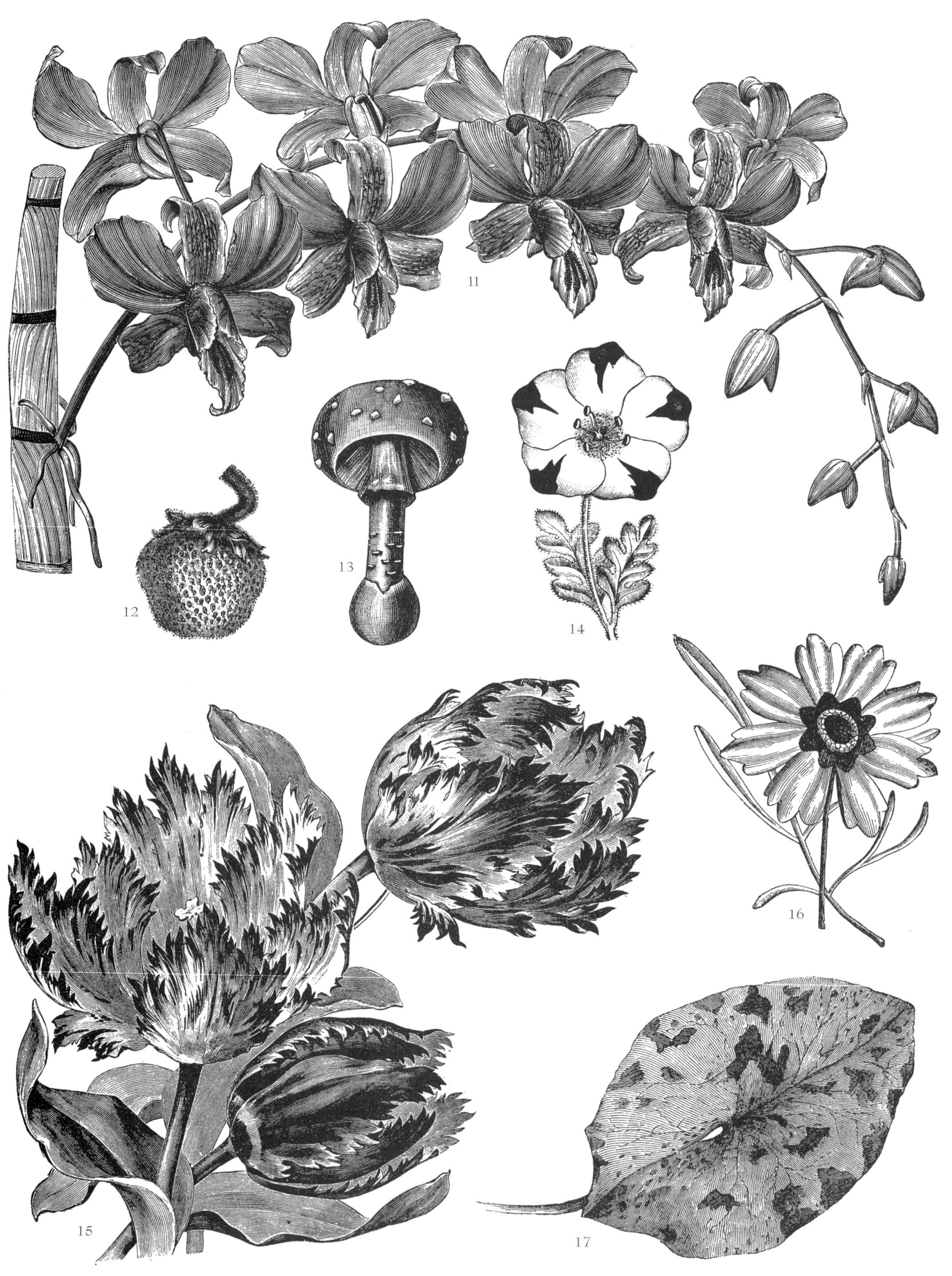
11
12
13
14
16
15
17

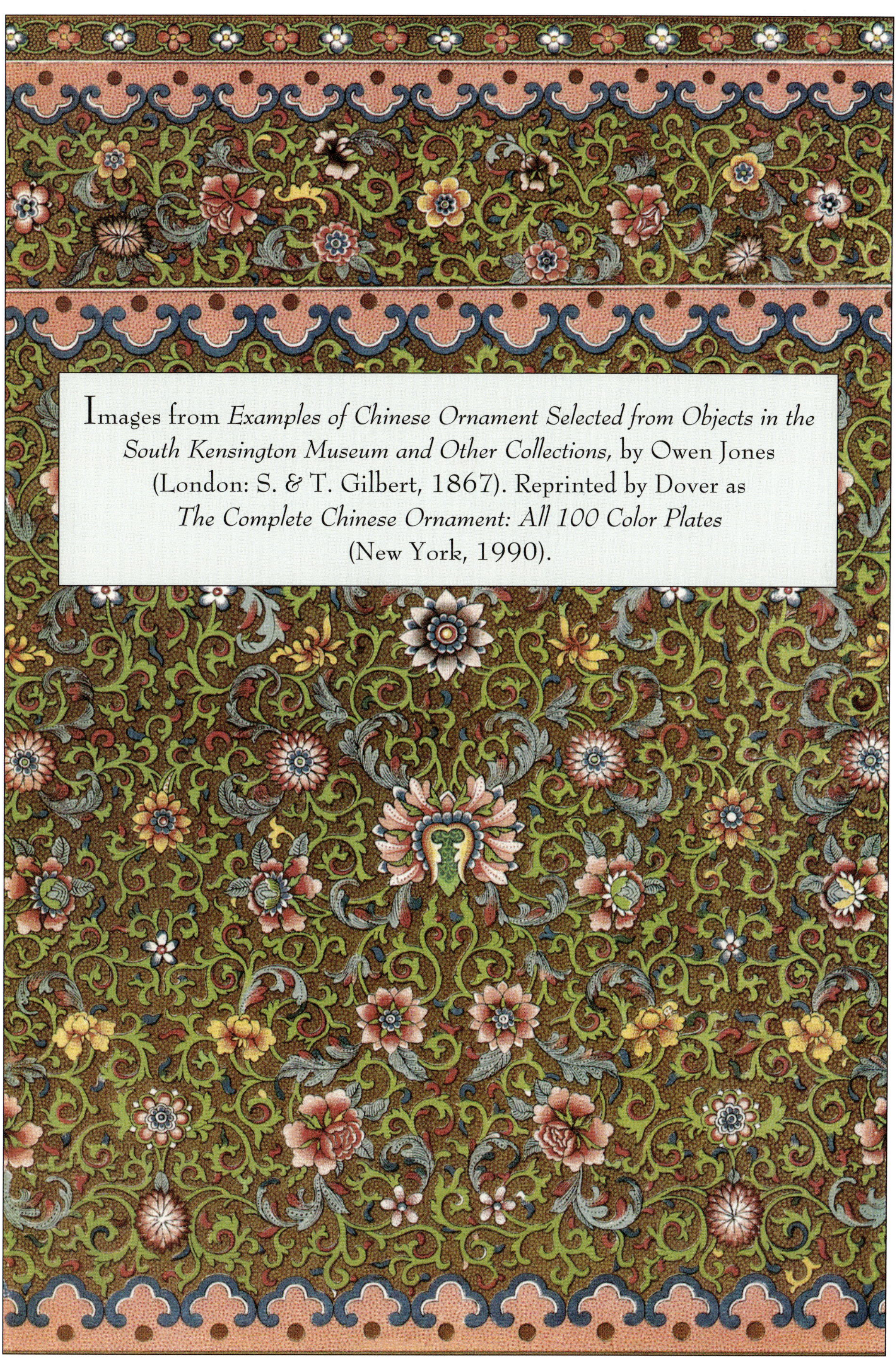

Images from *Examples of Chinese Ornament Selected from Objects in the South Kensington Museum and Other Collections,* by Owen Jones (London: S. & T. Gilbert, 1867). Reprinted by Dover as *The Complete Chinese Ornament: All 100 Color Plates* (New York, 1990).

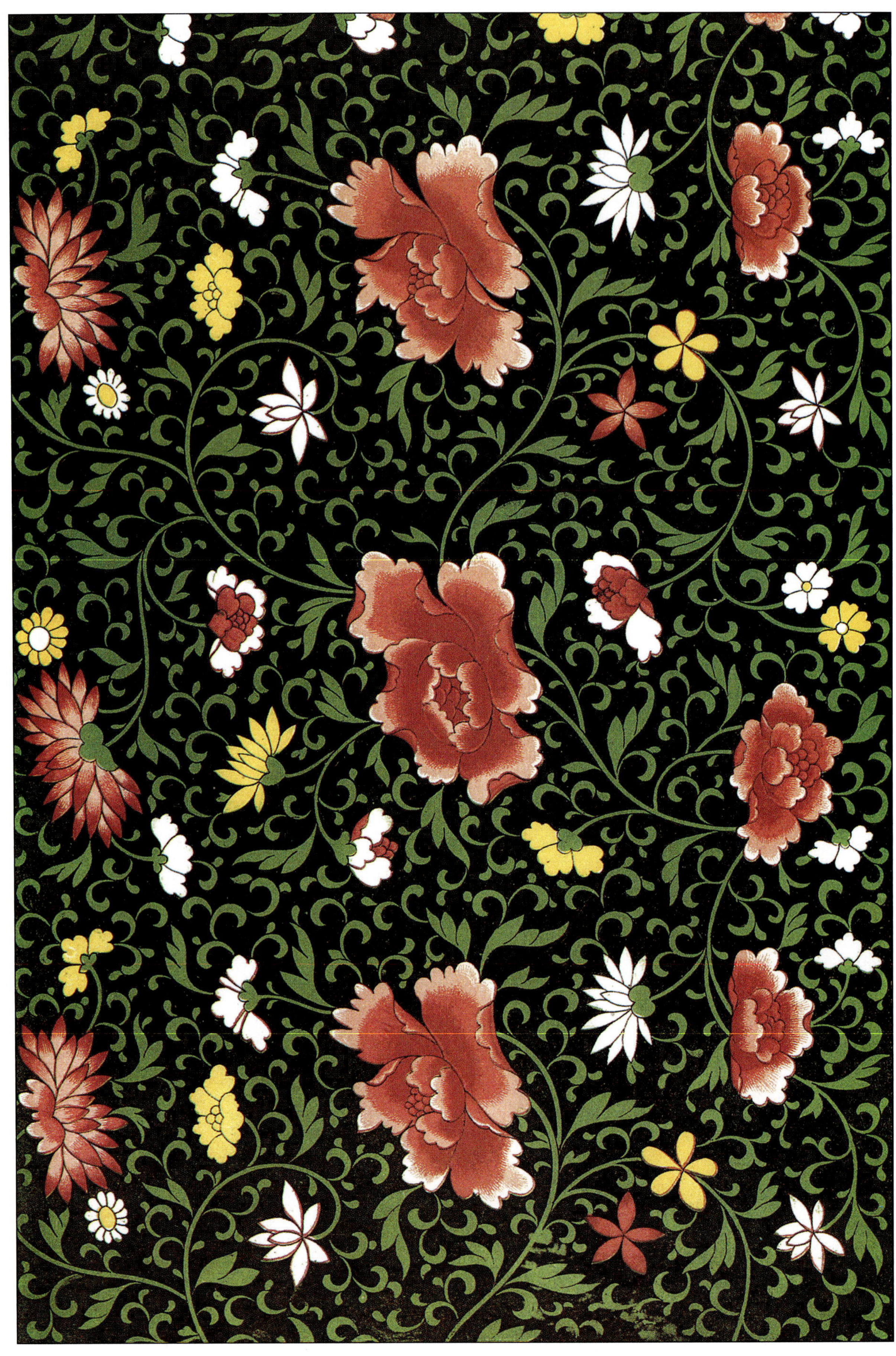

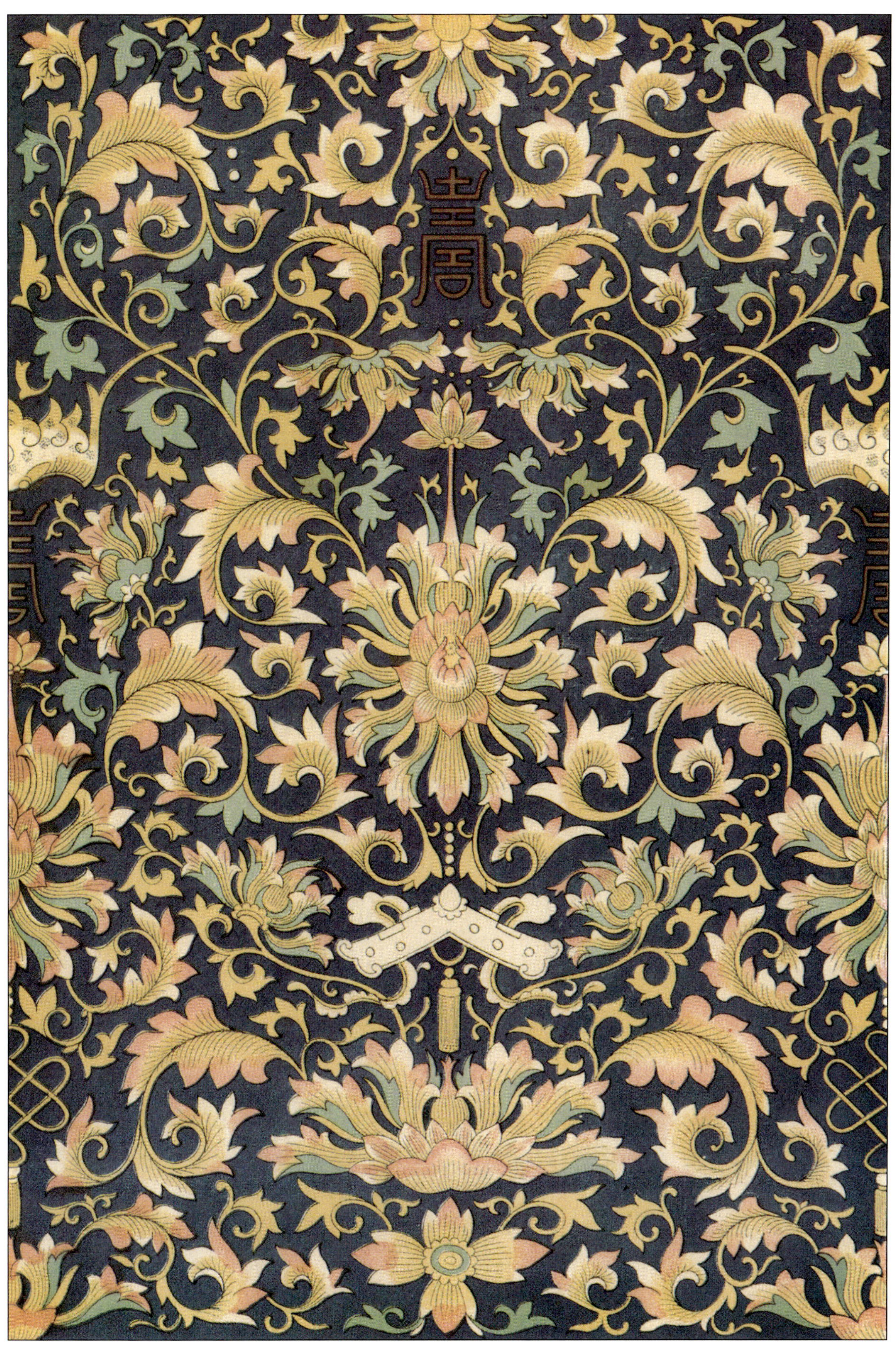

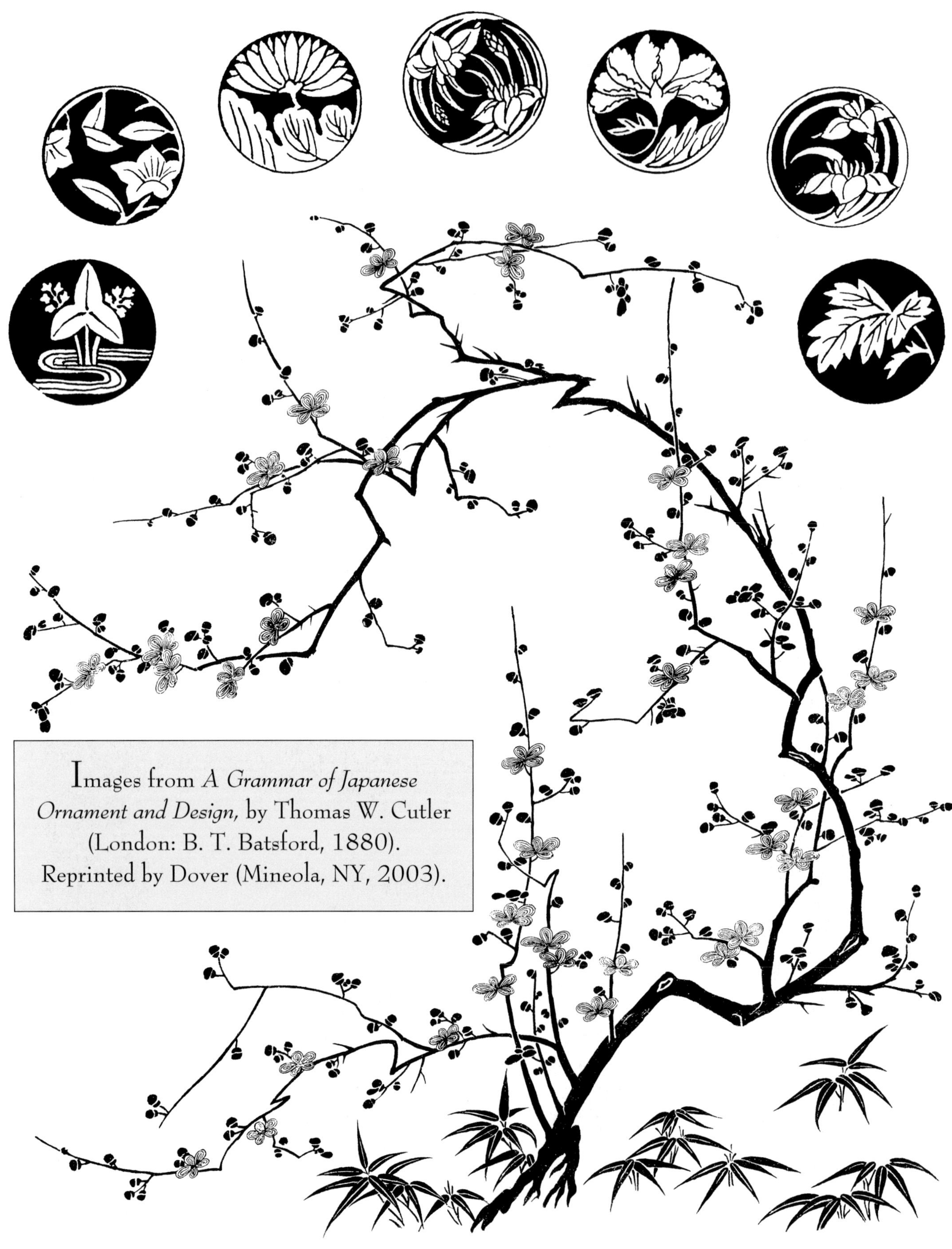

Images from *A Grammar of Japanese Ornament and Design*, by Thomas W. Cutler (London: B. T. Batsford, 1880). Reprinted by Dover (Mineola, NY, 2003).

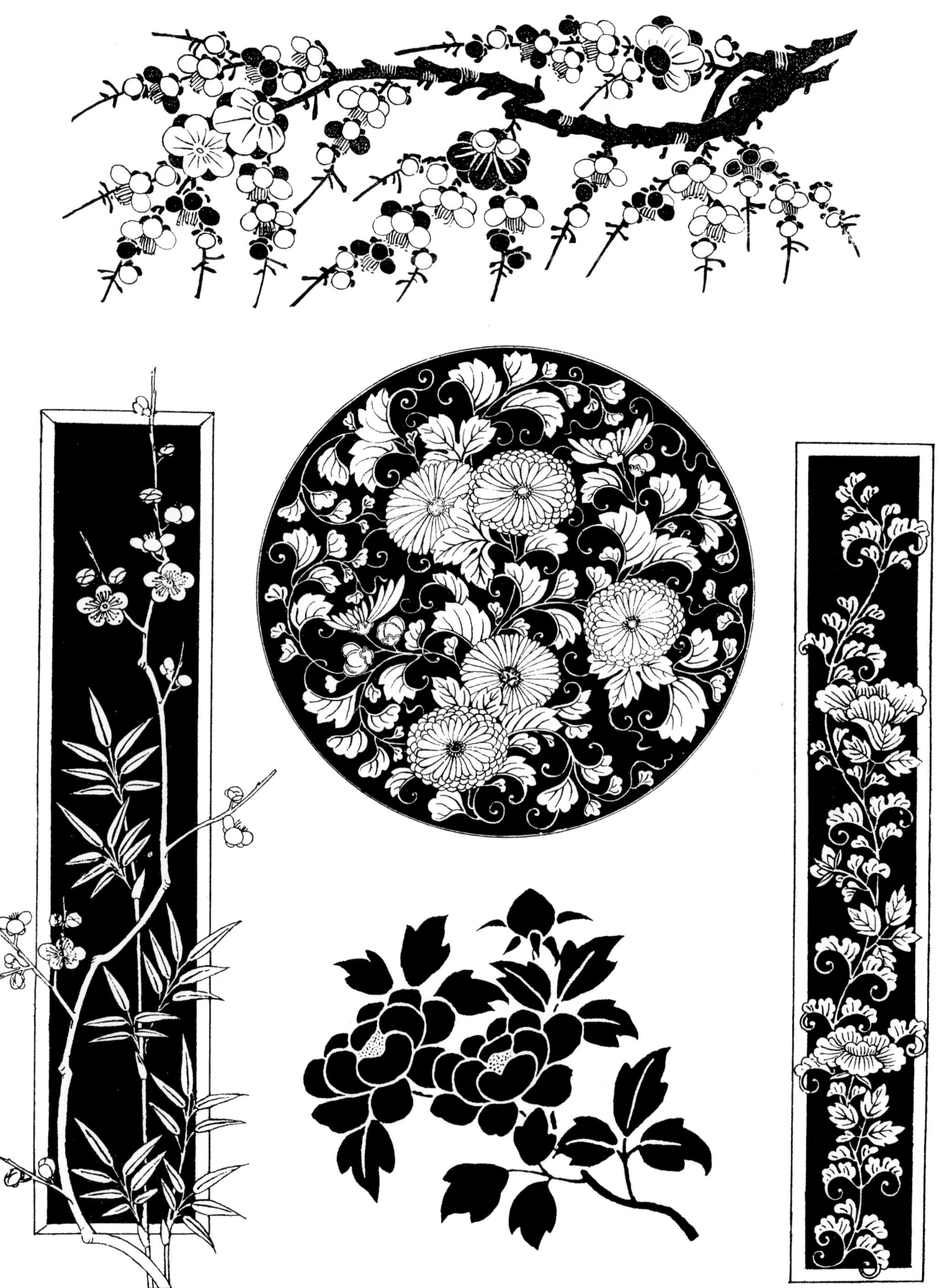

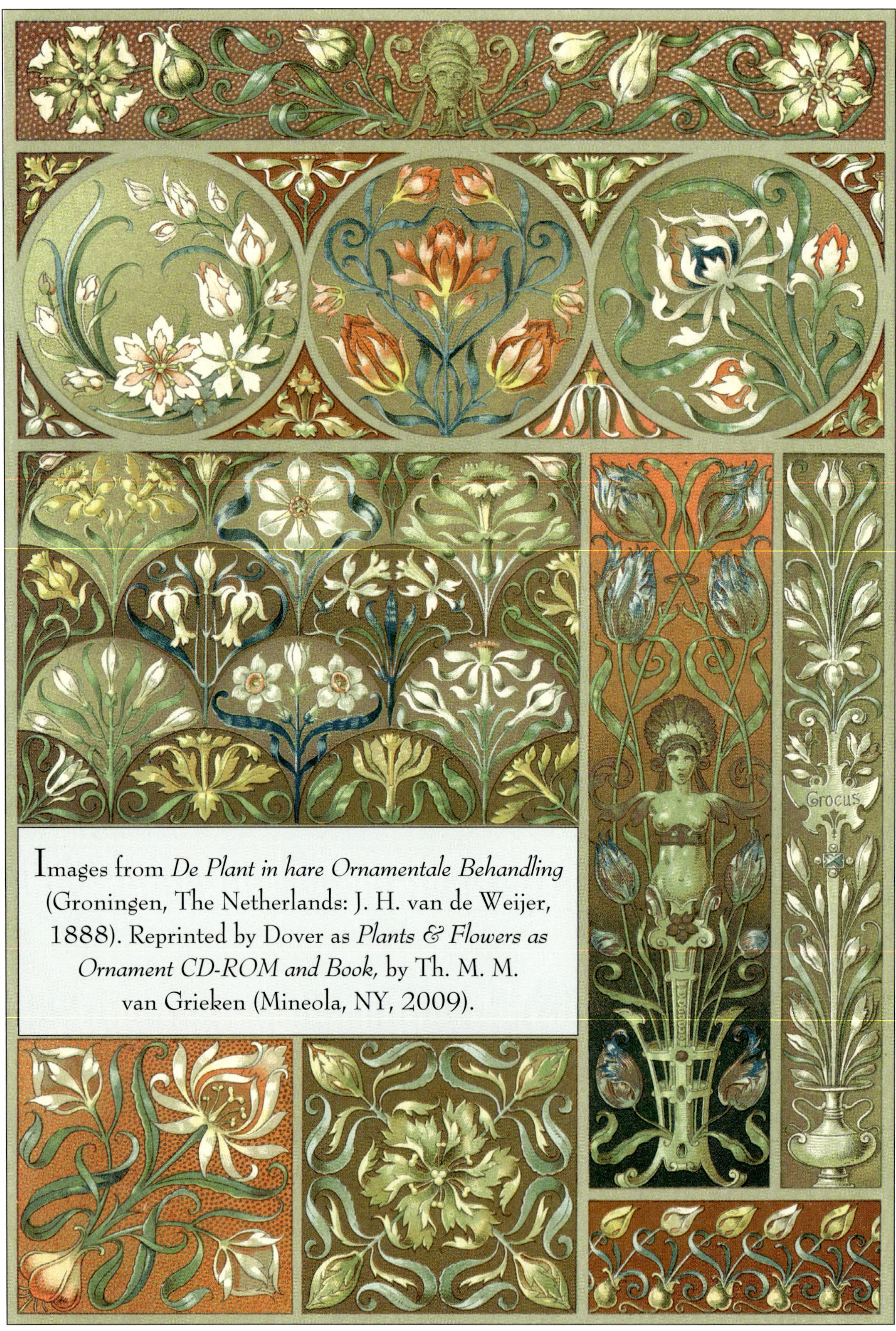

Images from *De Plant in hare Ornamentale Behandling* (Groningen, The Netherlands: J. H. van de Weijer, 1888). Reprinted by Dover as *Plants & Flowers as Ornament CD-ROM and Book,* by Th. M. M. van Grieken (Mineola, NY, 2009).

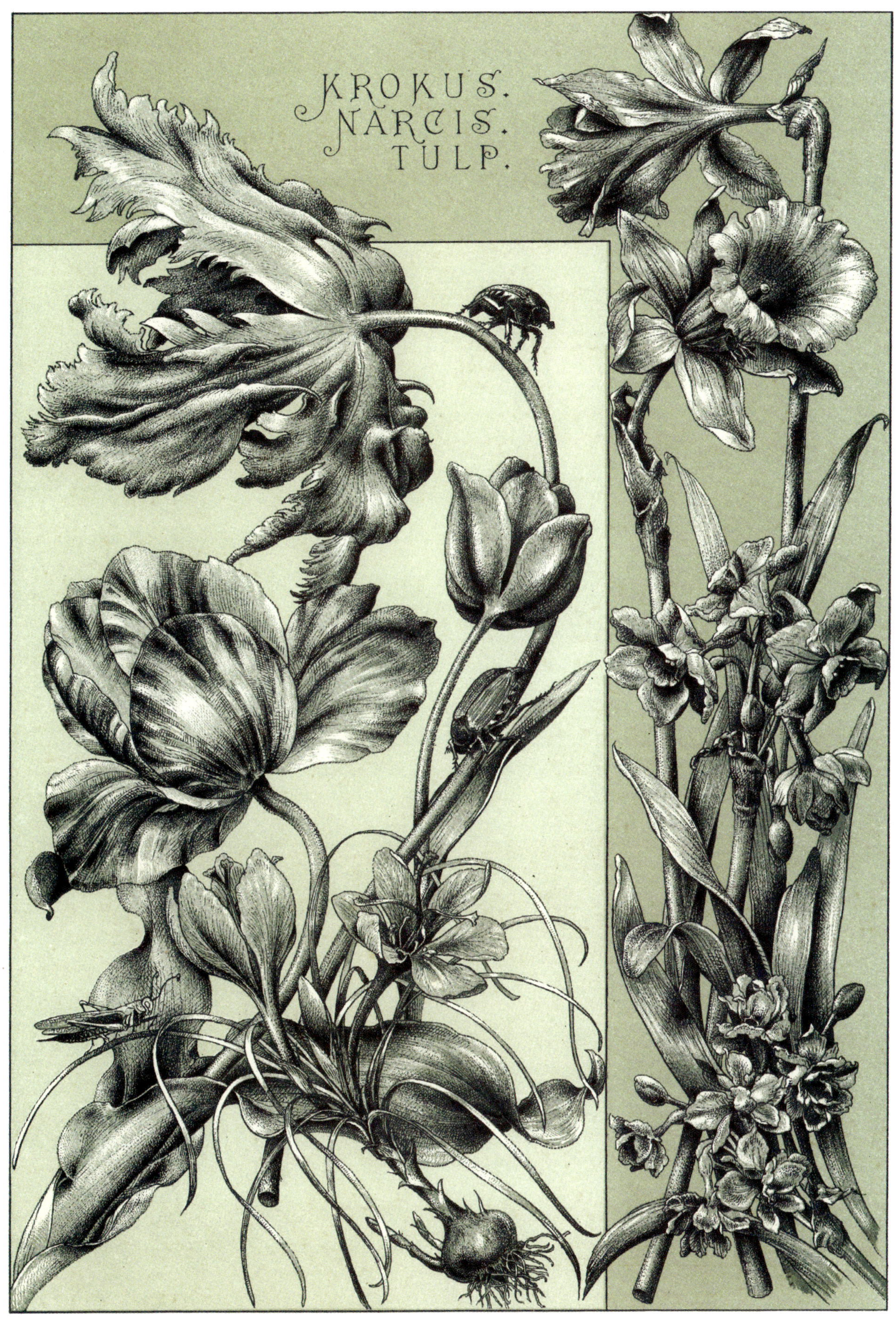
KROKUS.
NARCIS.
TULP.

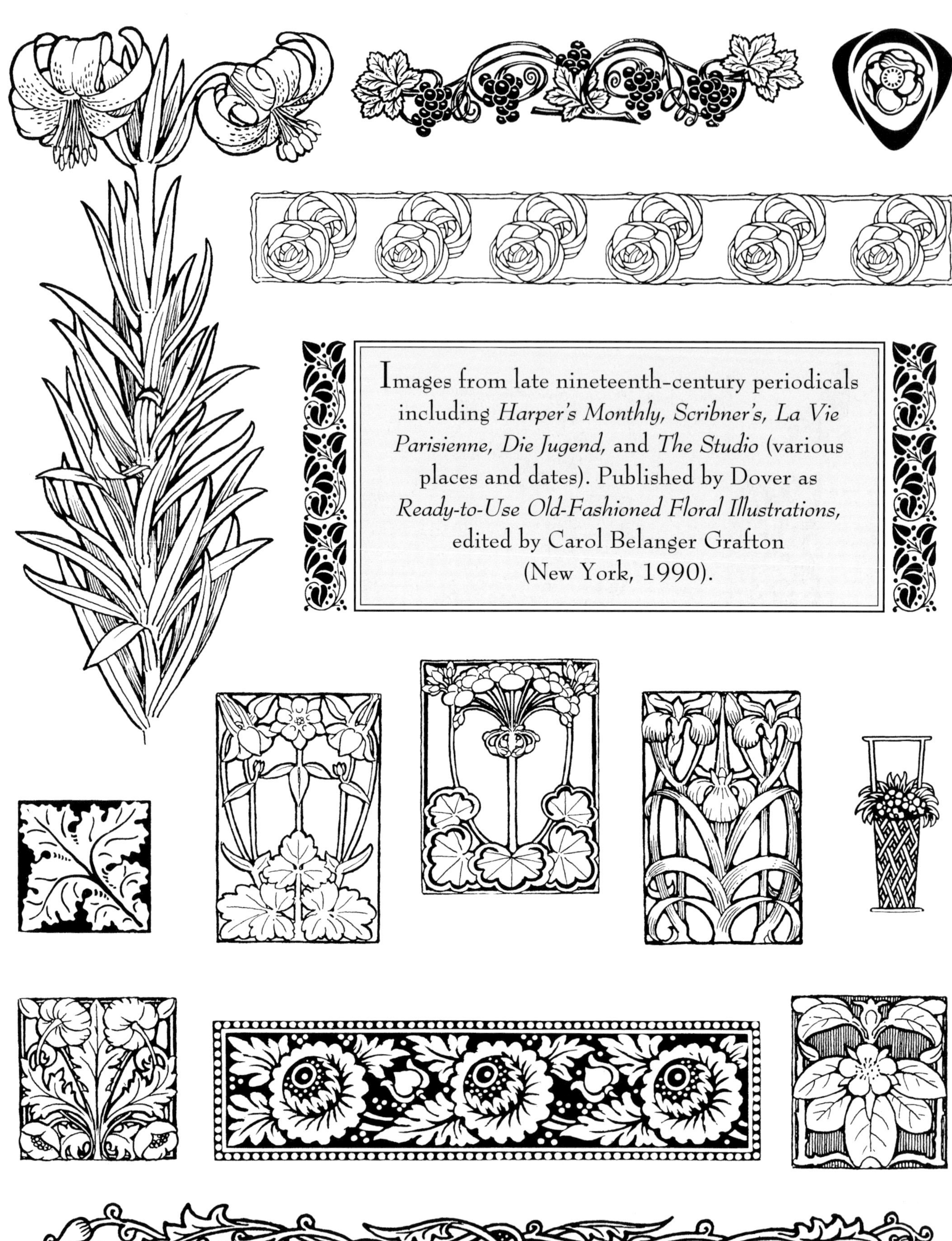

Images from late nineteenth-century periodicals including *Harper's Monthly, Scribner's, La Vie Parisienne, Die Jugend,* and *The Studio* (various places and dates). Published by Dover as *Ready-to-Use Old-Fashioned Floral Illustrations,* edited by Carol Belanger Grafton (New York, 1990).

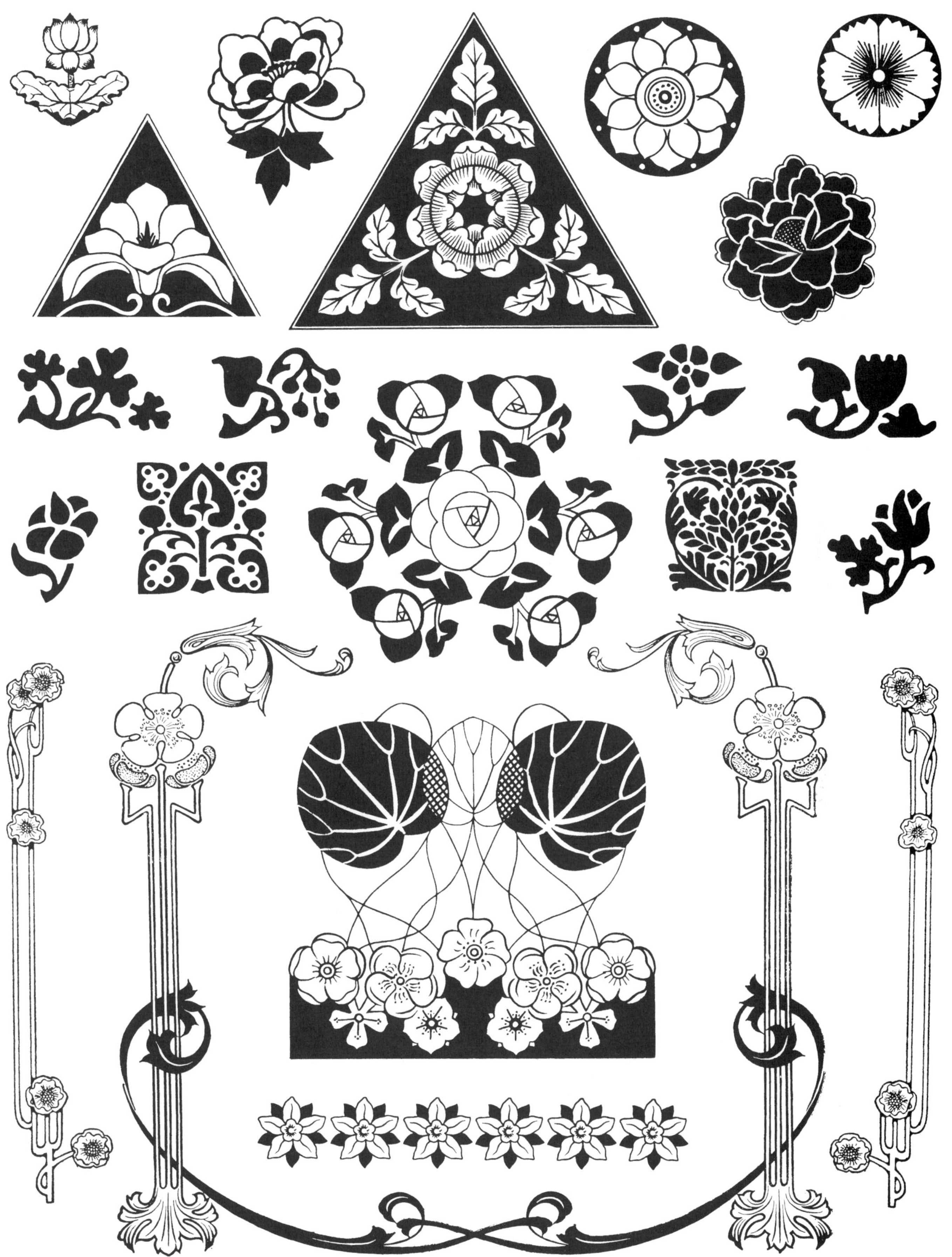

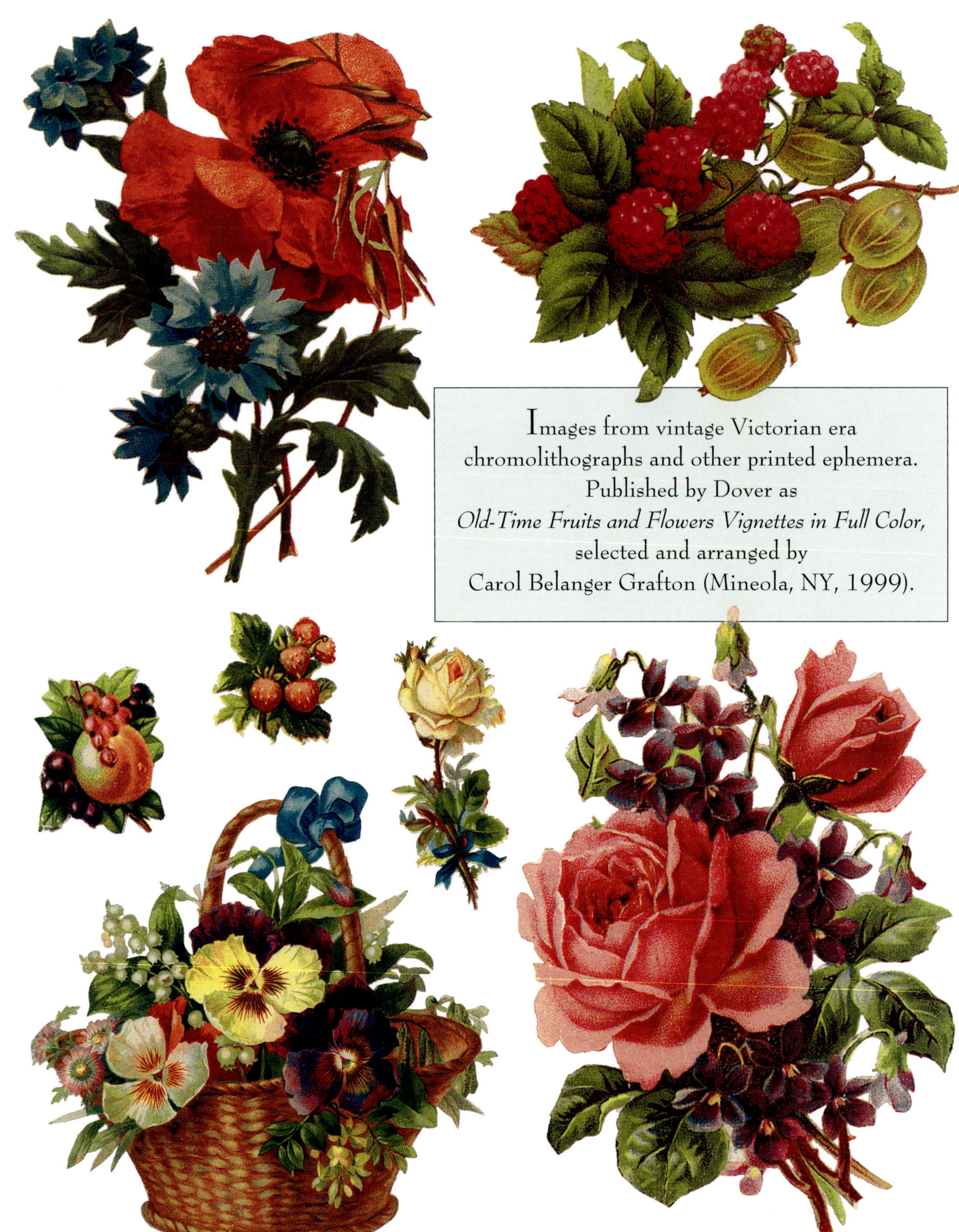

Images from vintage Victorian era chromolithographs and other printed ephemera. Published by Dover as *Old-Time Fruits and Flowers Vignettes in Full Color,* selected and arranged by Carol Belanger Grafton (Mineola, NY, 1999).

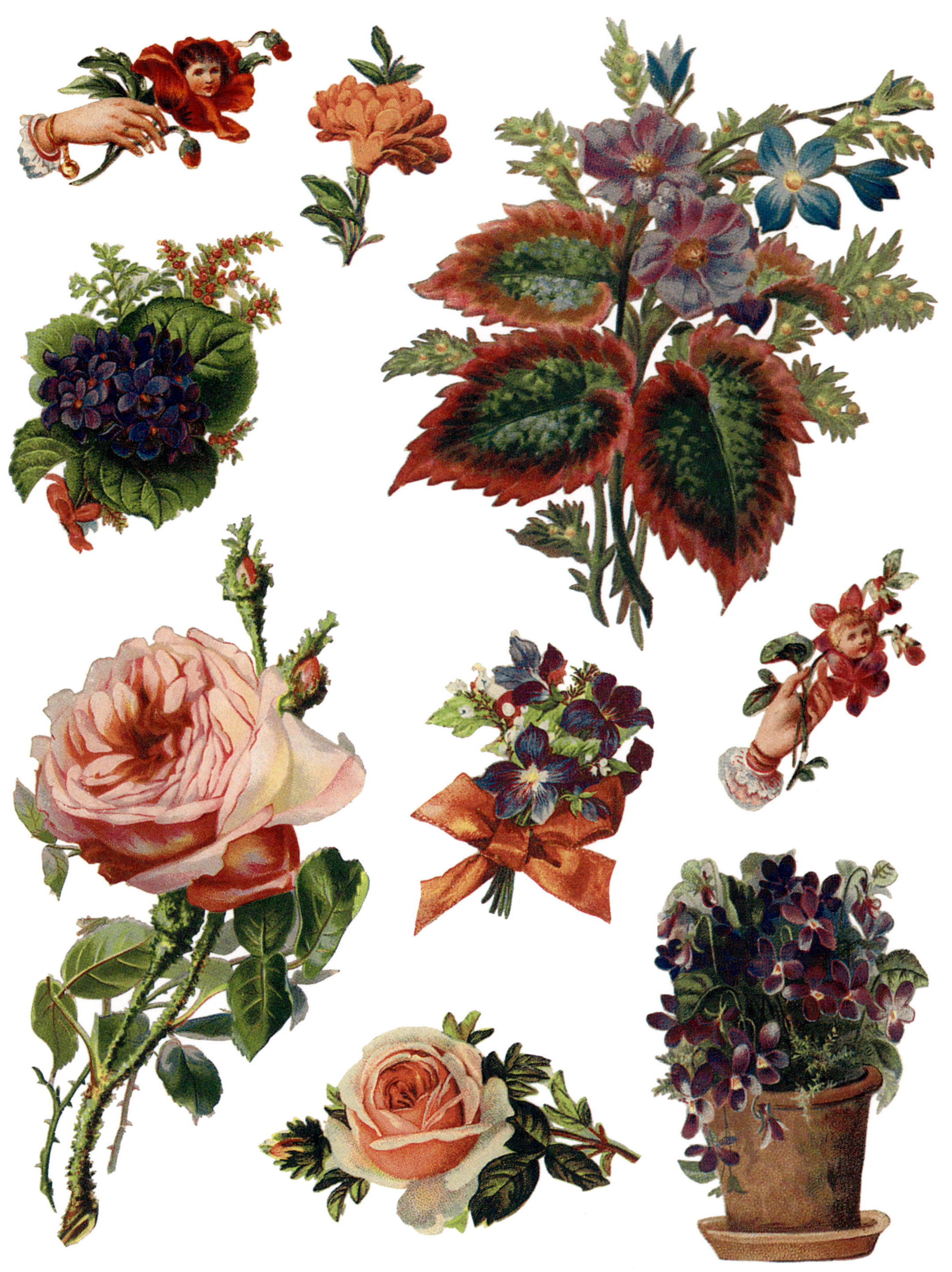

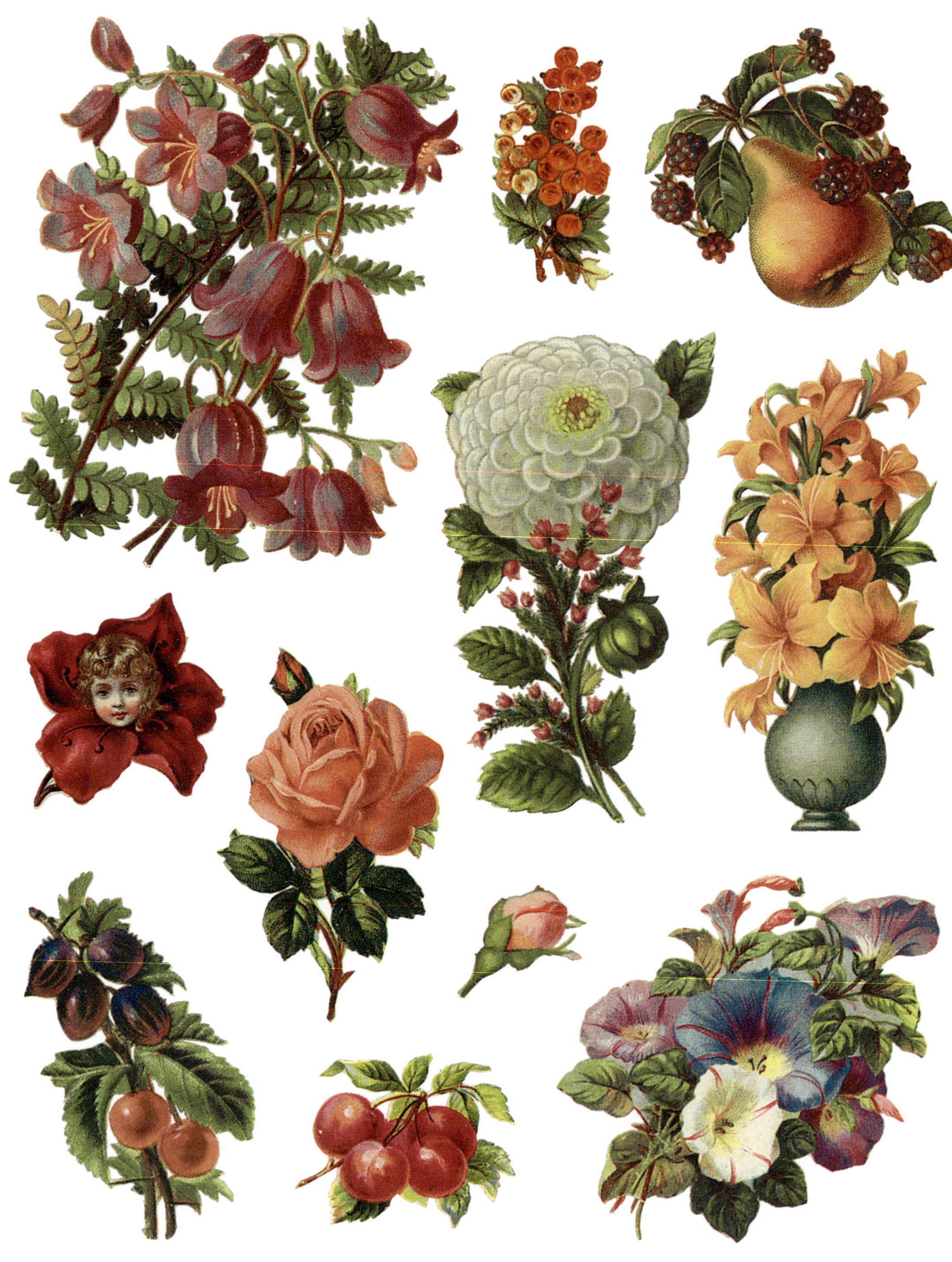

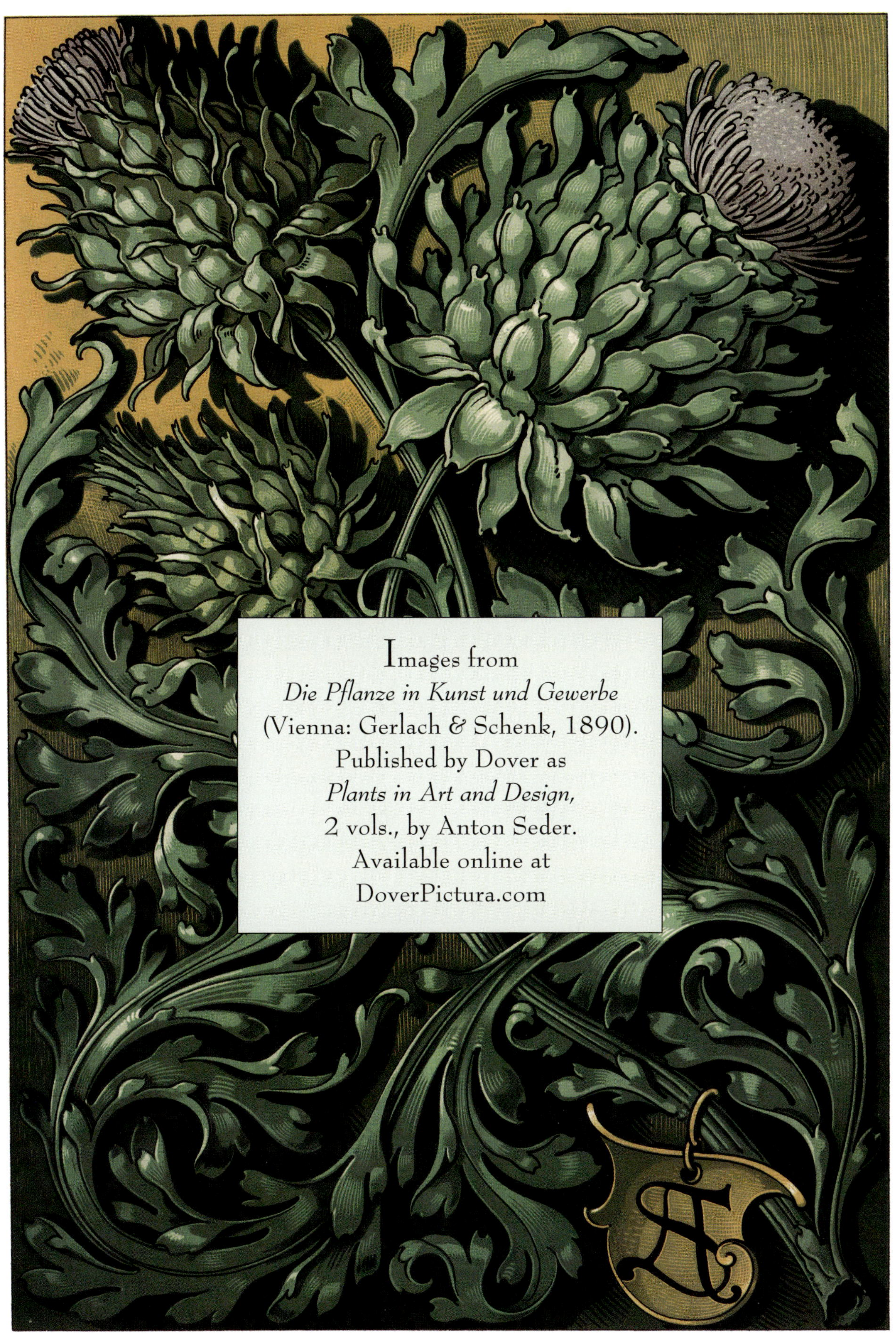
Images from
Die Pflanze in Kunst und Gewerbe
(Vienna: Gerlach & Schenk, 1890).
Published by Dover as
Plants in Art and Design,
2 vols., by Anton Seder.
Available online at
DoverPictura.com

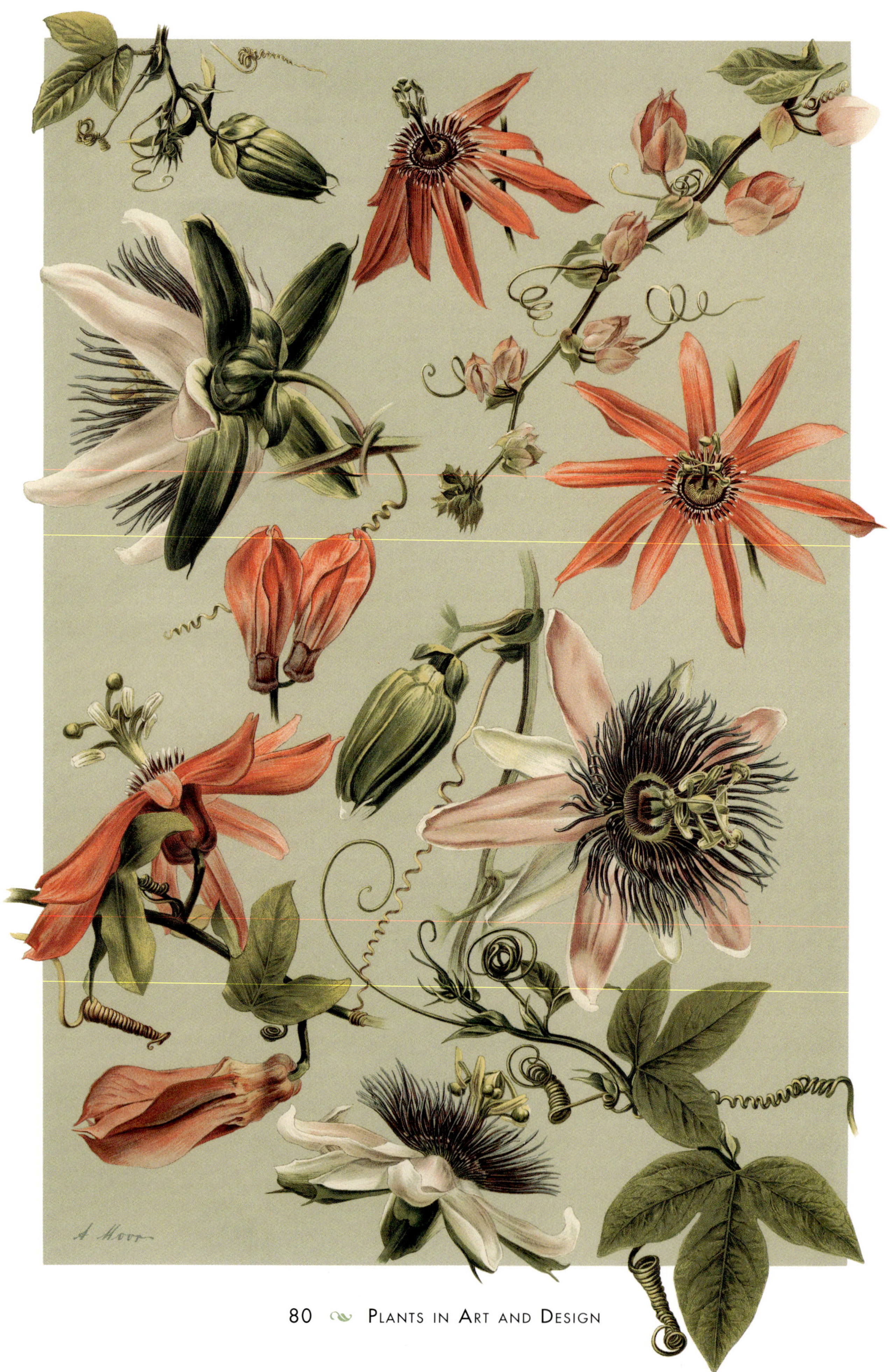
A. Moor

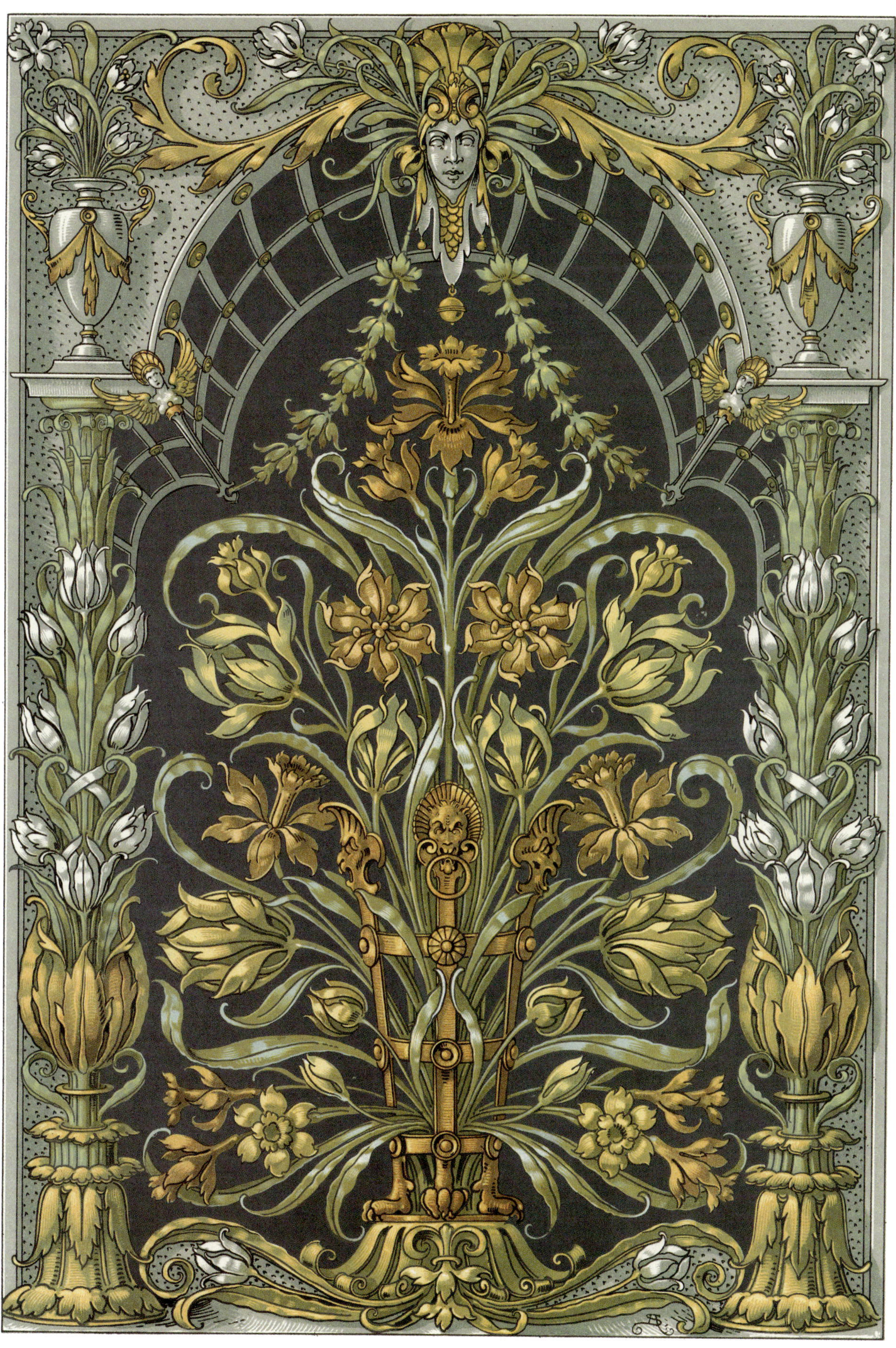

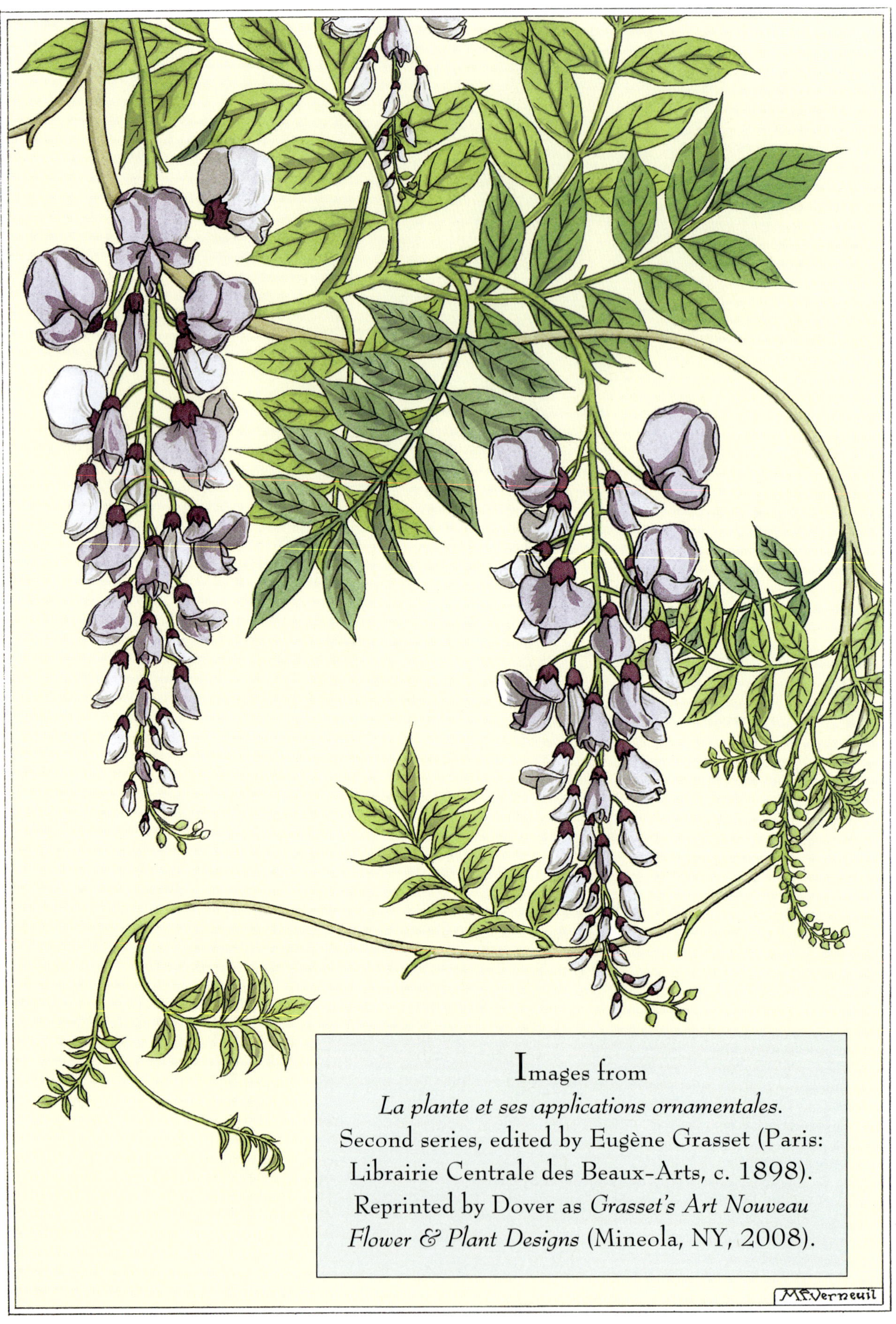

Images from
La plante et ses applications ornamentales.
Second series, edited by Eugène Grasset (Paris: Librairie Centrale des Beaux-Arts, c. 1898).
Reprinted by Dover as *Grasset's Art Nouveau Flower & Plant Designs* (Mineola, NY, 2008).

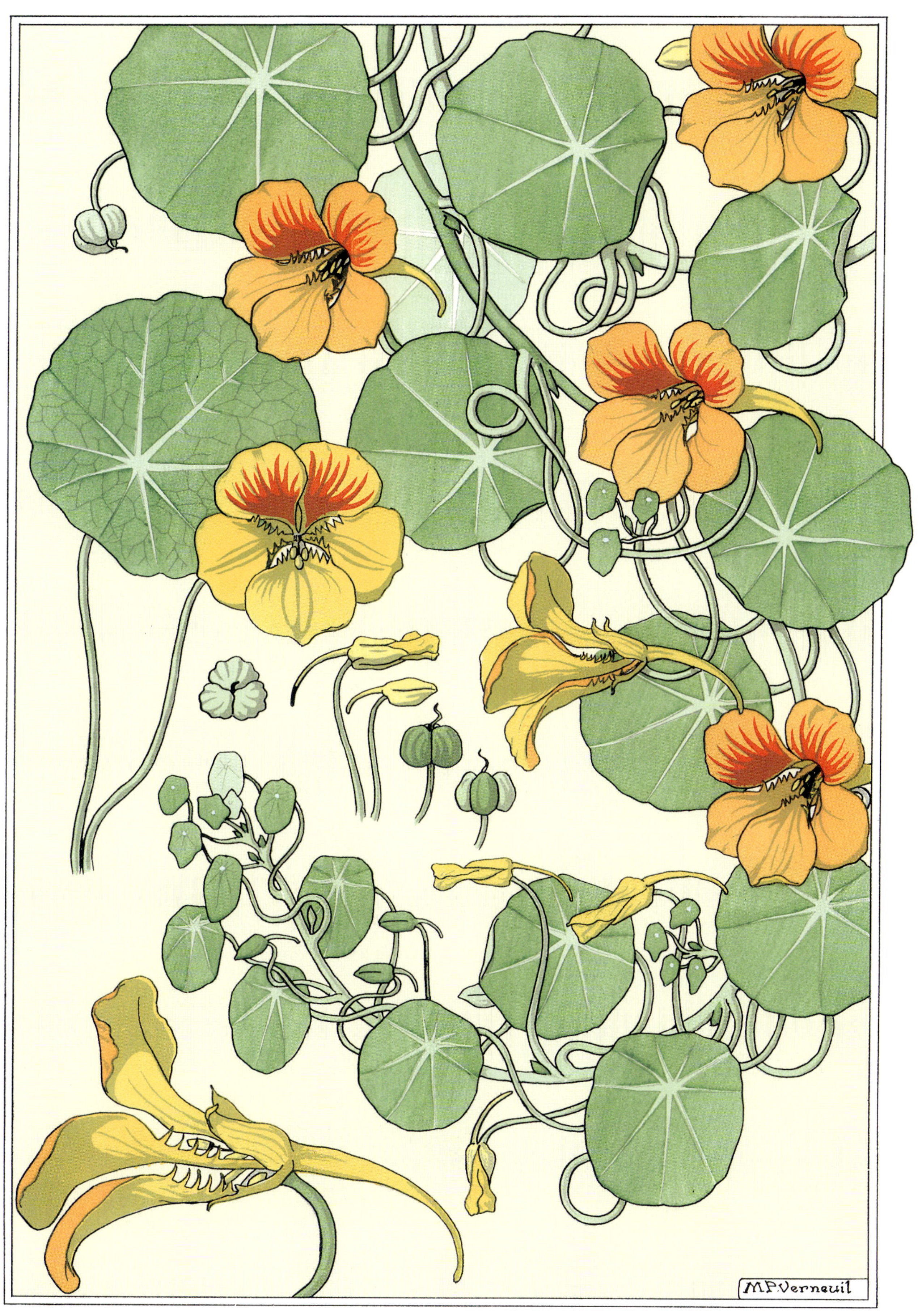
M.P.Verneuil

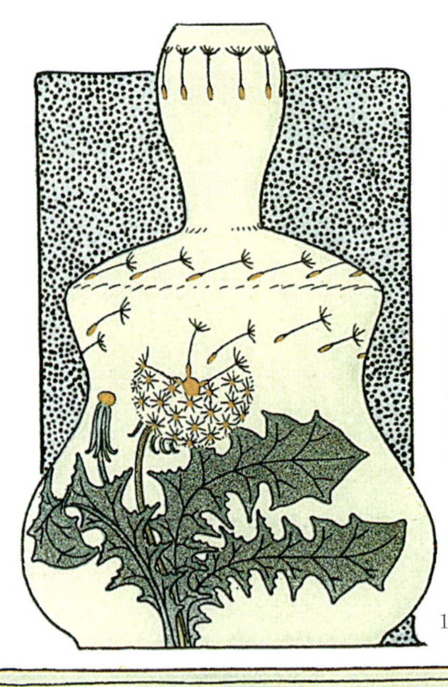

Images from *Étude de la Plante: son application aux industries d'art* (Paris: Librairie Centrale des Beaux-Arts, c. 1900), and *L'ornementation par le Pochoir* (Paris: Schmid and Laurens, n.d.). Reprinted by Dover as *Art Nouveau Floral Patterns & Stencil Designs in Full Color*, by M. P. Verneuil (Mineola, NY, 1998).

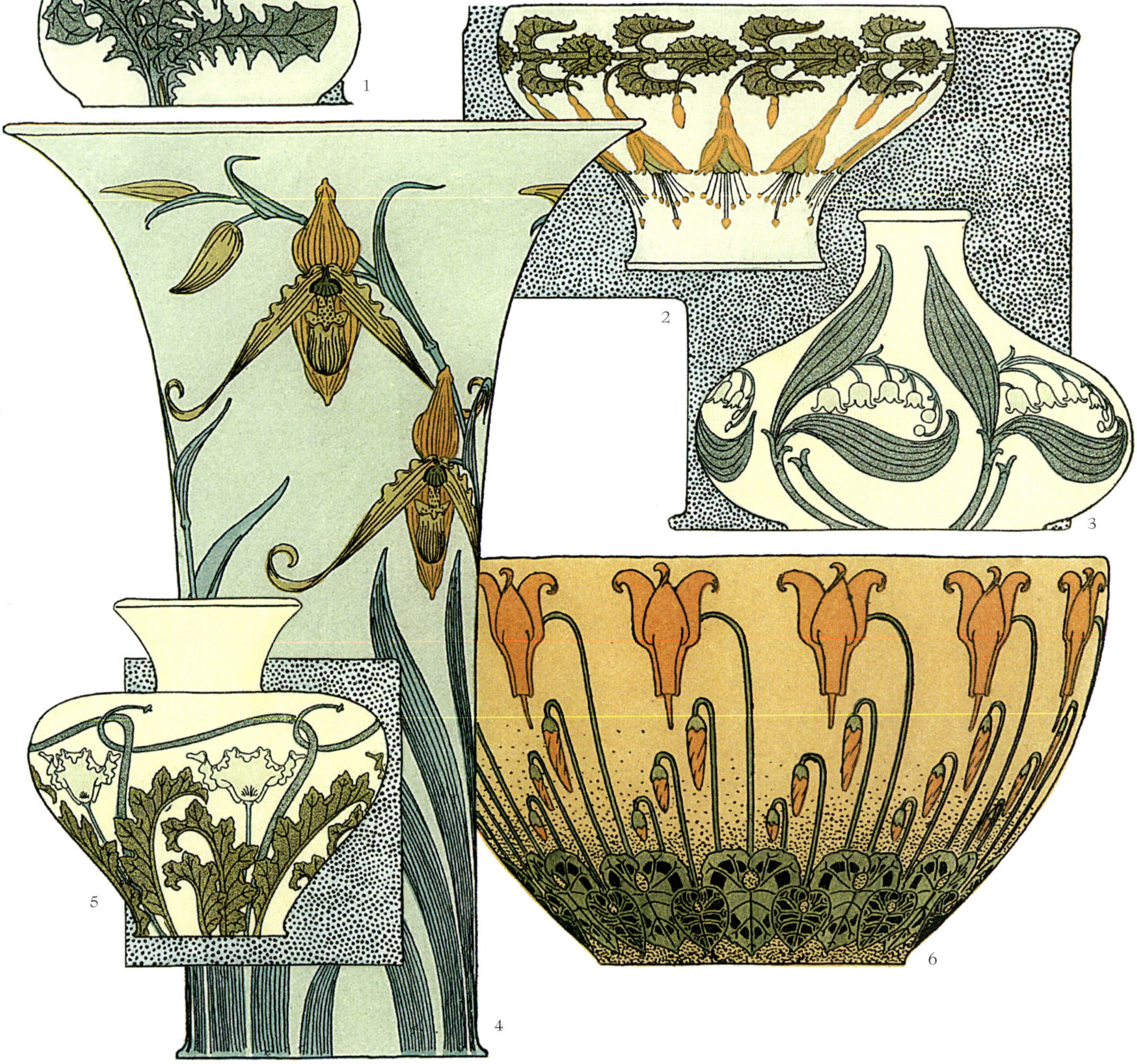

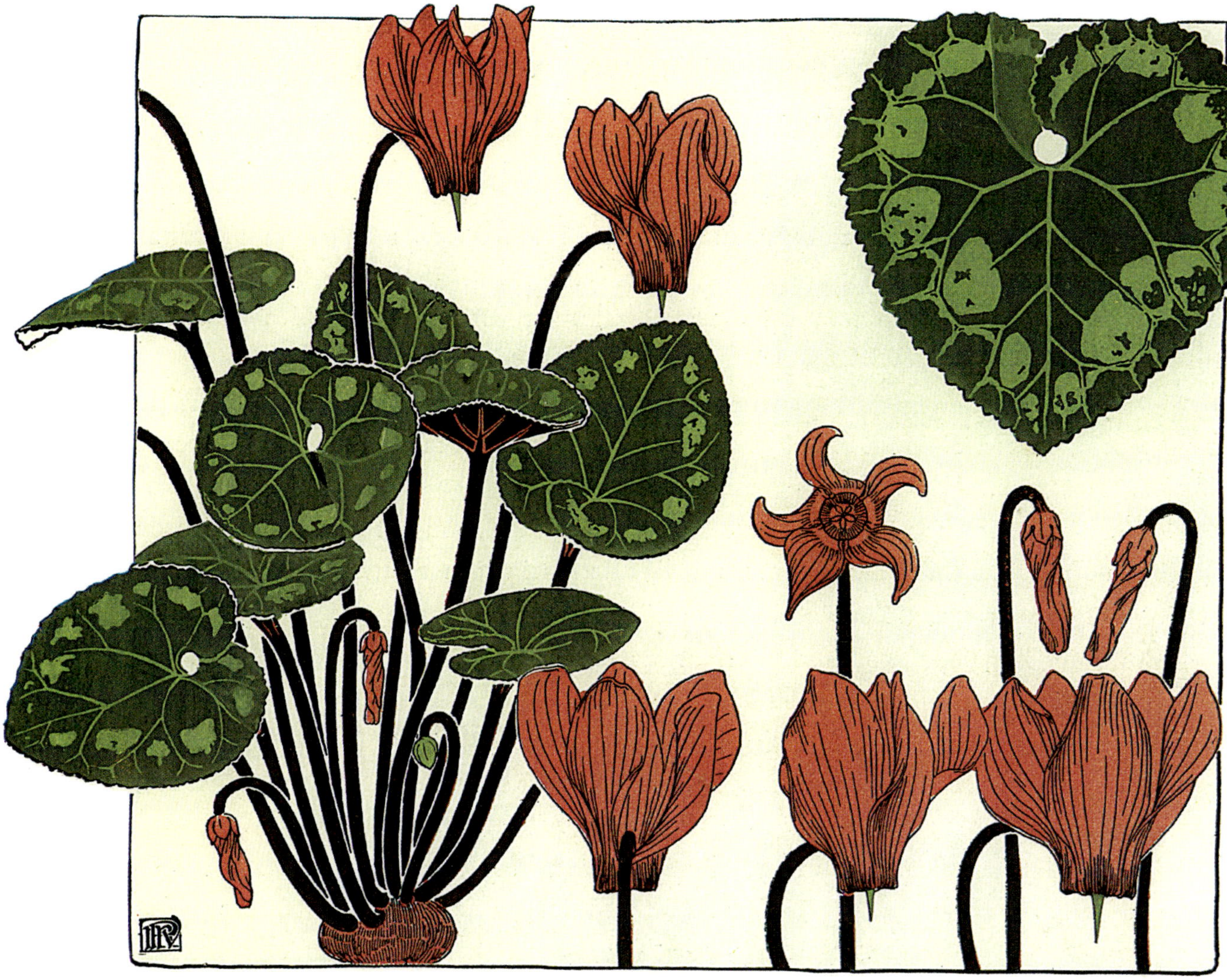

7

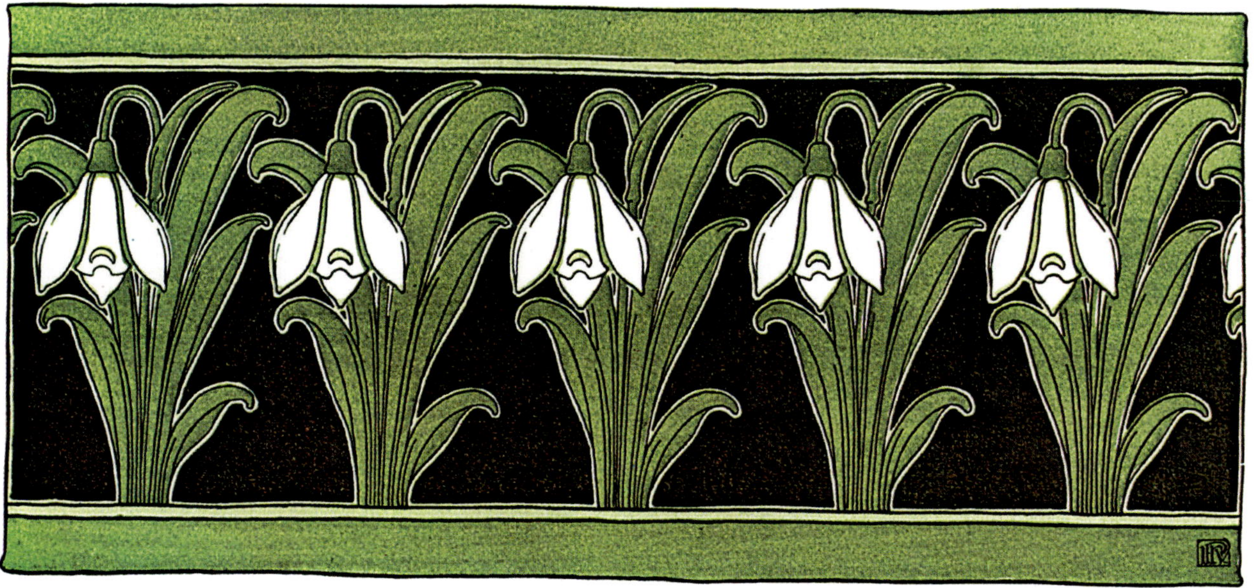

8

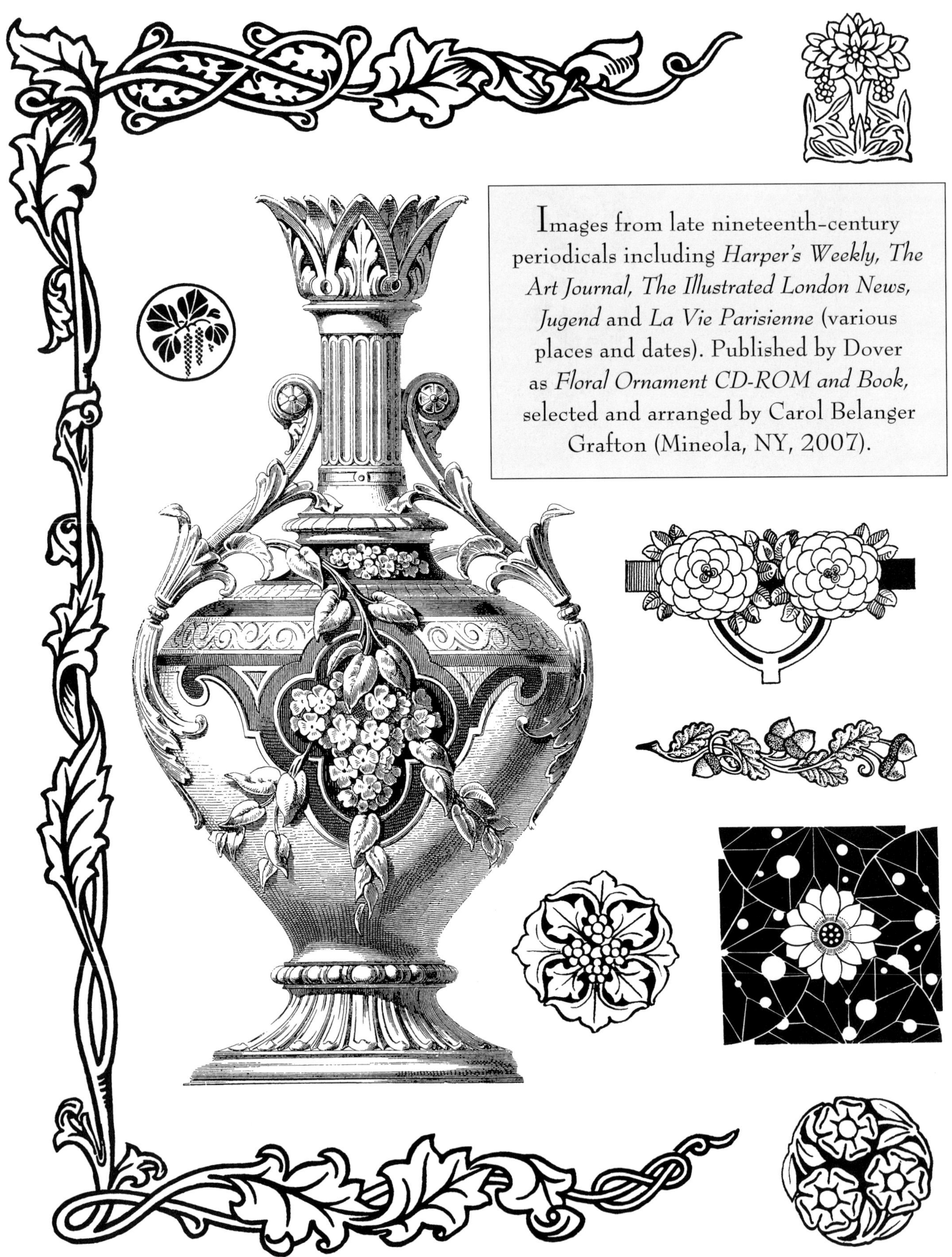

Images from late nineteenth-century periodicals including *Harper's Weekly*, *The Art Journal*, *The Illustrated London News*, *Jugend* and *La Vie Parisienne* (various places and dates). Published by Dover as *Floral Ornament CD-ROM and Book*, selected and arranged by Carol Belanger Grafton (Mineola, NY, 2007).

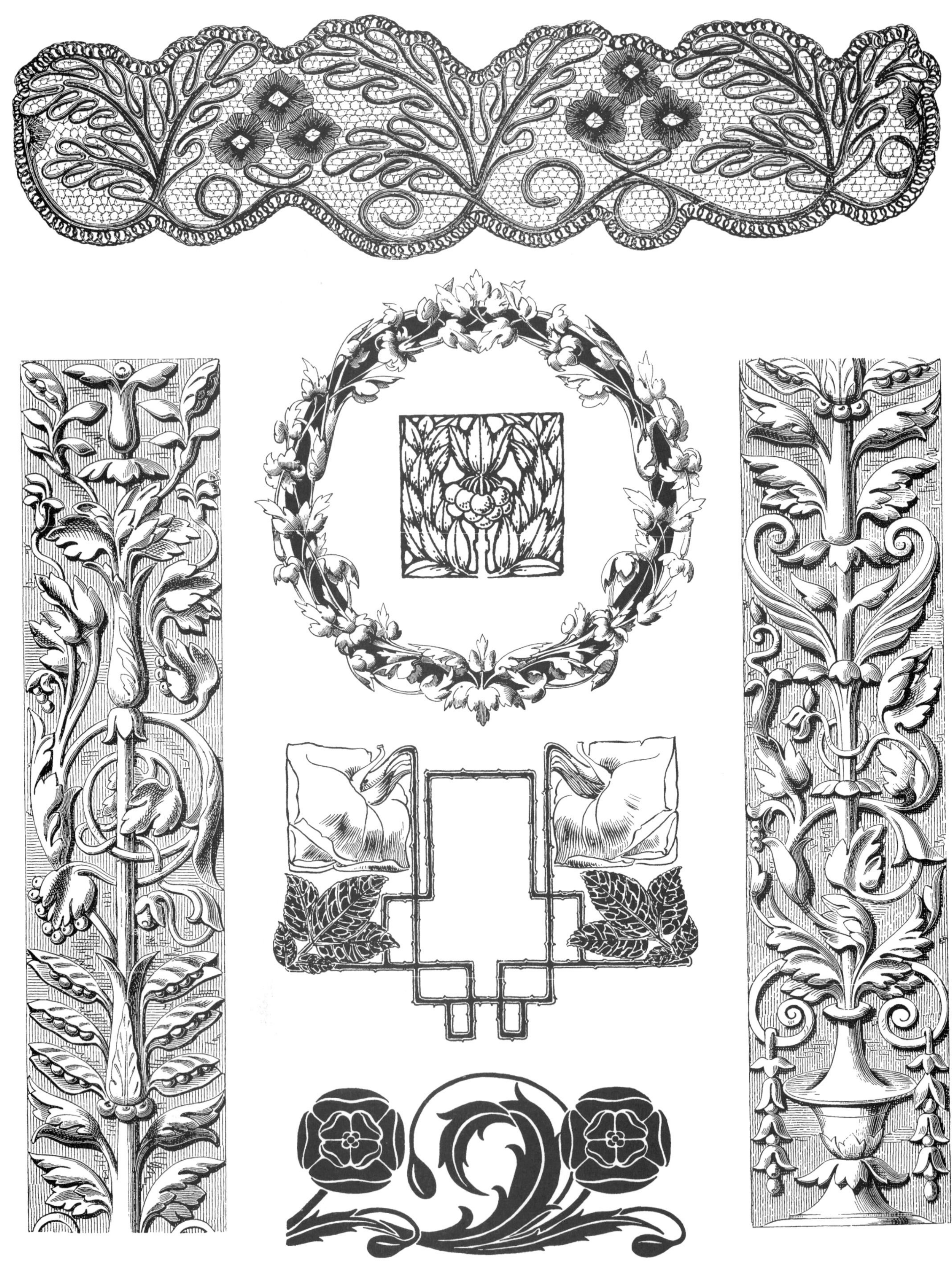

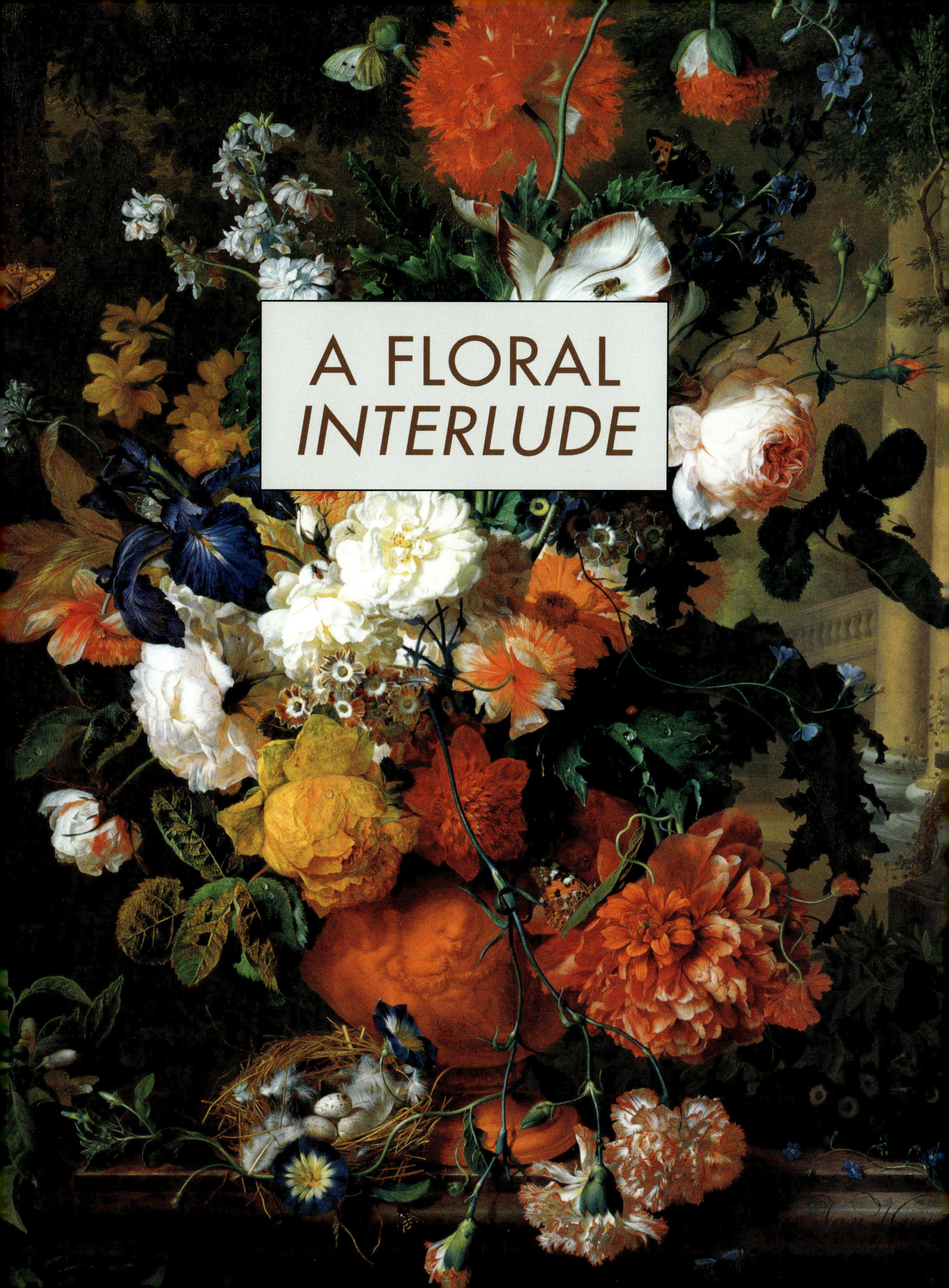
A FLORAL
INTERLUDE

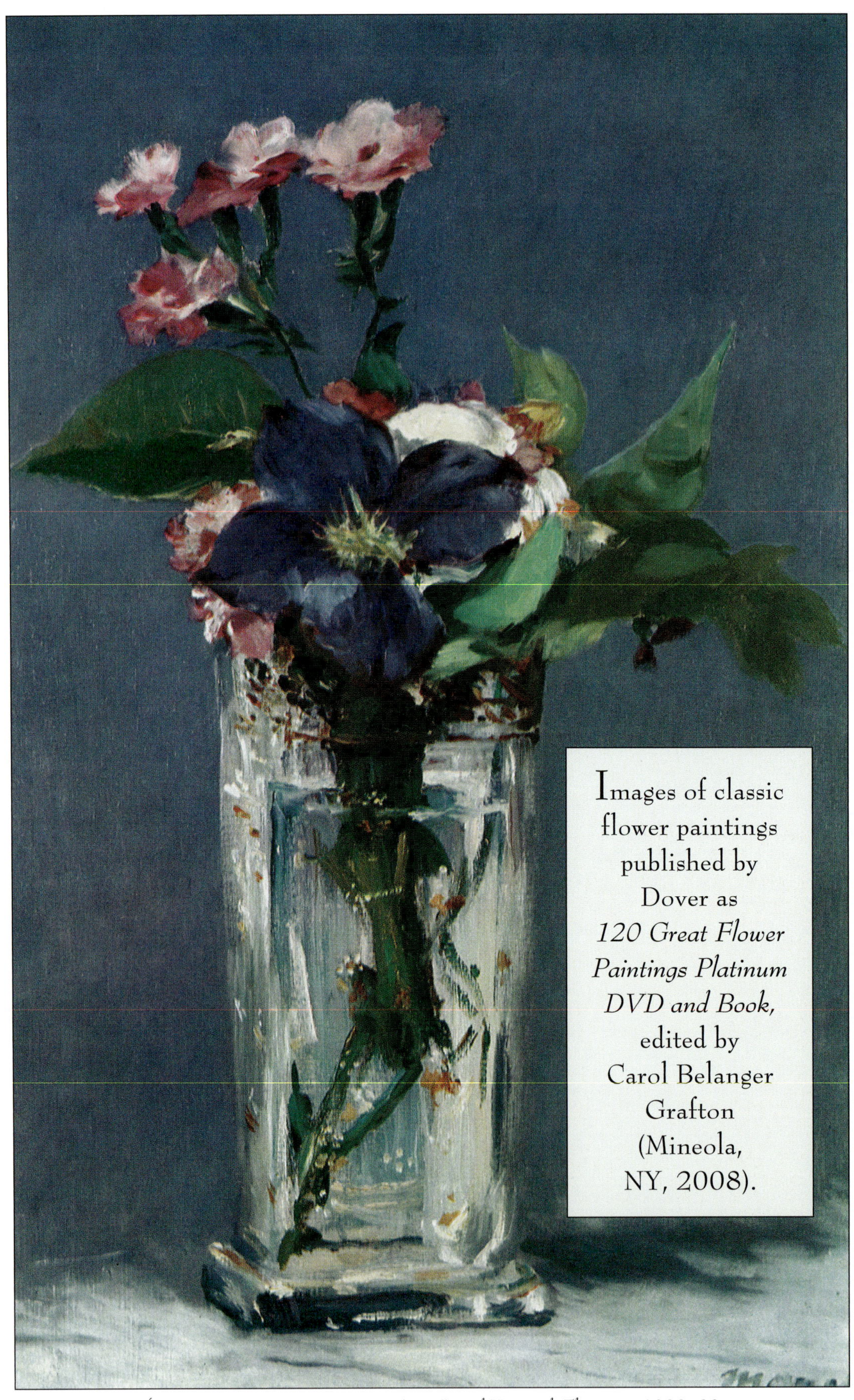

ÉDOUARD MANET (1832–1883) / *Crystal Vase with Flowers*, c. 1880–83

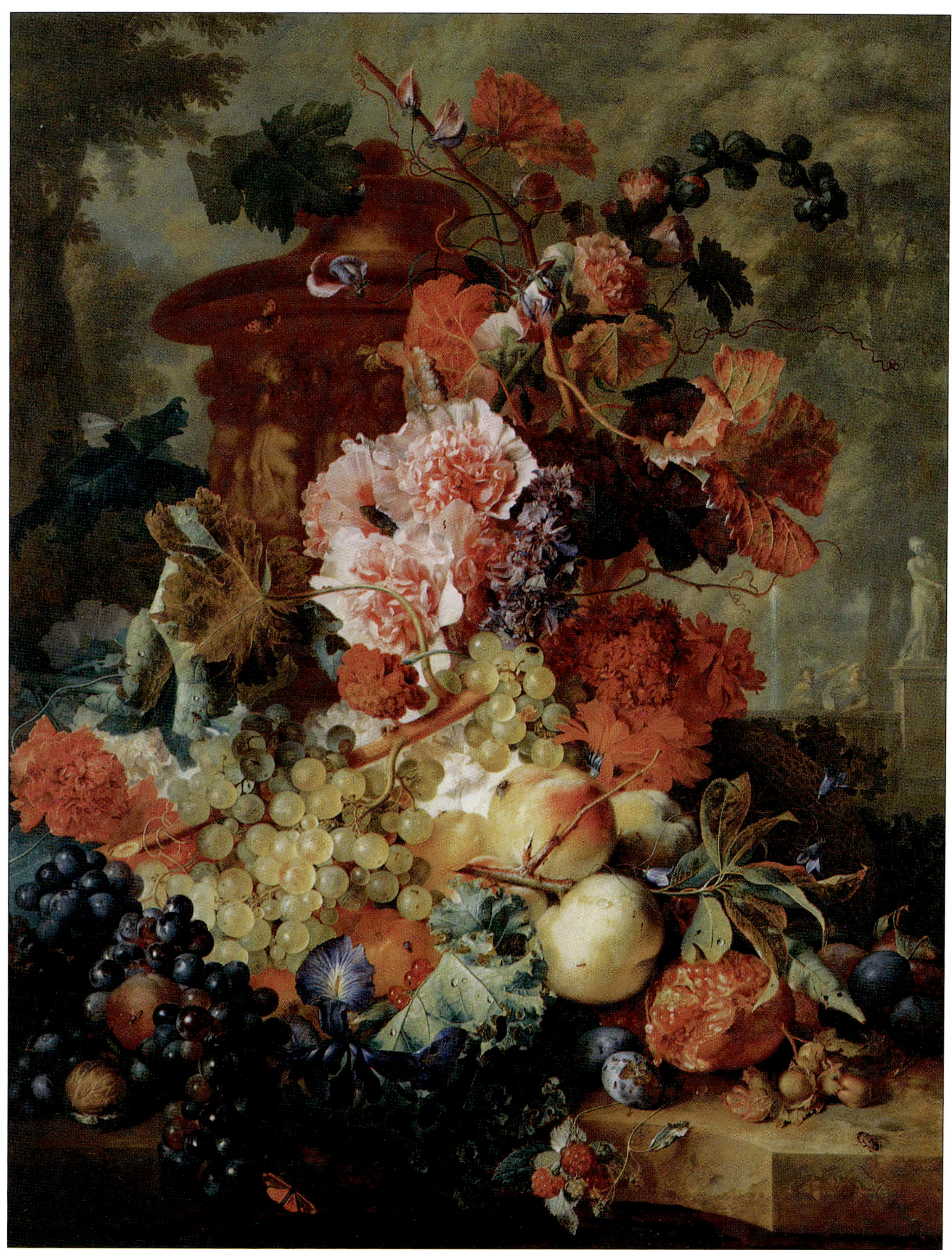

Jan van Huysum (1682–1749) / *Flower and Fruit Piece*, 1722

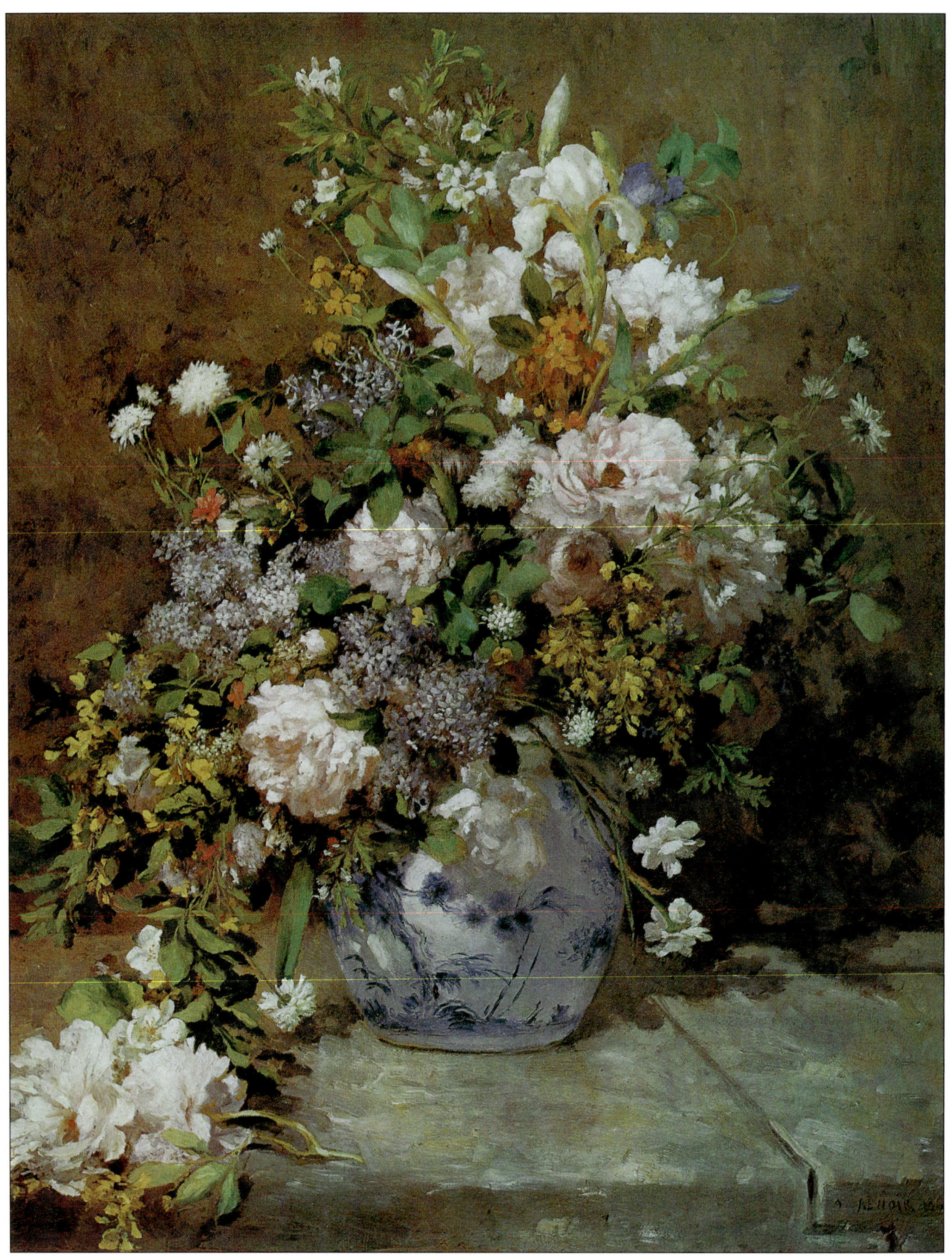

Pierre-Auguste Renoir (1841–1919) / *Spring Bouquet,* 1866

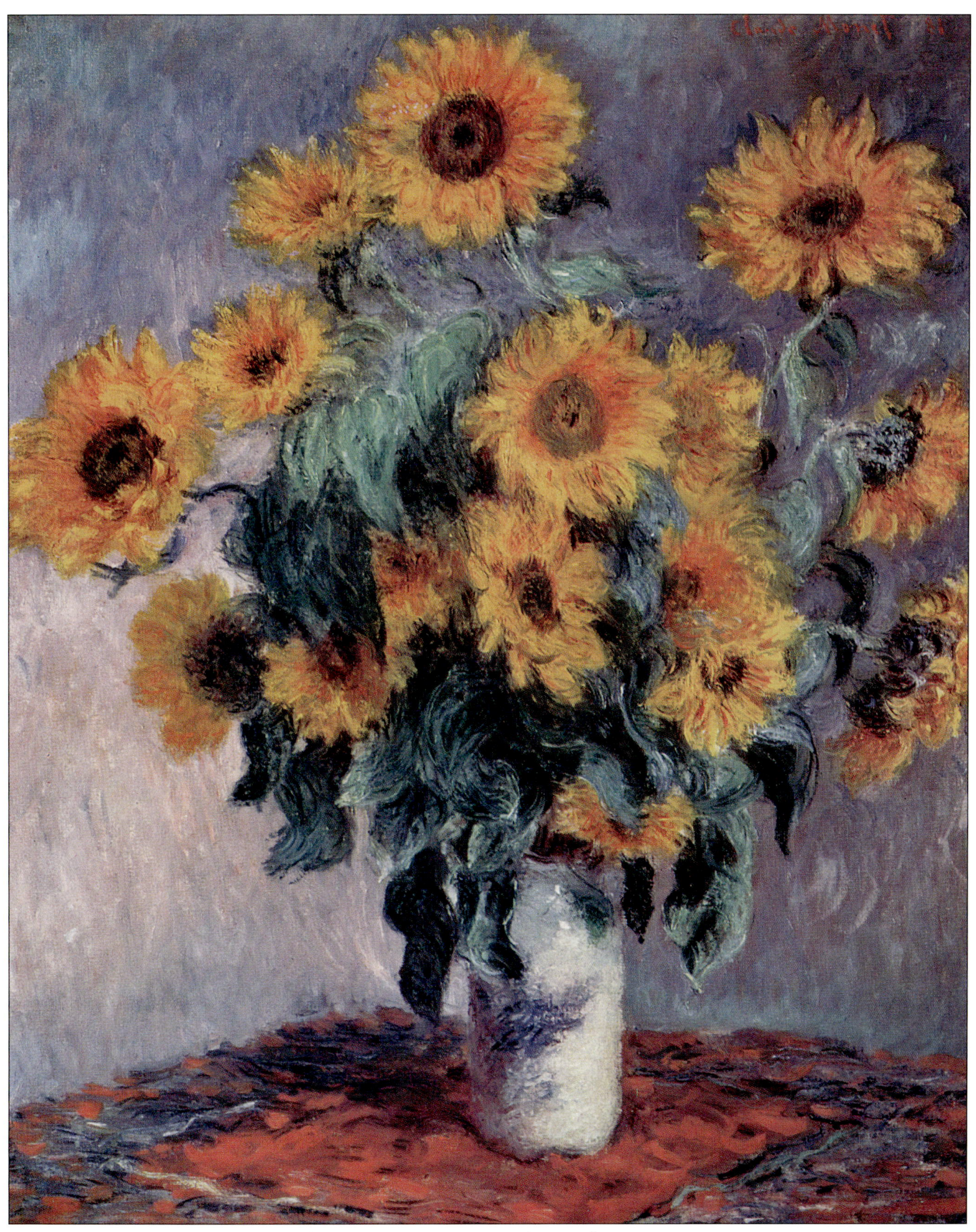

CLAUDE MONET (1840–1926) / *Sunflowers,* 1881

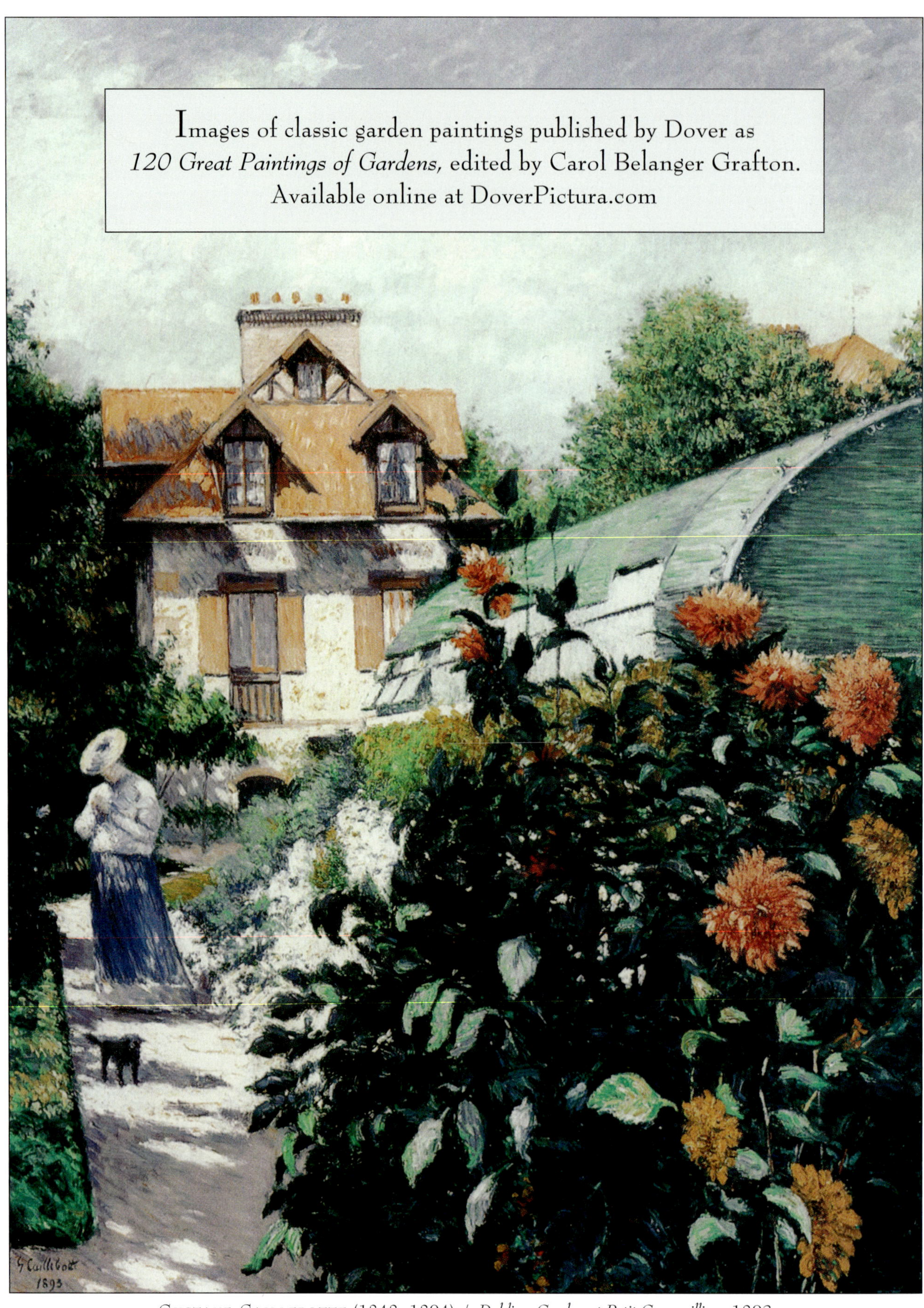

GUSTAVE CAILLEBOTTE (1848–1894) / *Dahlias, Garden at Petit Gennevilliers*, 1893

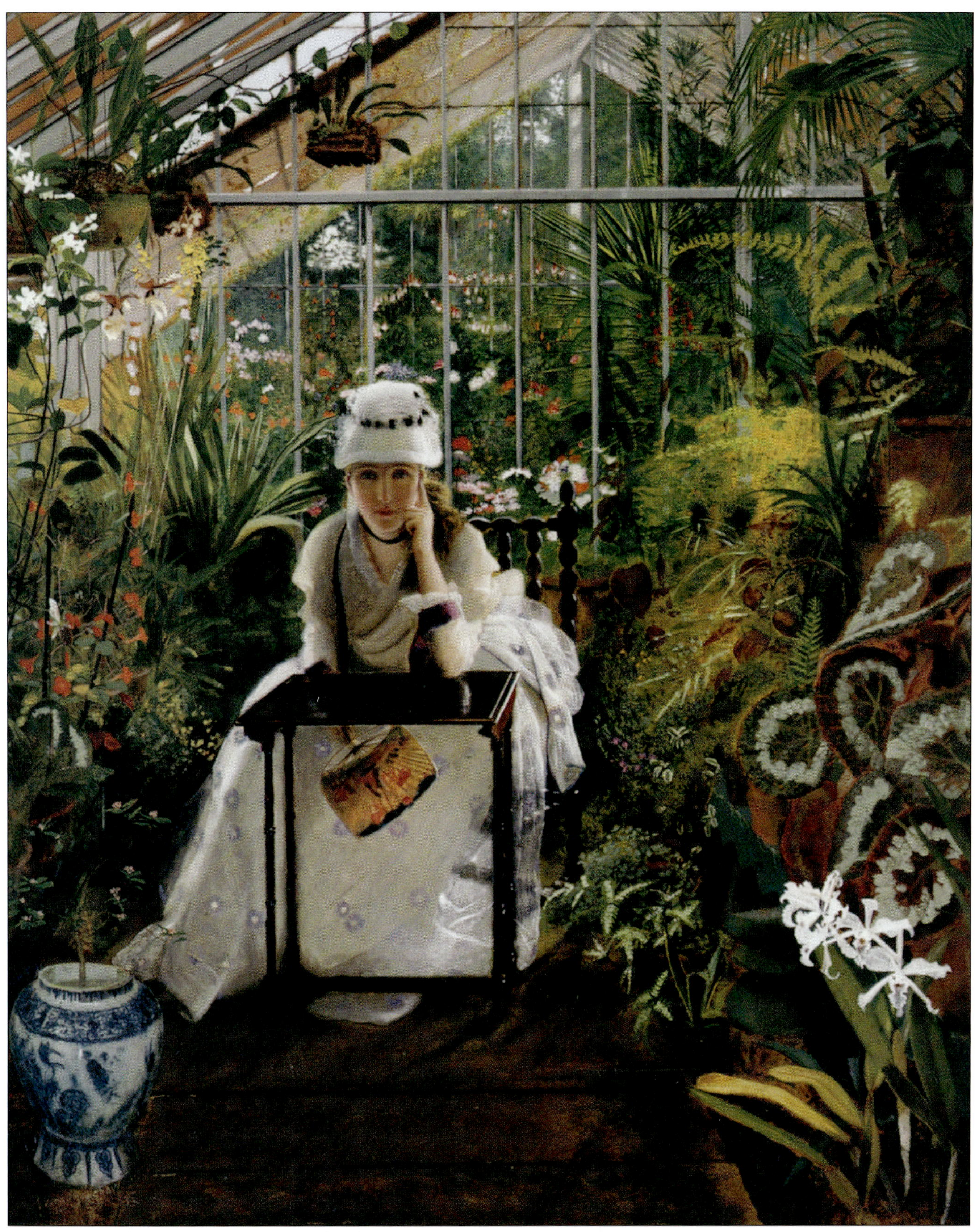

John Atkinson Grimshaw (1836–1893) / *Il Penseroso,* 1875

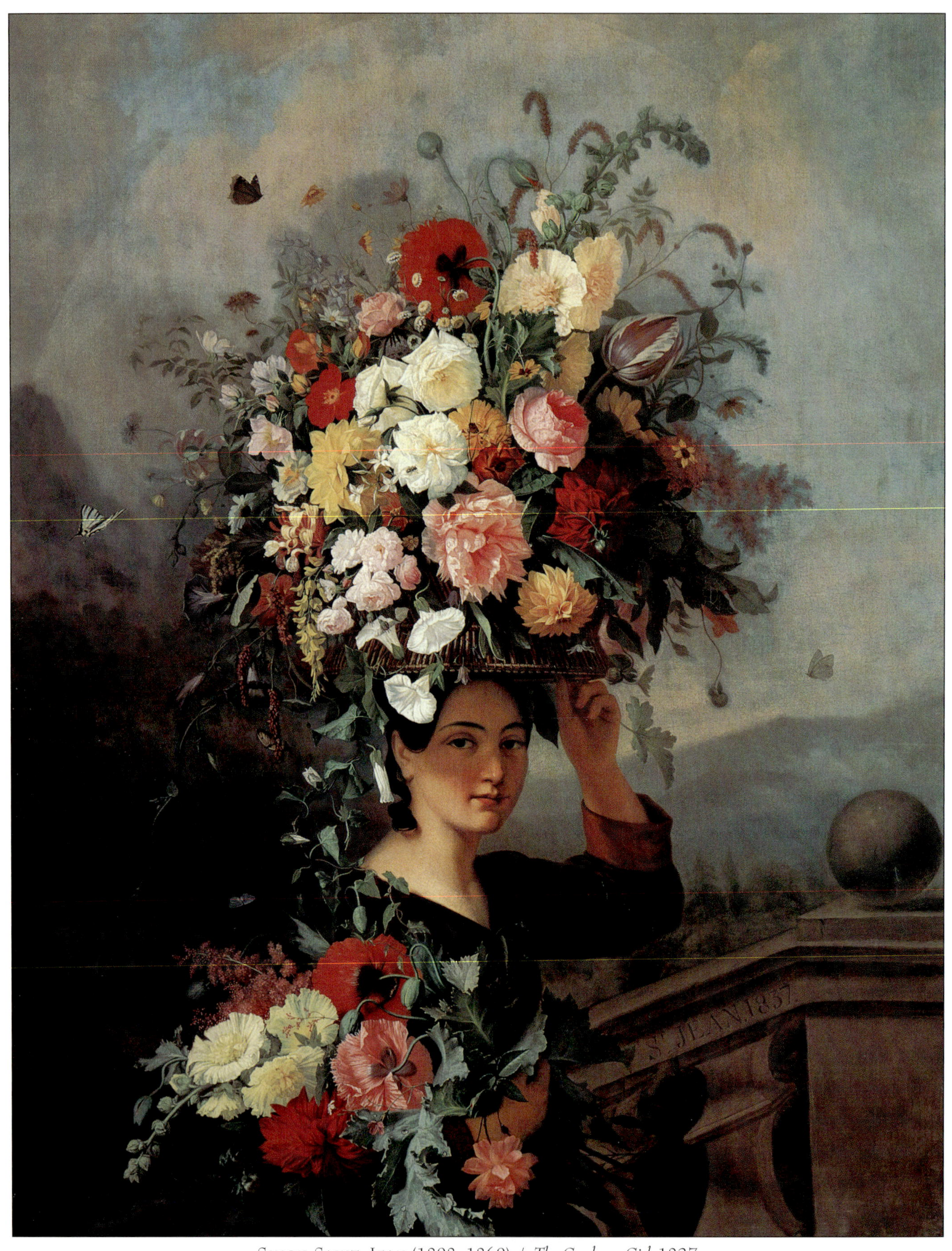

Simon Saint-Jean (1808–1860) / *The Gardener-Girl*, 1837

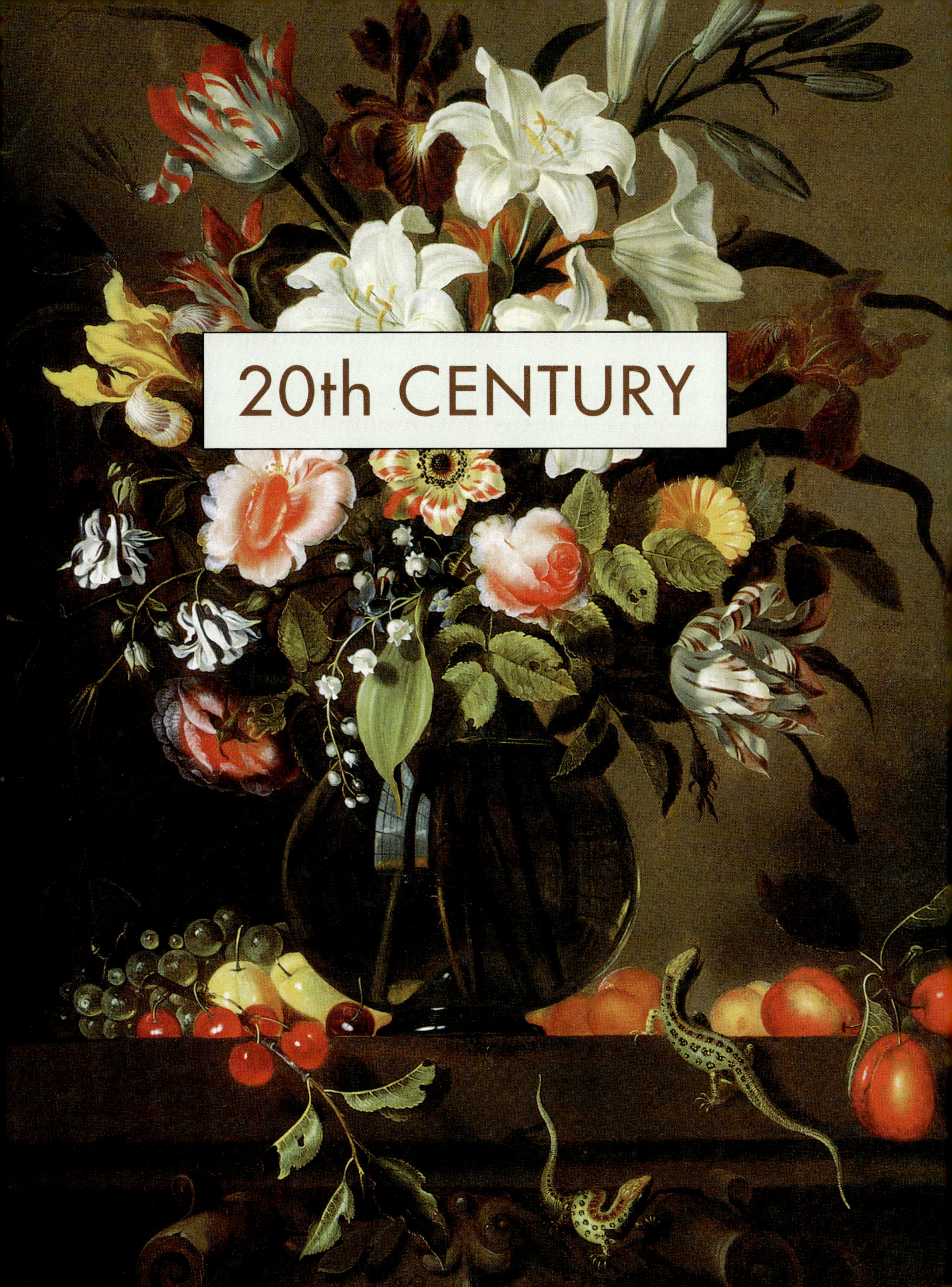

20th CENTURY

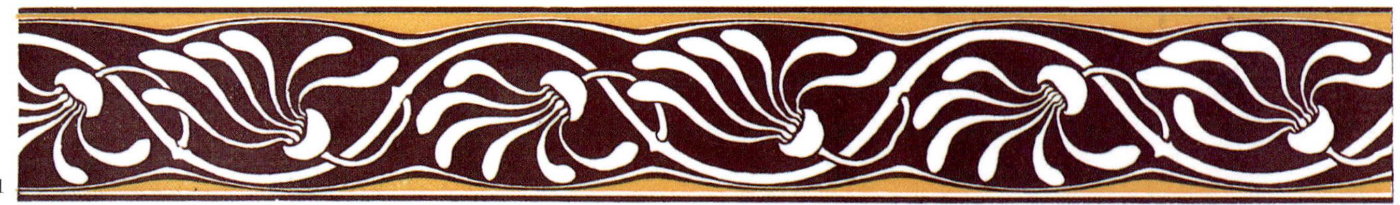

1

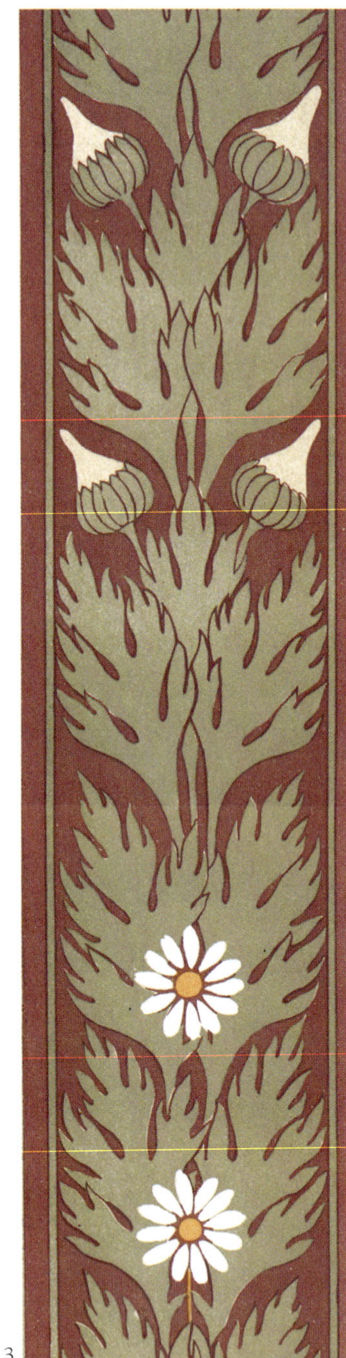

3

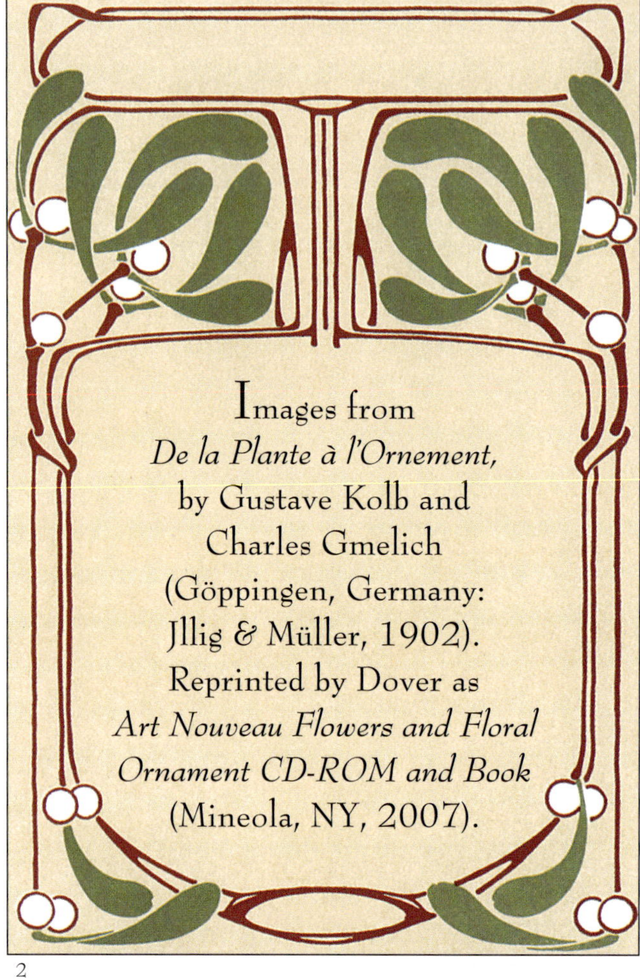
Images from
De la Plante à l'Ornement,
by Gustave Kolb and
Charles Gmelich
(Göppingen, Germany:
Jllig & Müller, 1902).
Reprinted by Dover as
Art Nouveau Flowers and Floral
Ornament CD-ROM and Book
(Mineola, NY, 2007).

2

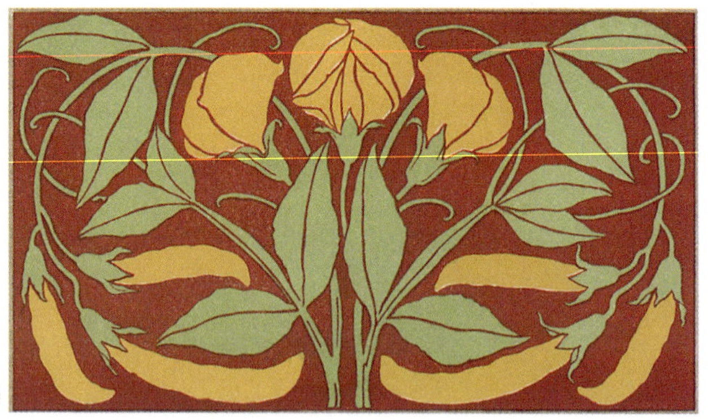

4

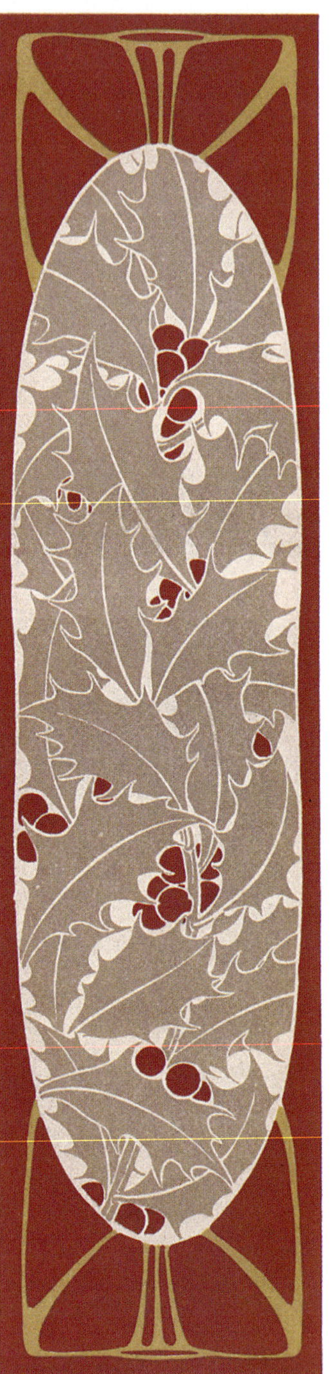

5

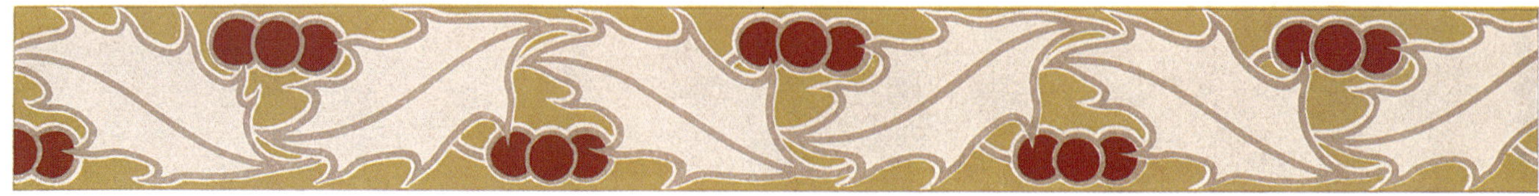

6

8

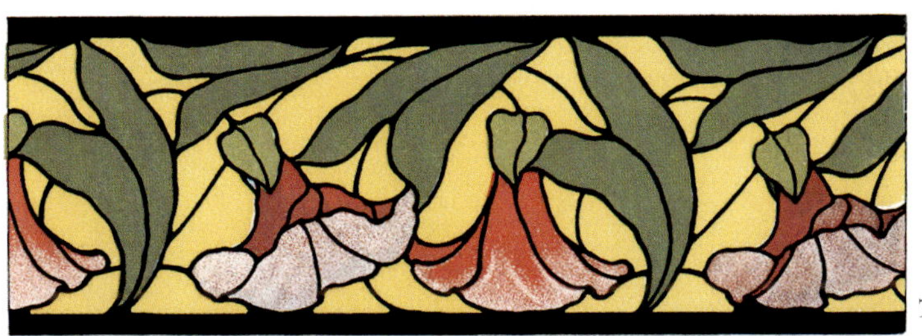
7

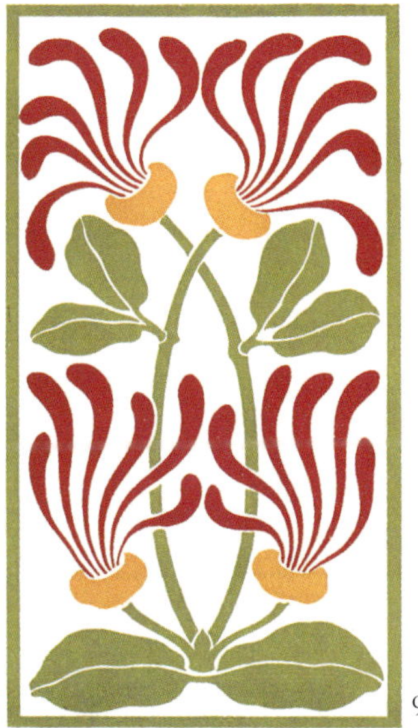
9

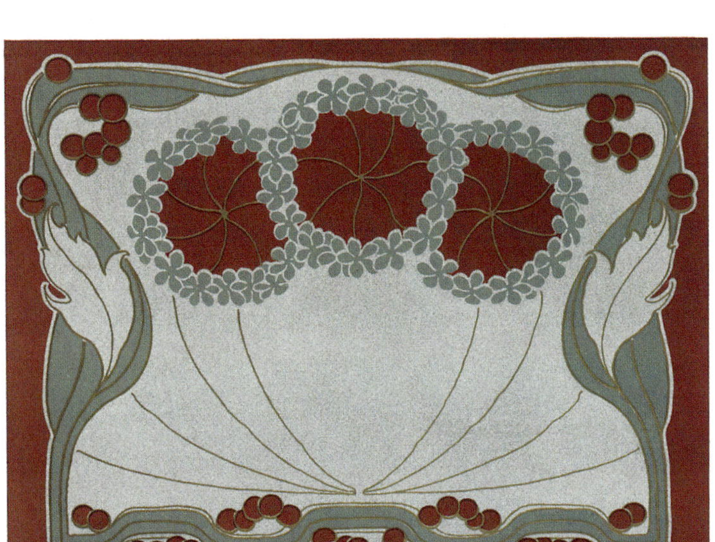
10

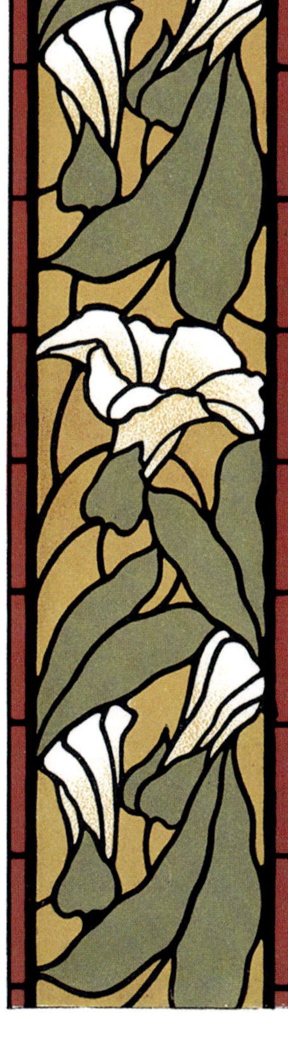
13

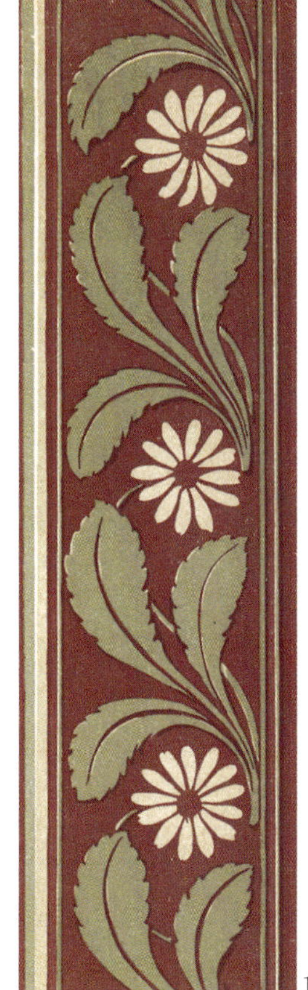
11

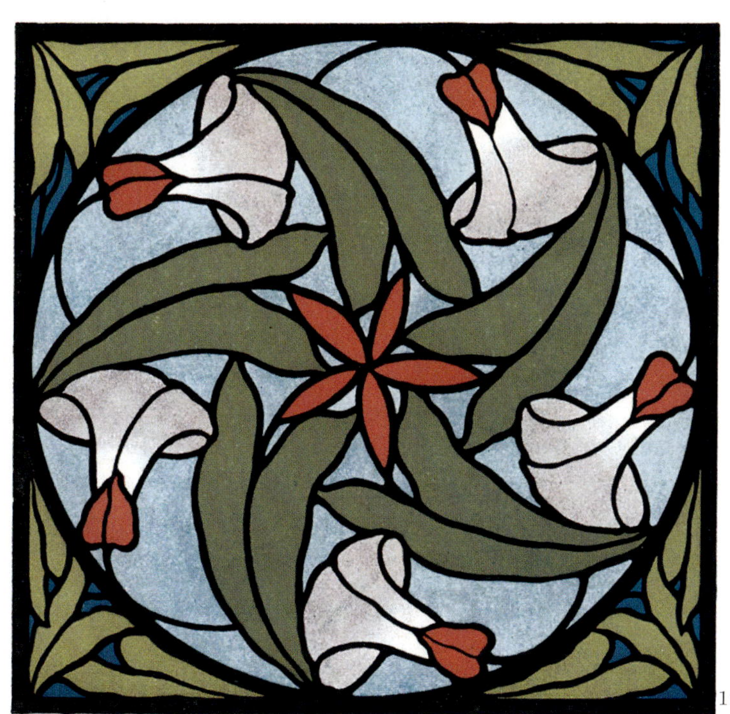
12

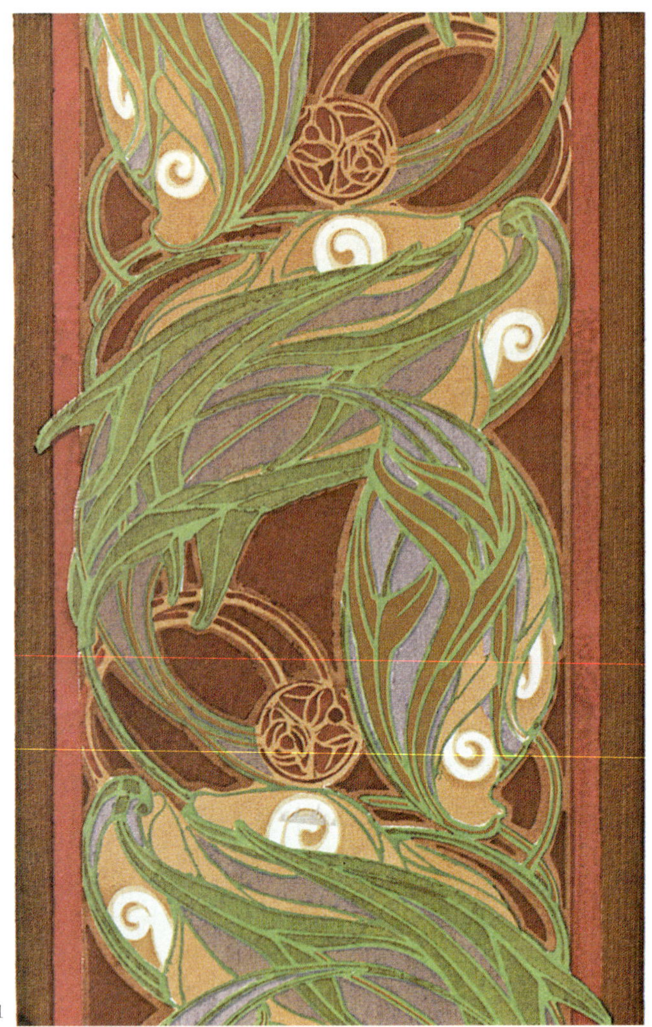

1

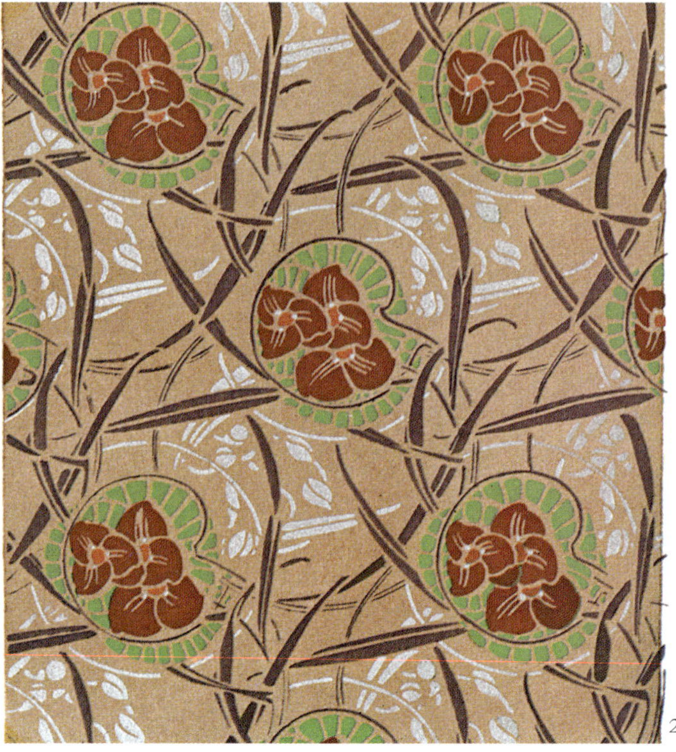

2

Images from
Les fleurs et leurs applications décoratives
by E. A. Seguy (Paris: Librairie des Arts Décoratifs, A. Calavas, c. 1902). Reprinted by Dover as *Full-Color Floral Designs in the Art Nouveau Style*, edited by Charles Rahn Fry (New York, 1977).

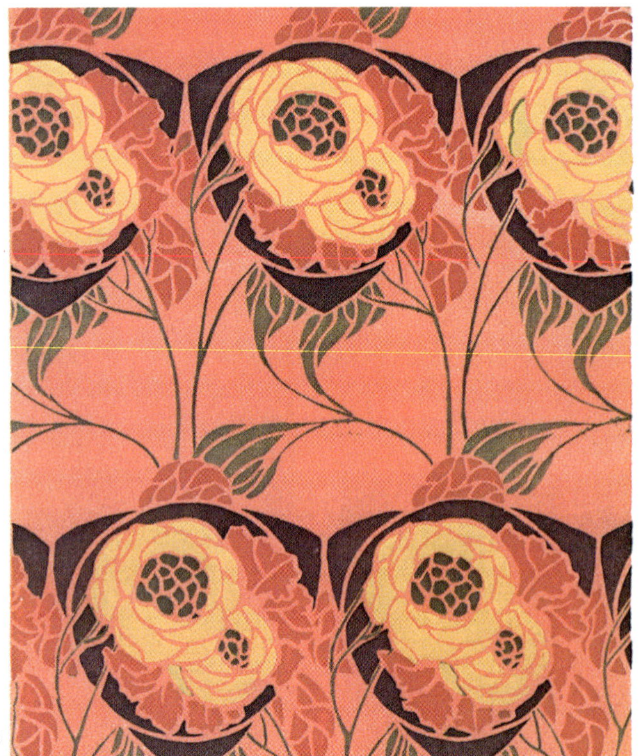

3

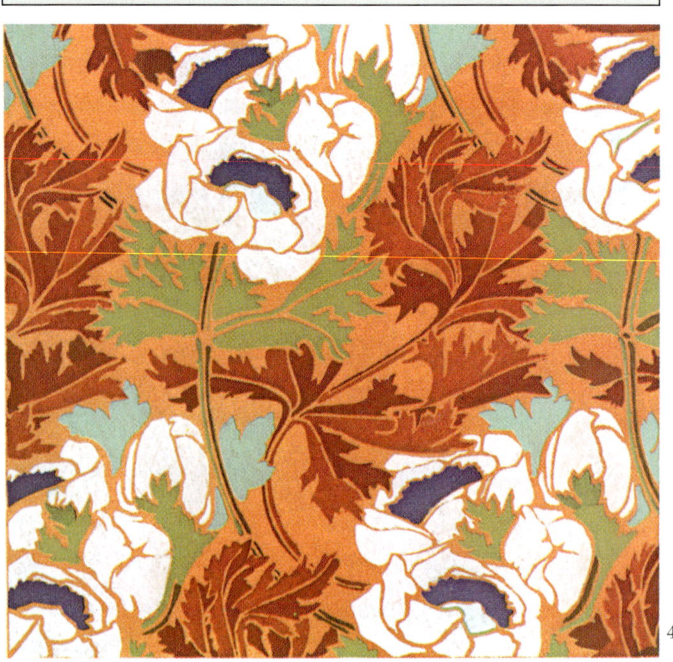

4

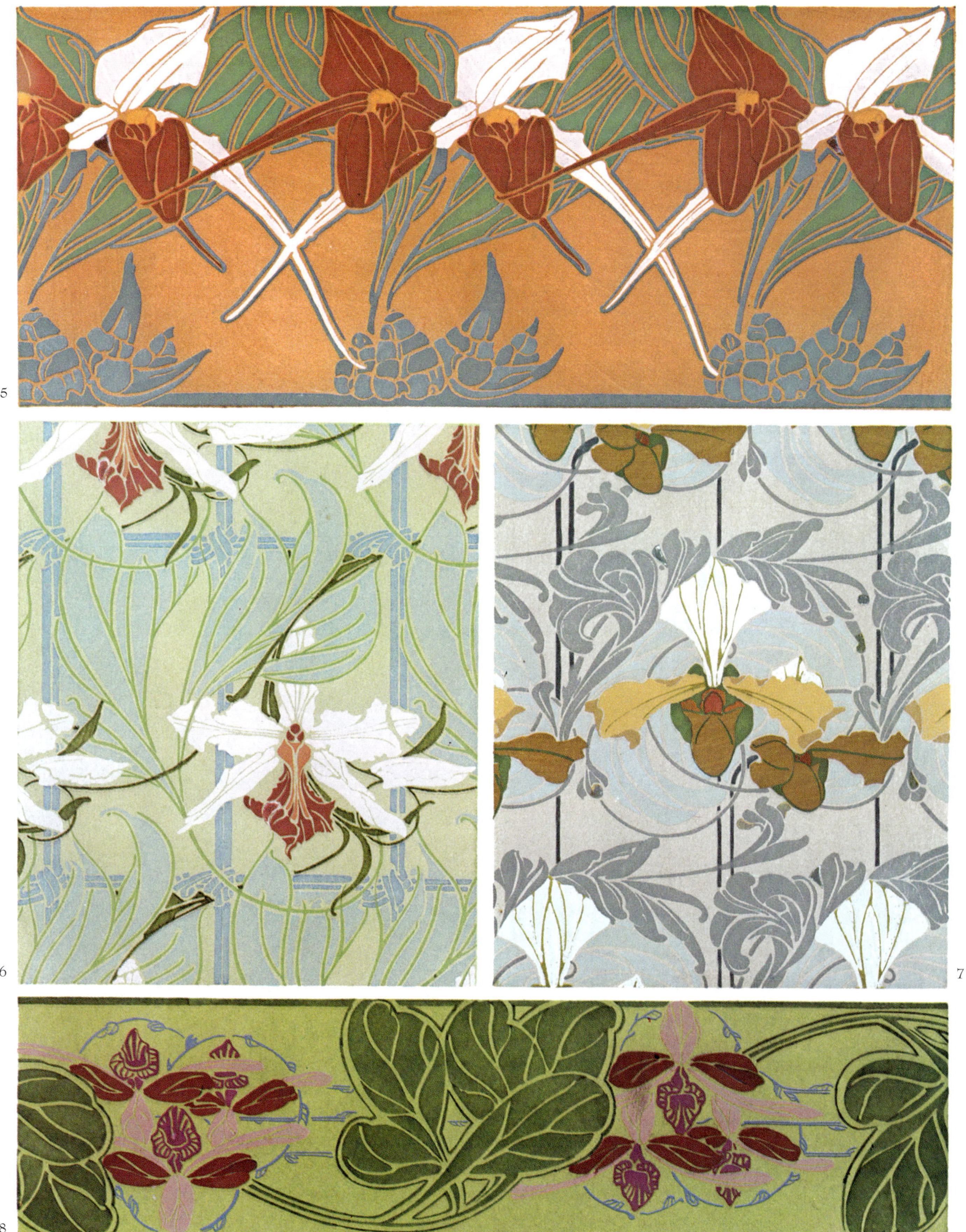

5

6

7

8

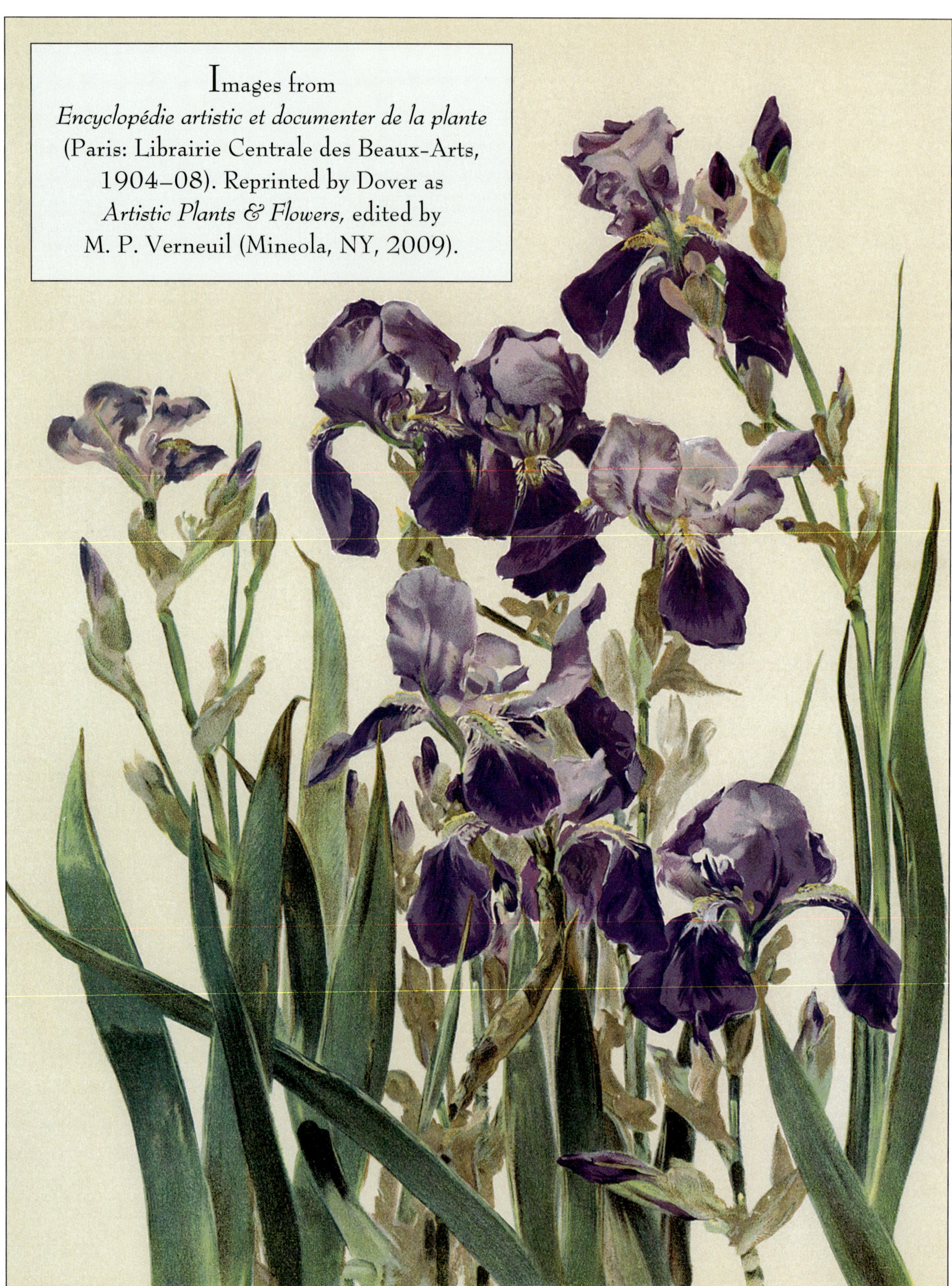

Images from
Encyclopédie artistic et documenter de la plante
(Paris: Librairie Centrale des Beaux-Arts, 1904–08). Reprinted by Dover as *Artistic Plants & Flowers,* edited by M. P. Verneuil (Mineola, NY, 2009).

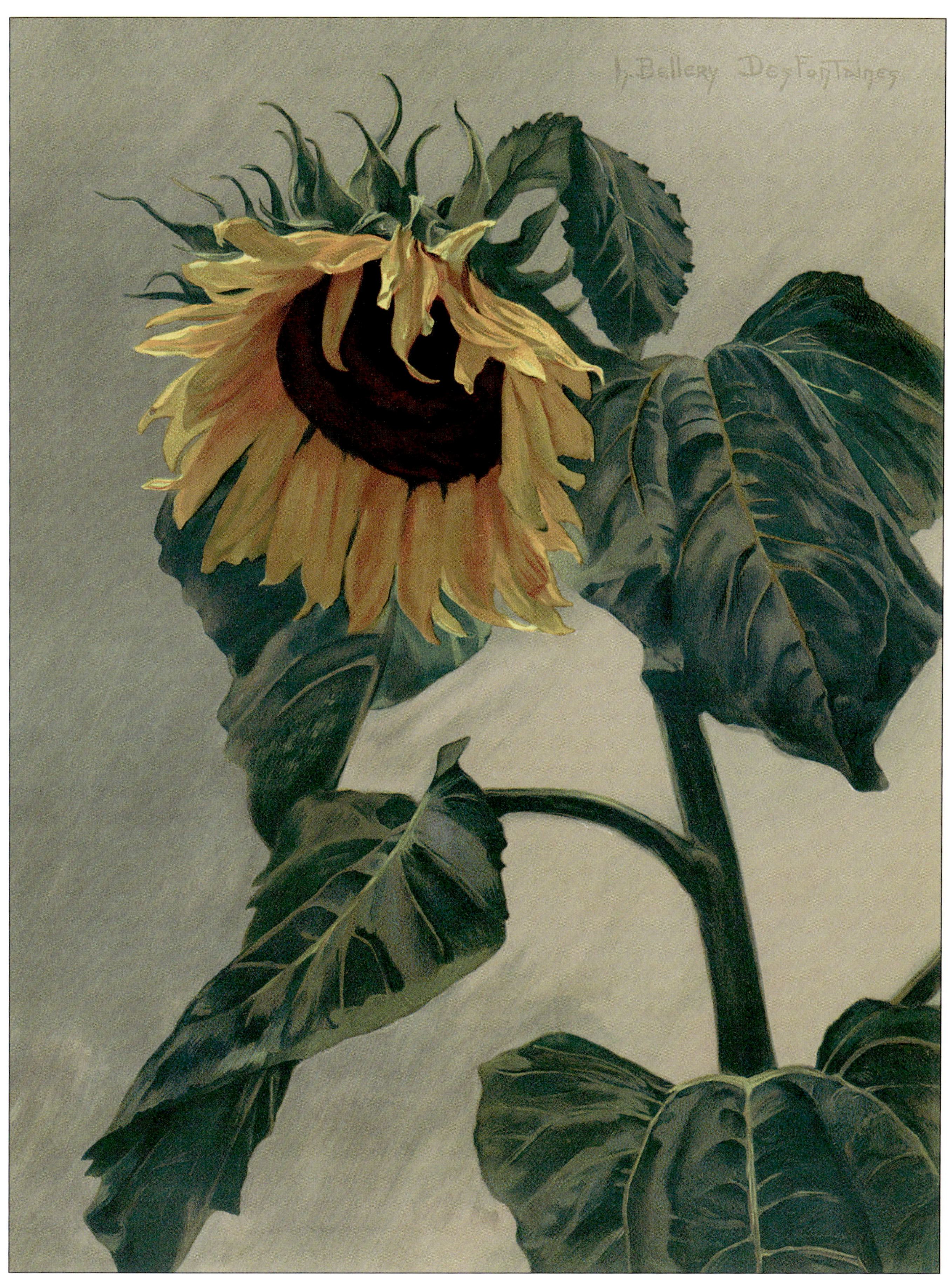
H. Bellery DesFontaines

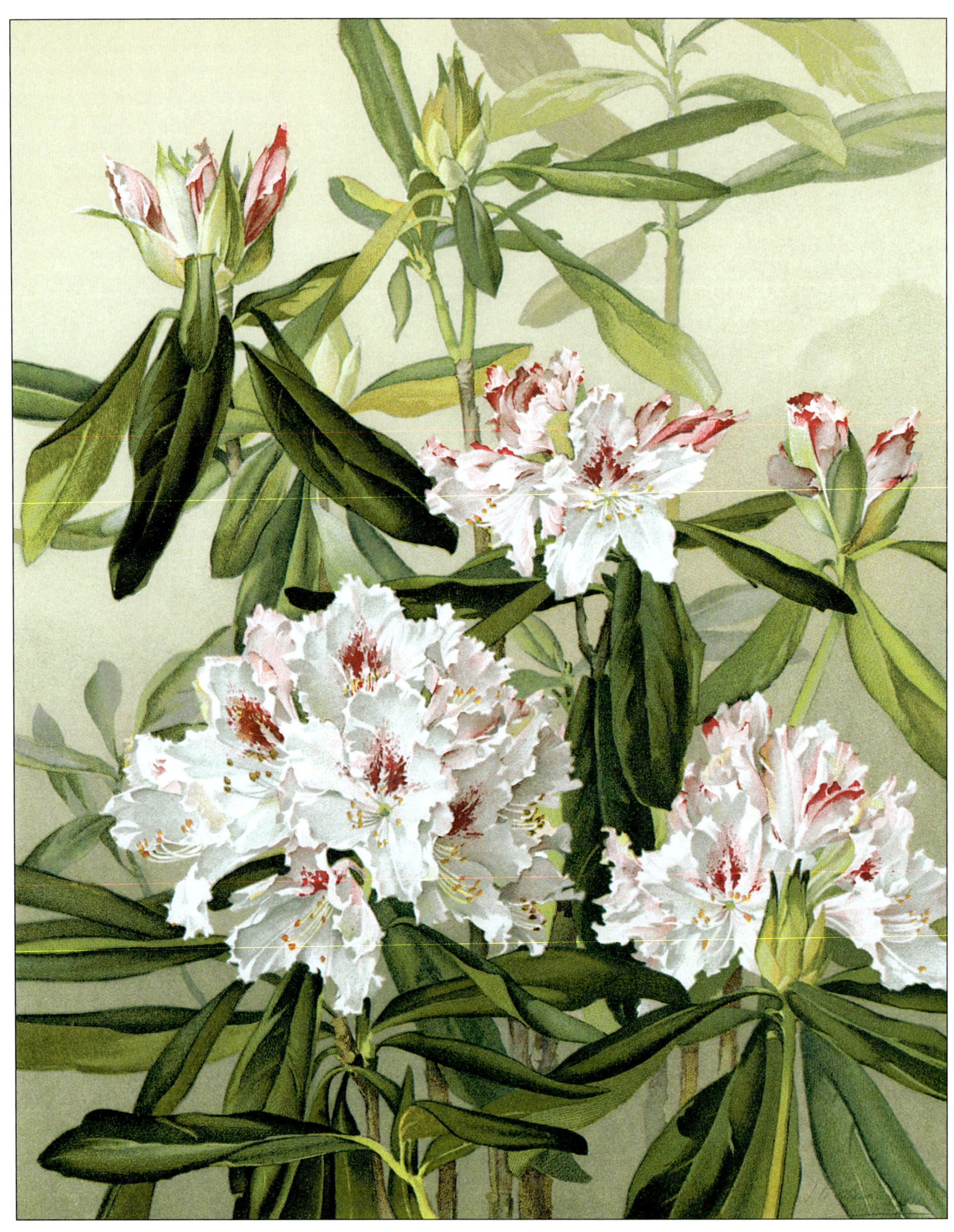

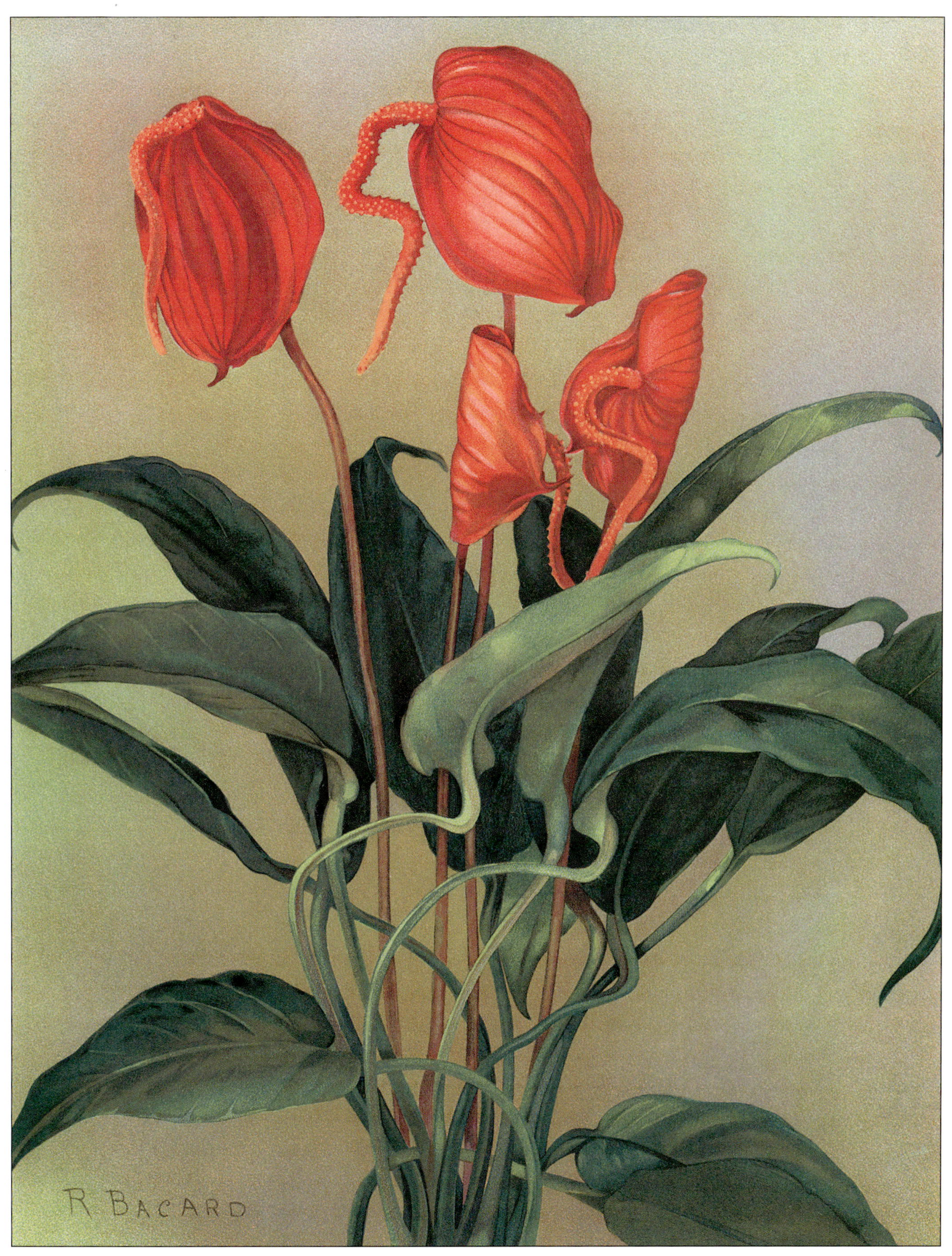
R. BACARD

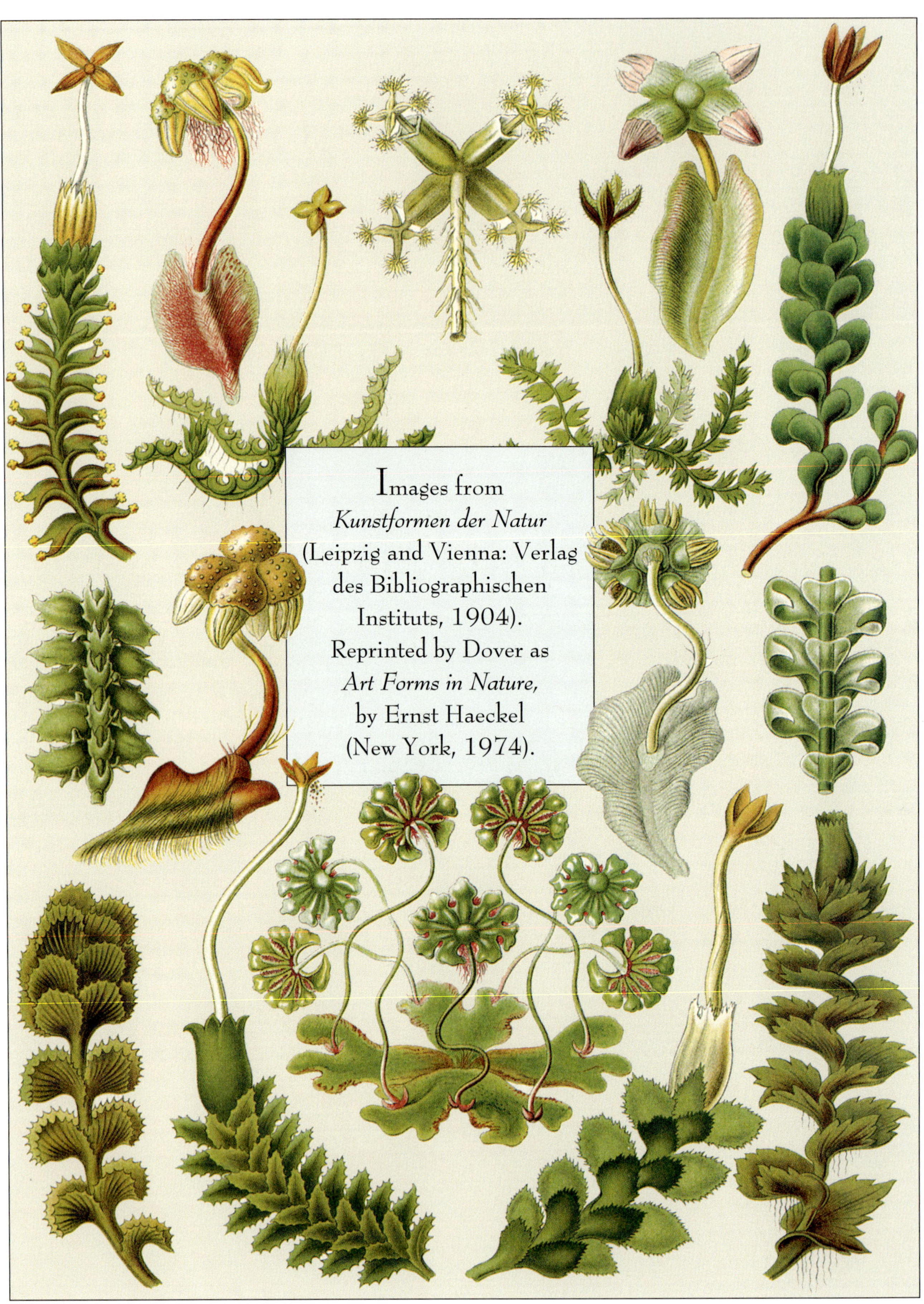

Images from
Kunstformen der Natur
(Leipzig and Vienna: Verlag
des Bibliographischen
Instituts, 1904).
Reprinted by Dover as
Art Forms in Nature,
by Ernst Haeckel
(New York, 1974).

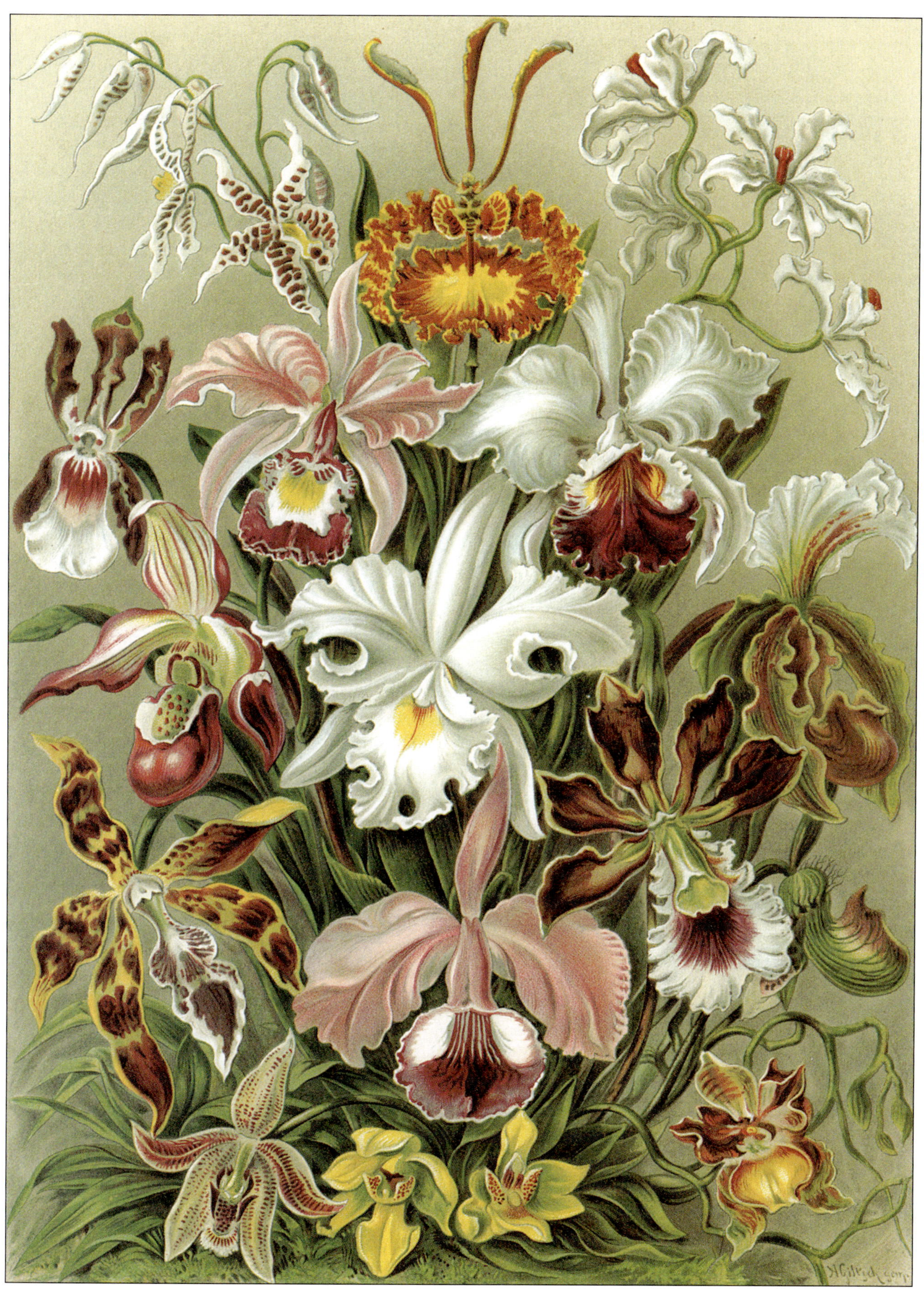

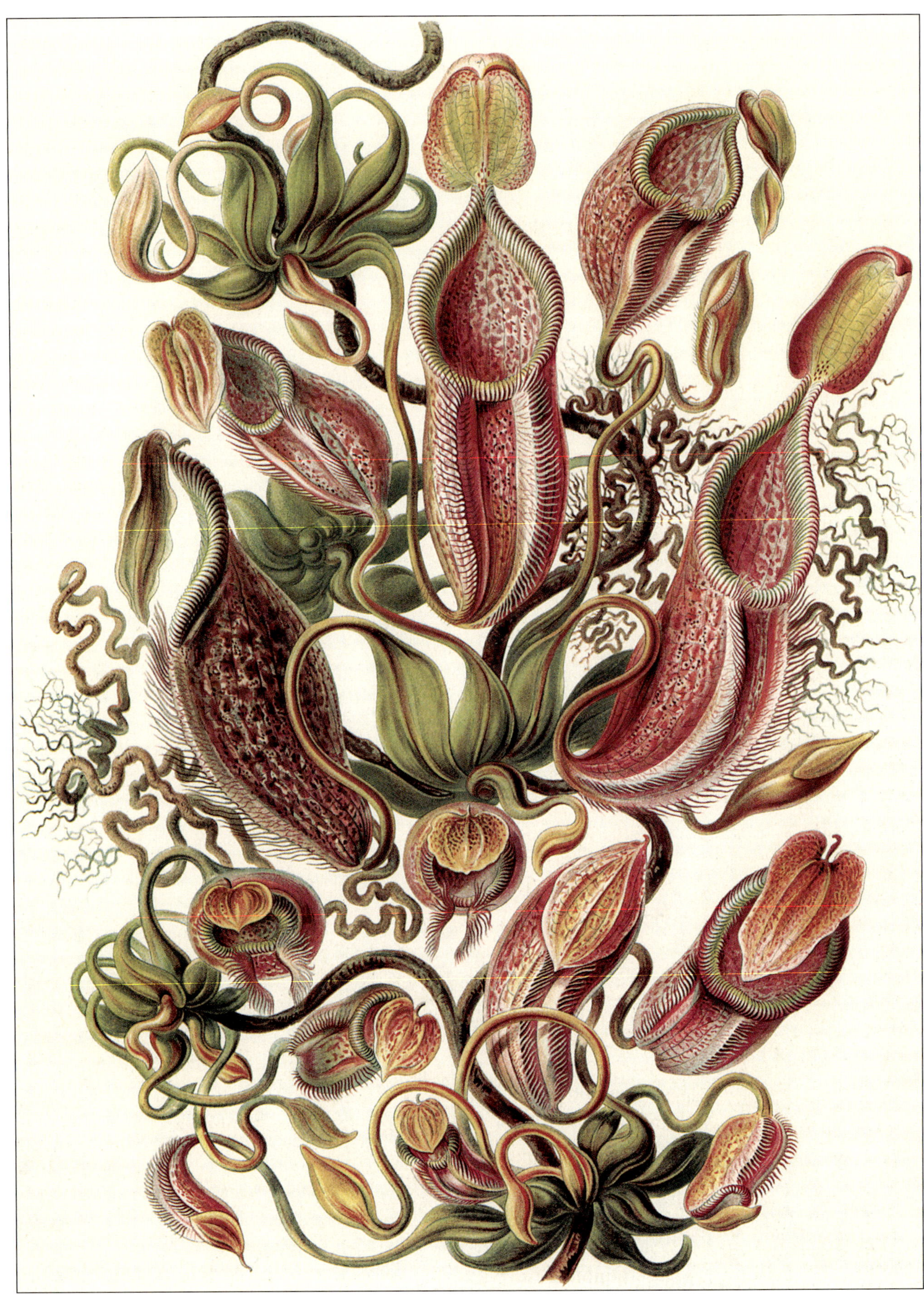

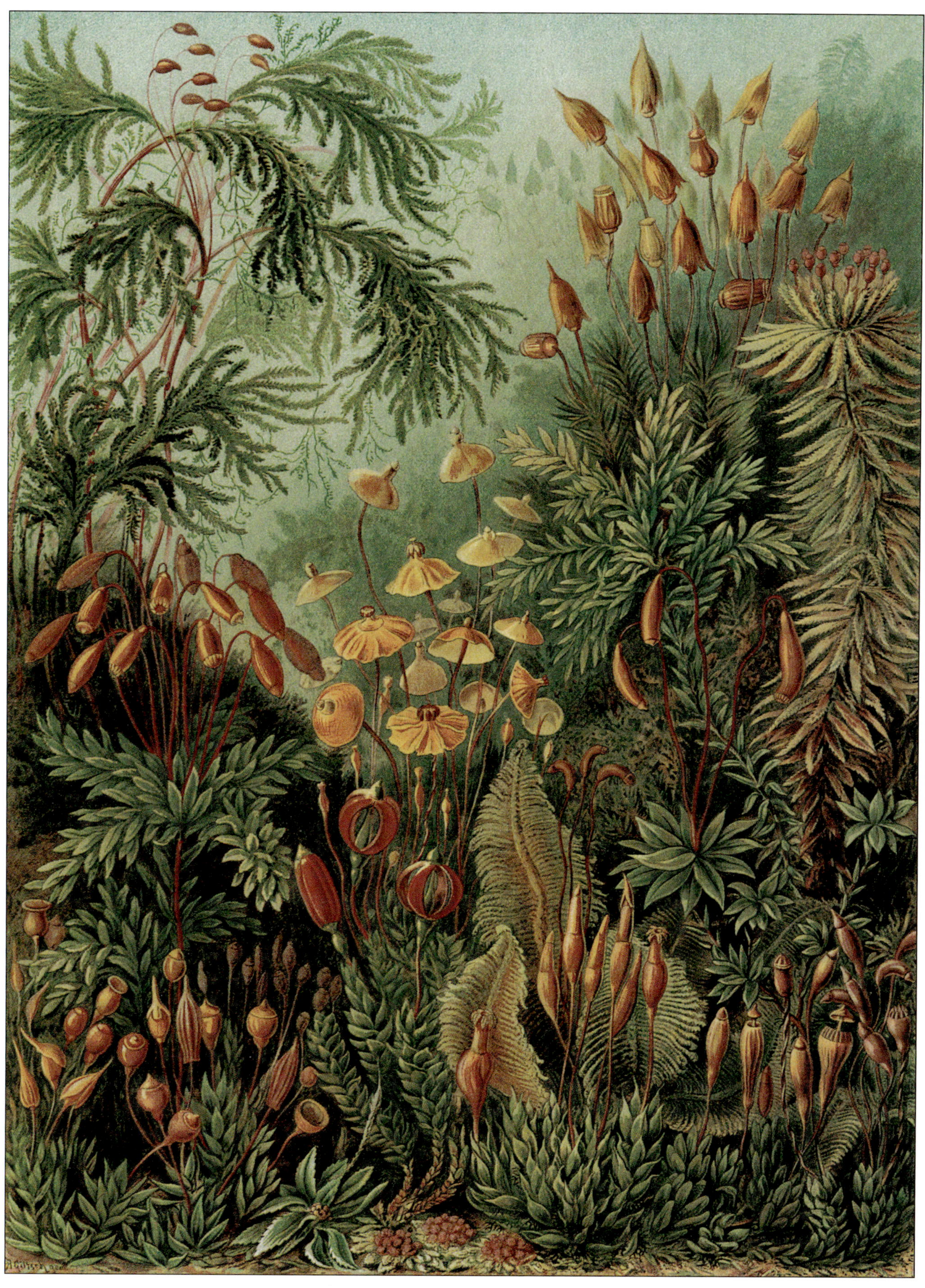

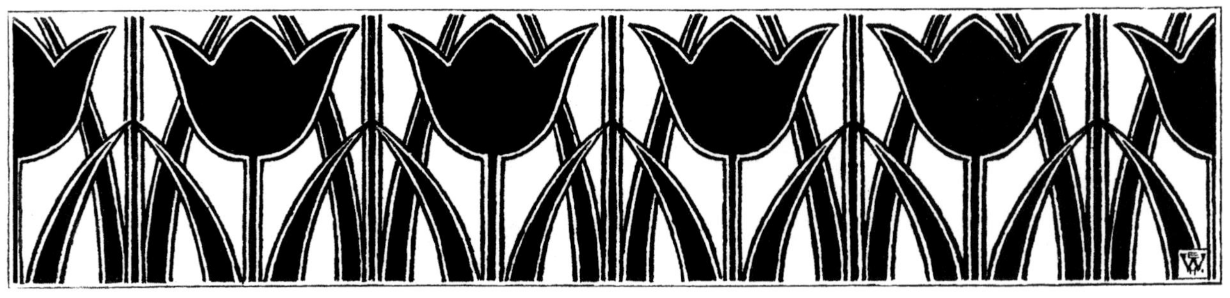

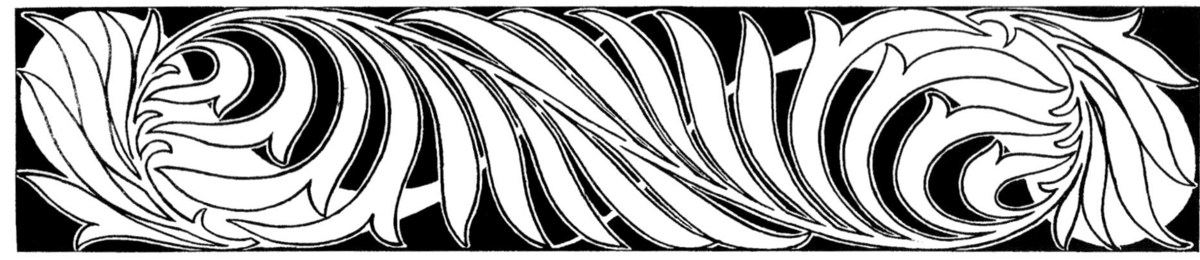

Images from *Motivenschatz für Modernes Kunstschaffen Studienblatter für Kuenstler* (Dresden: Verlag von Gerhard Kuehtmann). Published by Dover as *Early Twentieth Century Motifs from Nature,* available online at DoverPictura.com

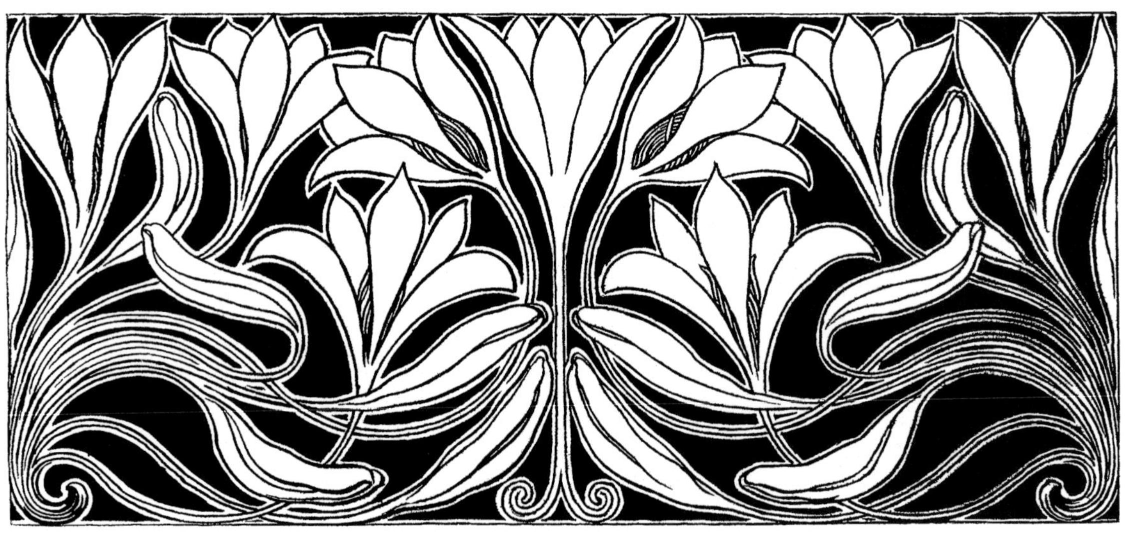

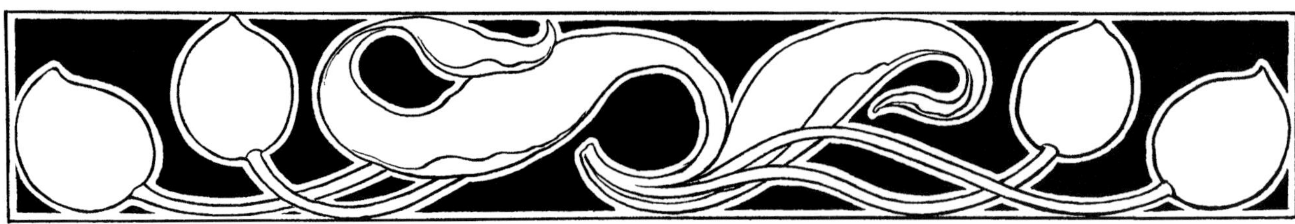

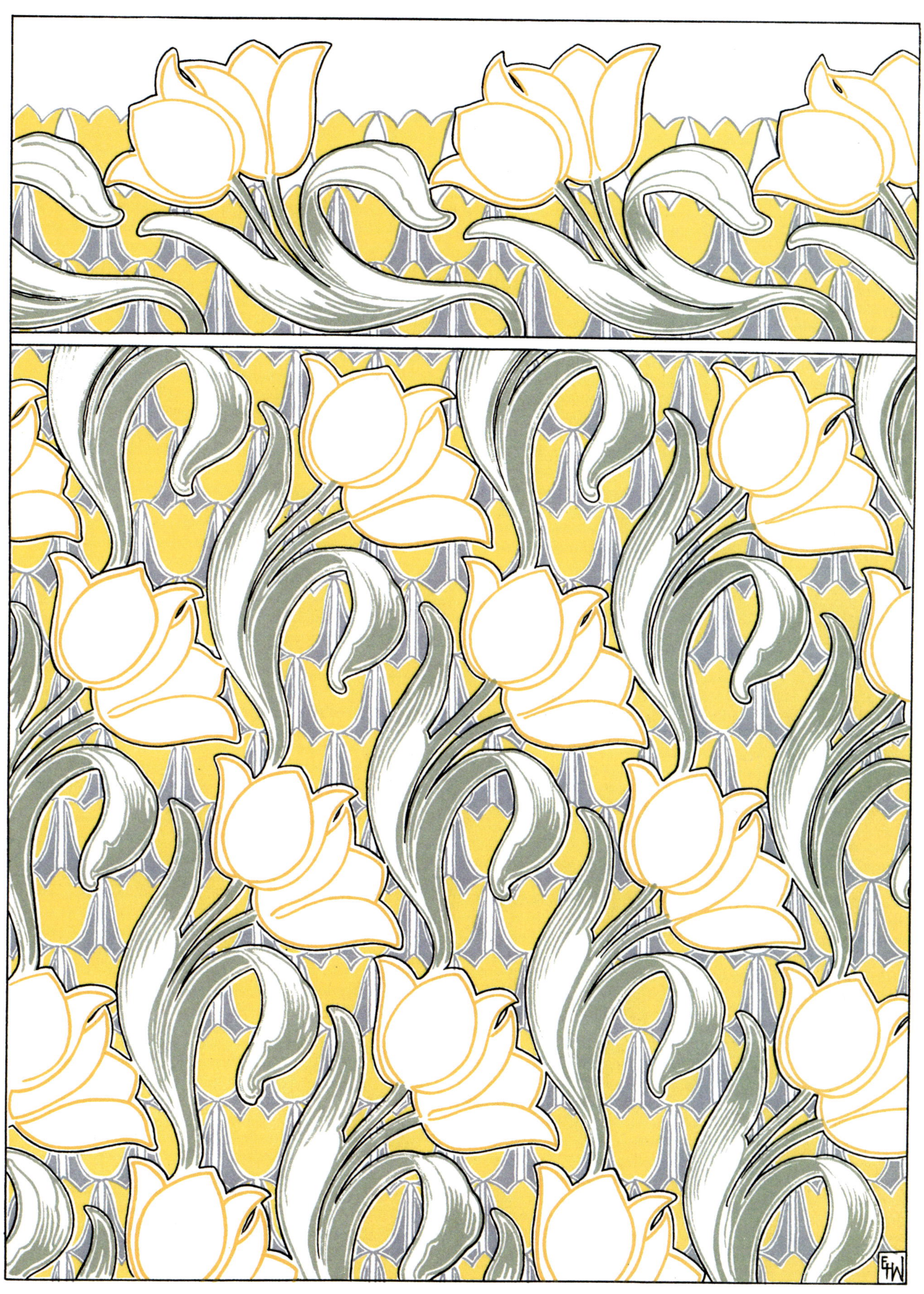

Images from the following three books by E. A. Seguy: *Primavera: Dessins & coloris nouveaux* (Plauen, Germany: Christian Stoll, n.d.), *Floréal: Dessins & coloris nouveaux* (Paris: A. Calavas, c. 1914), and *Samarkande: 20 compositions en couleurs dans le Style oriental* (Paris: Ch. Massin, c. 1920). Reprinted by Dover as *The Spectacular Color Floral Designs of E. A. Seguy* (New York, 1983).

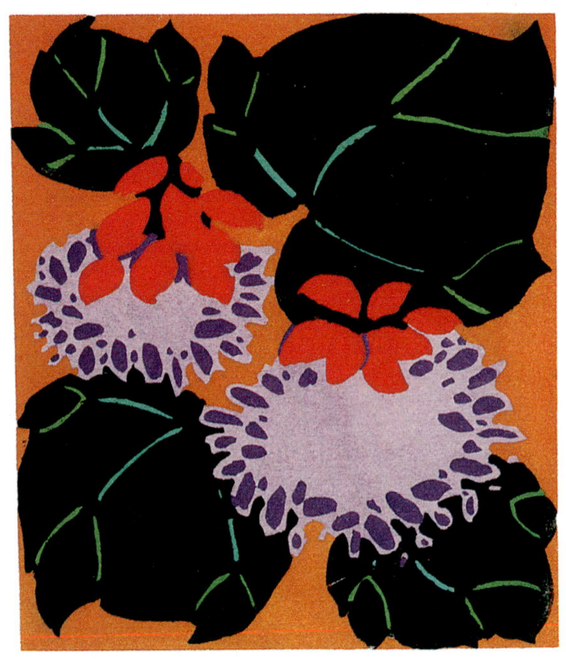

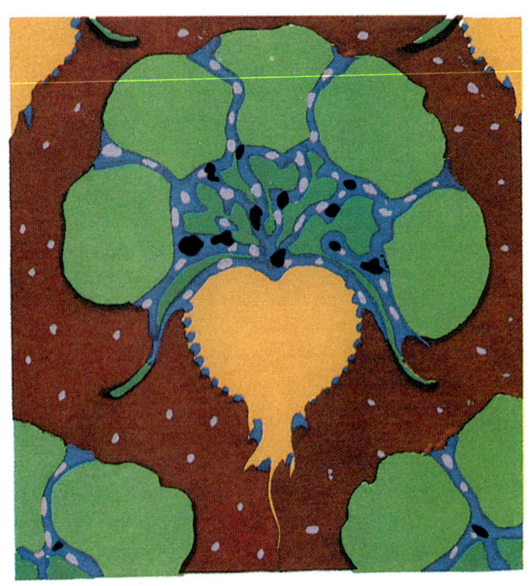

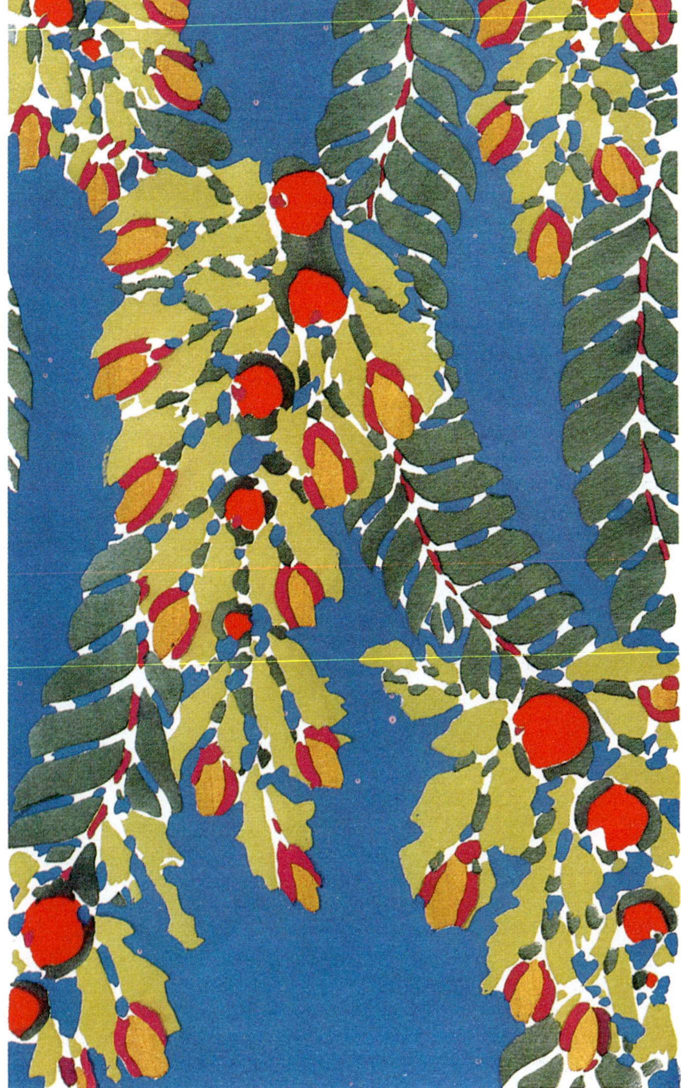

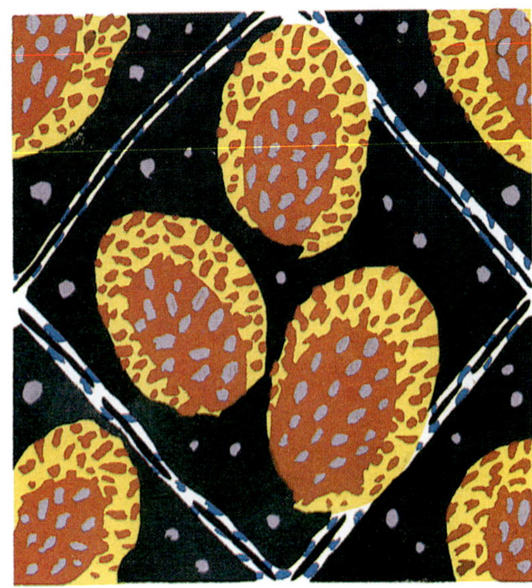

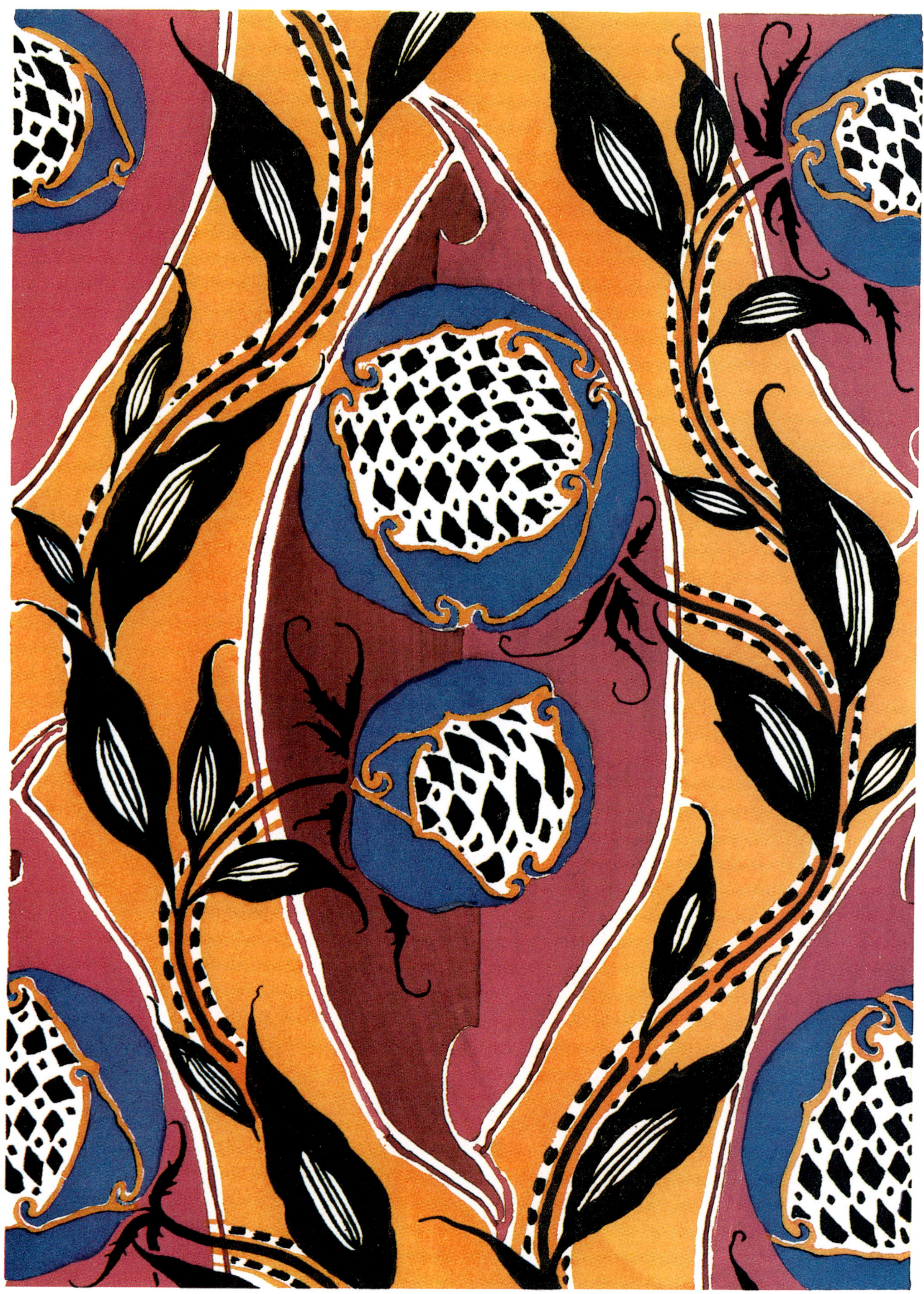

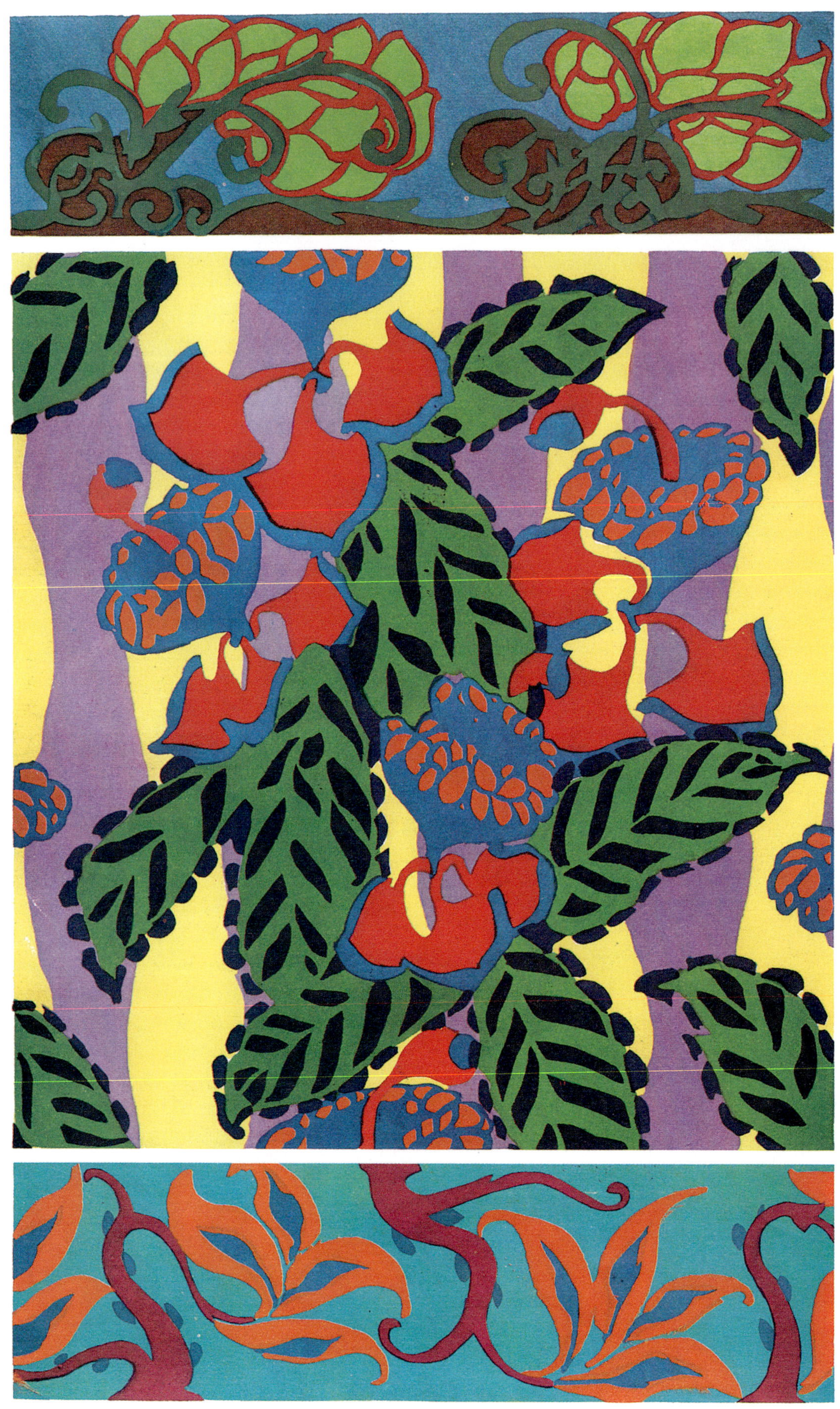

Images from
Seiyô Soka Zufu
(Kyoto: Unsôdô, c. 1917).
Published by Dover as
Japanese Woodblock Flower Prints,
by Tanigami Kônan
(Mineola, NY, 2008).

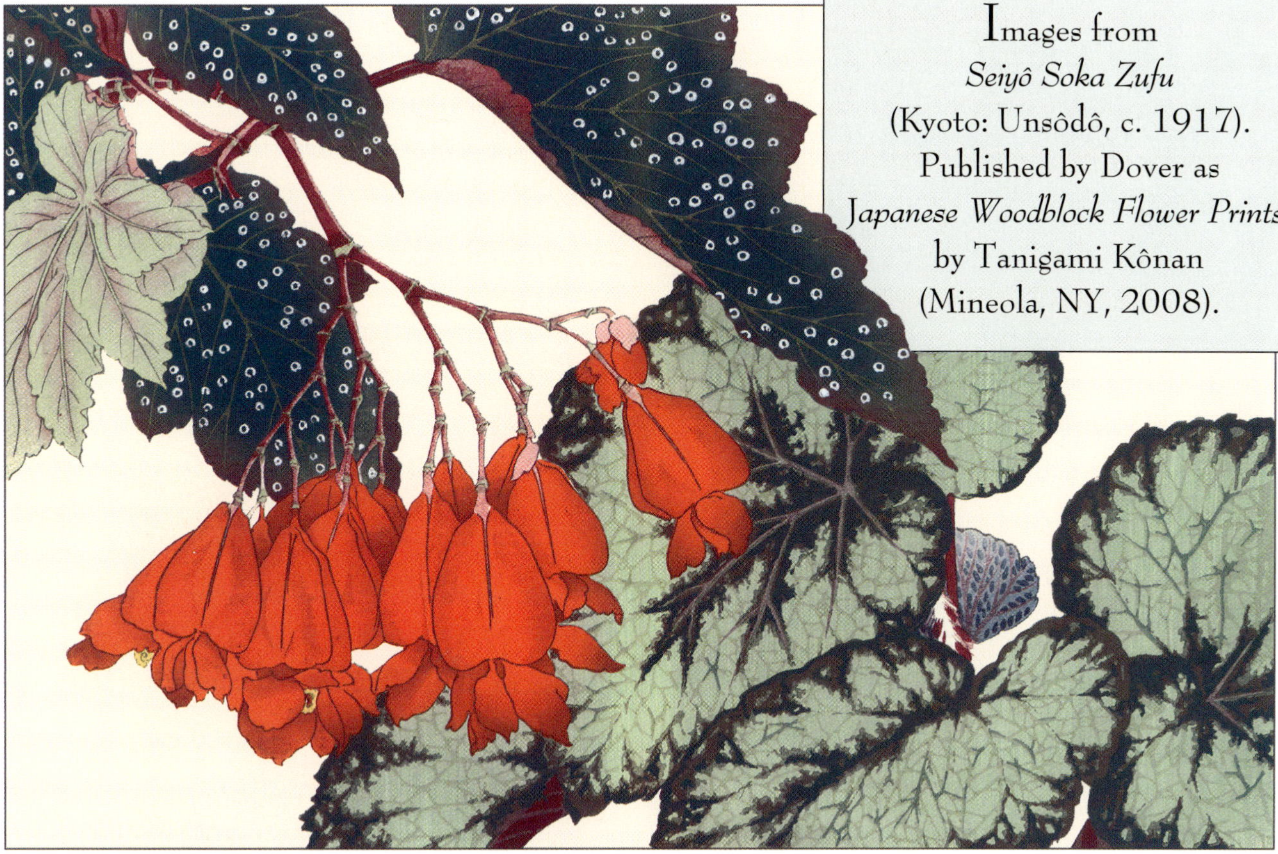

1

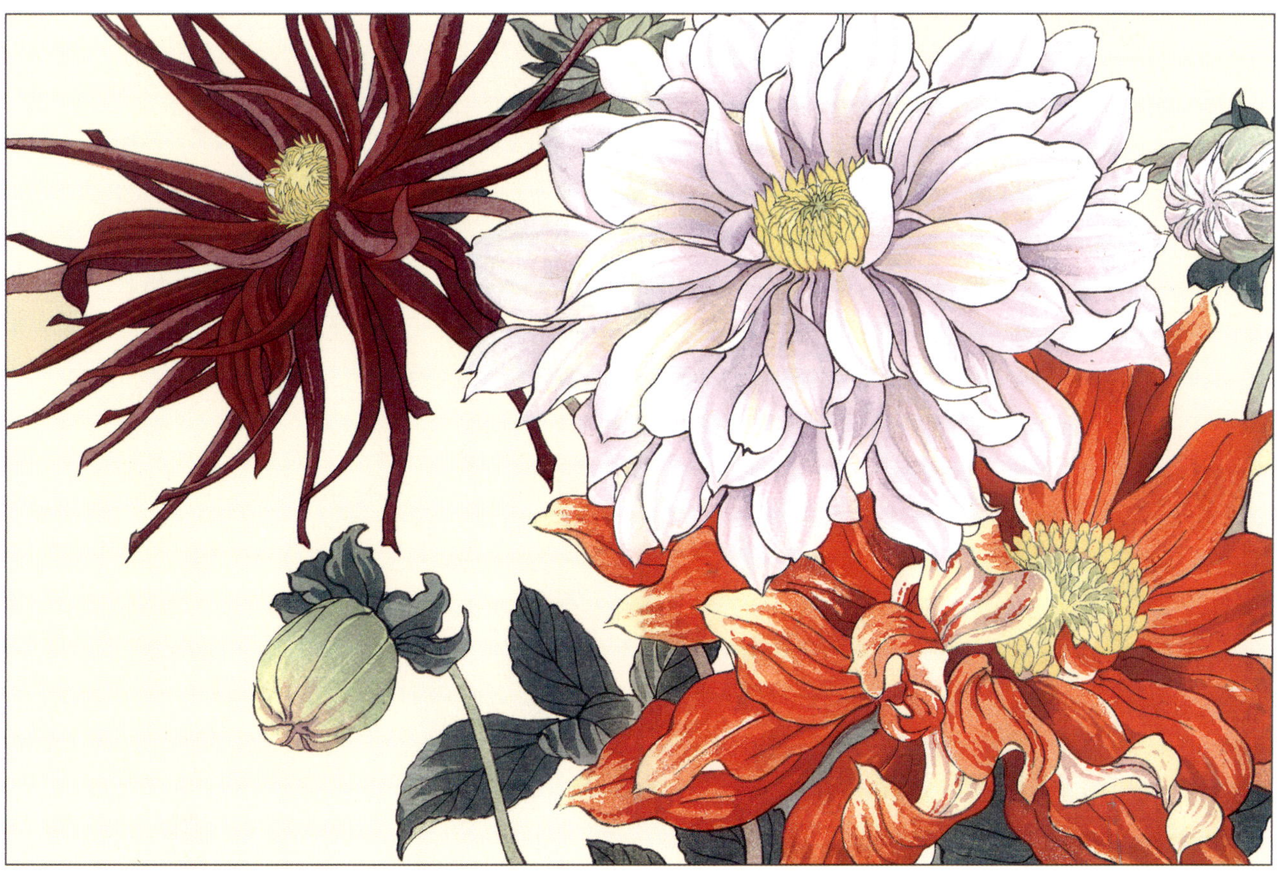

2

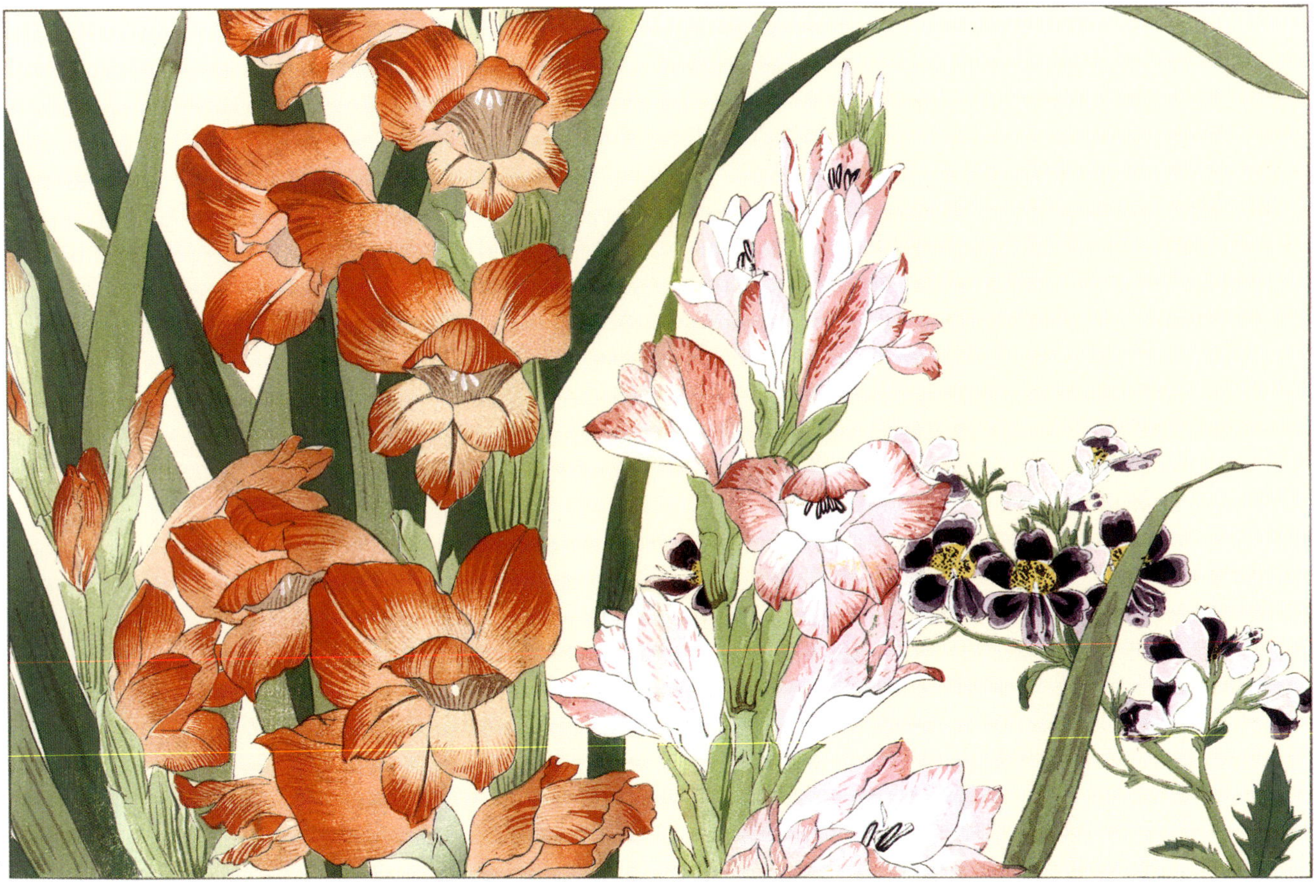

3

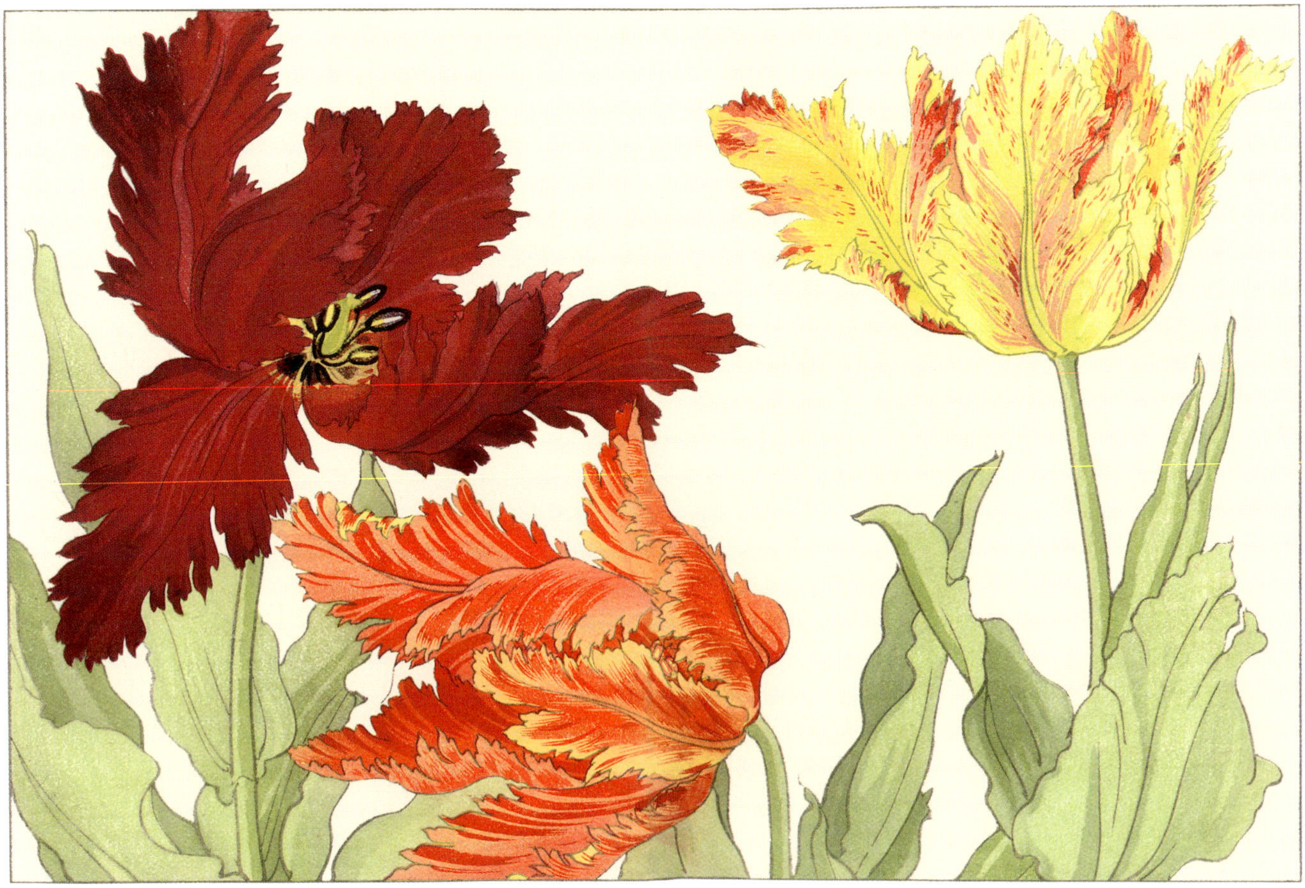

4

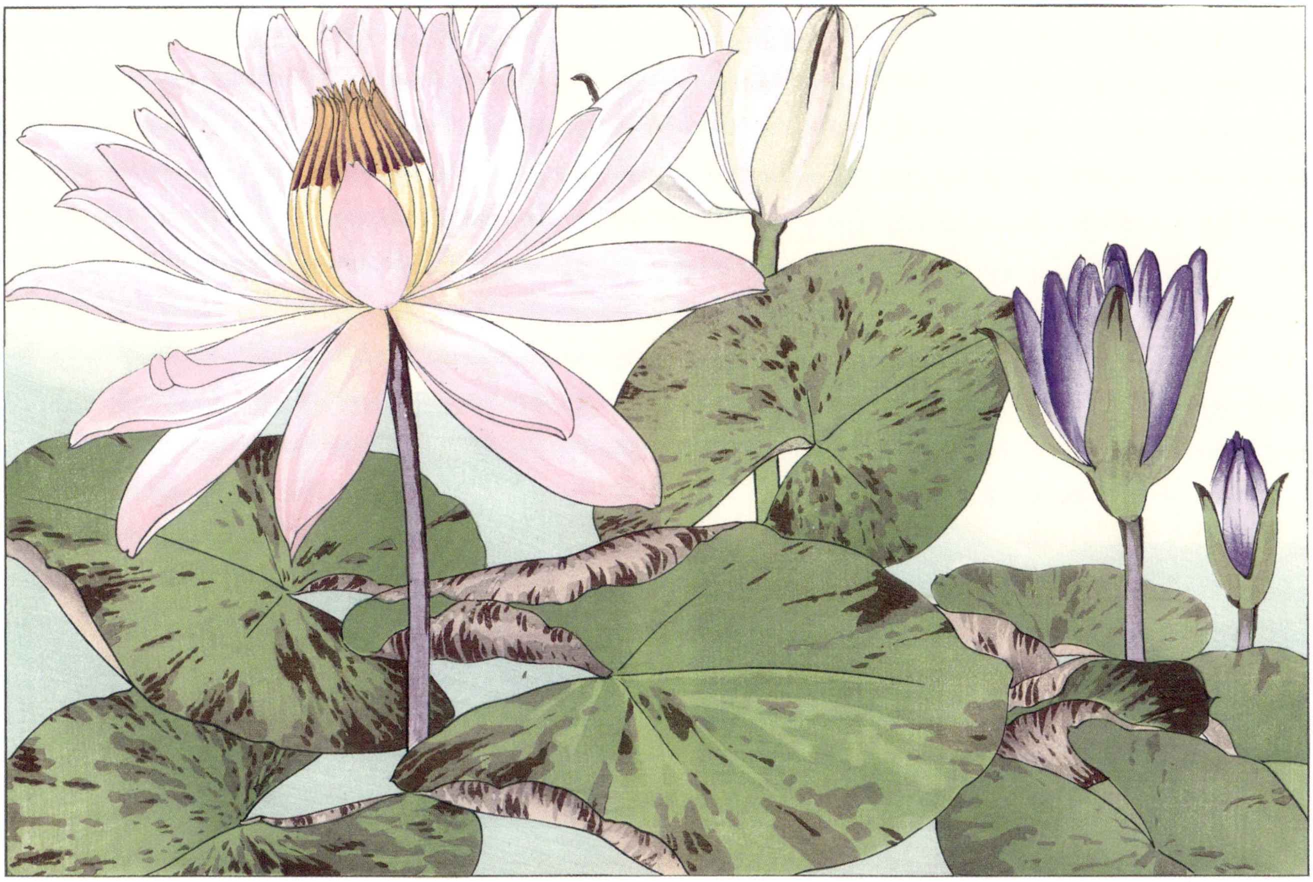

5

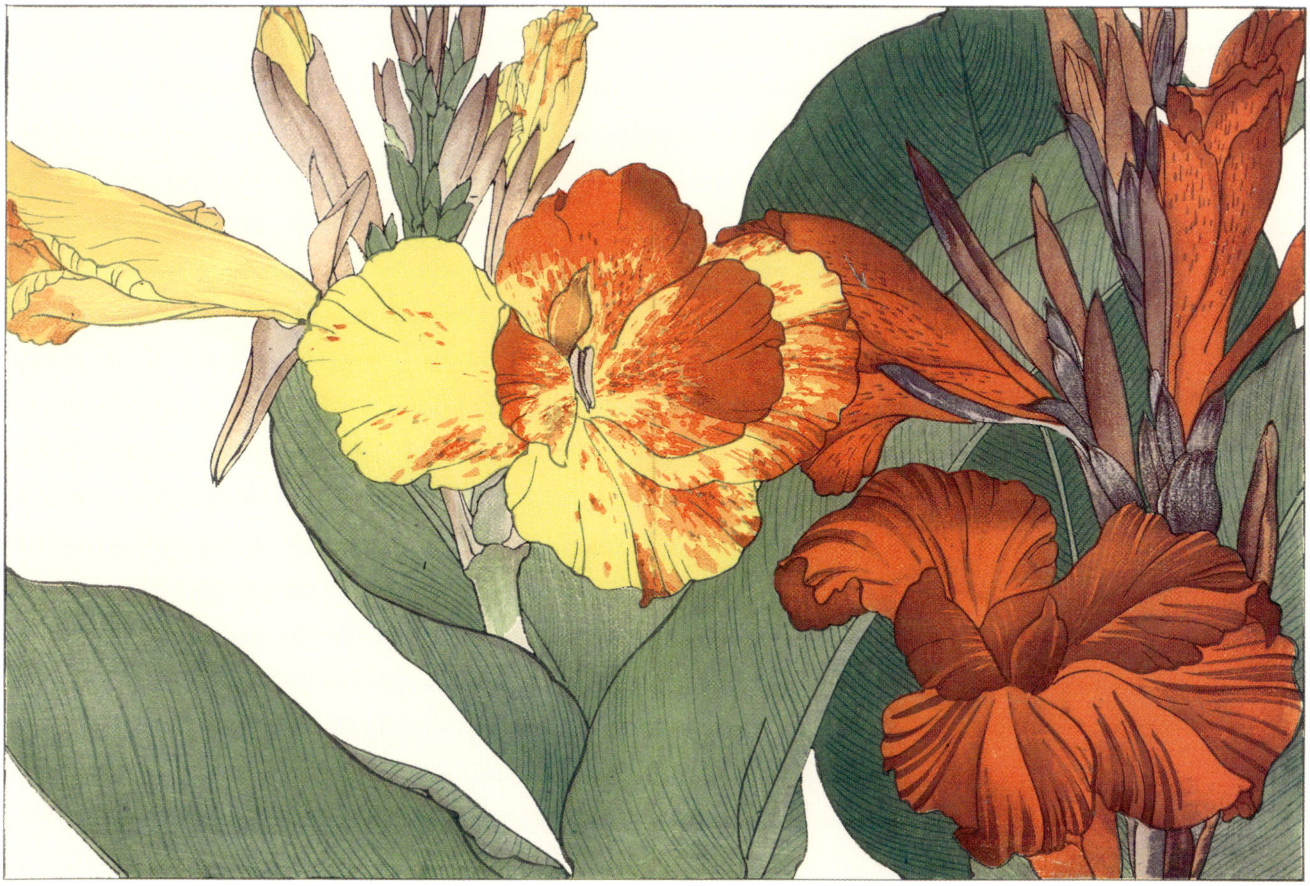

6

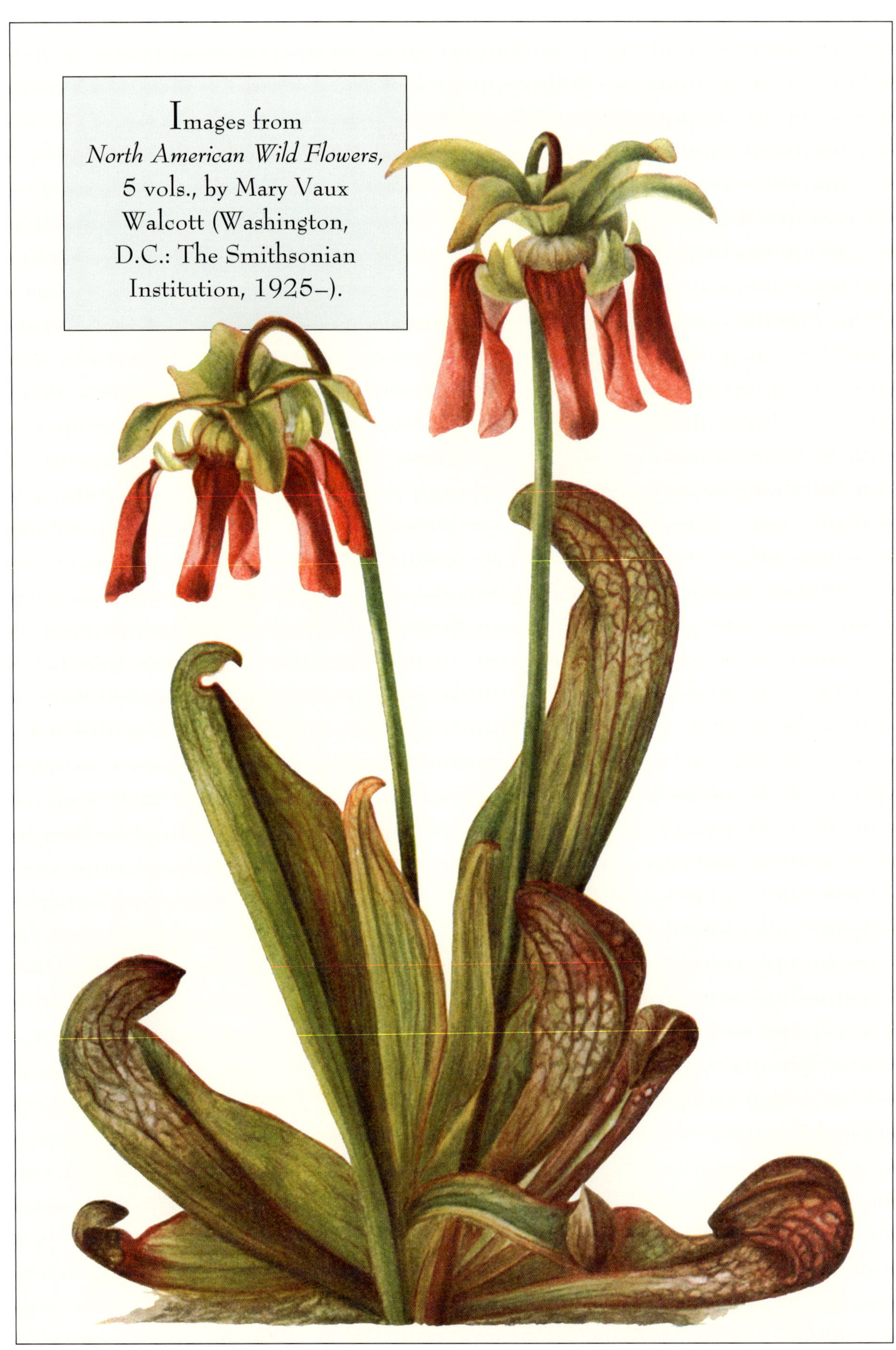

Images from
North American Wild Flowers,
5 vols., by Mary Vaux
Walcott (Washington,
D.C.: The Smithsonian
Institution, 1925–).

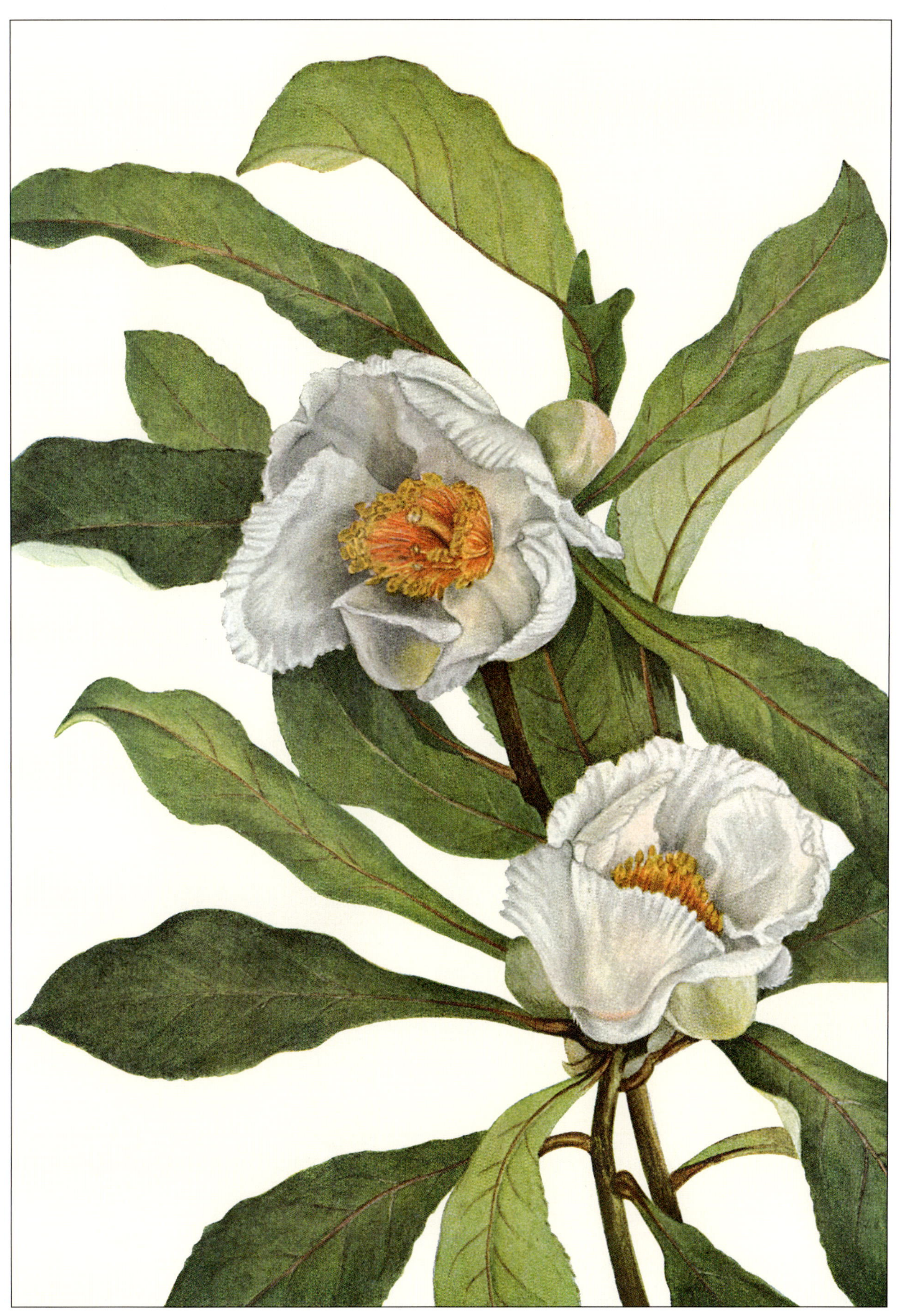

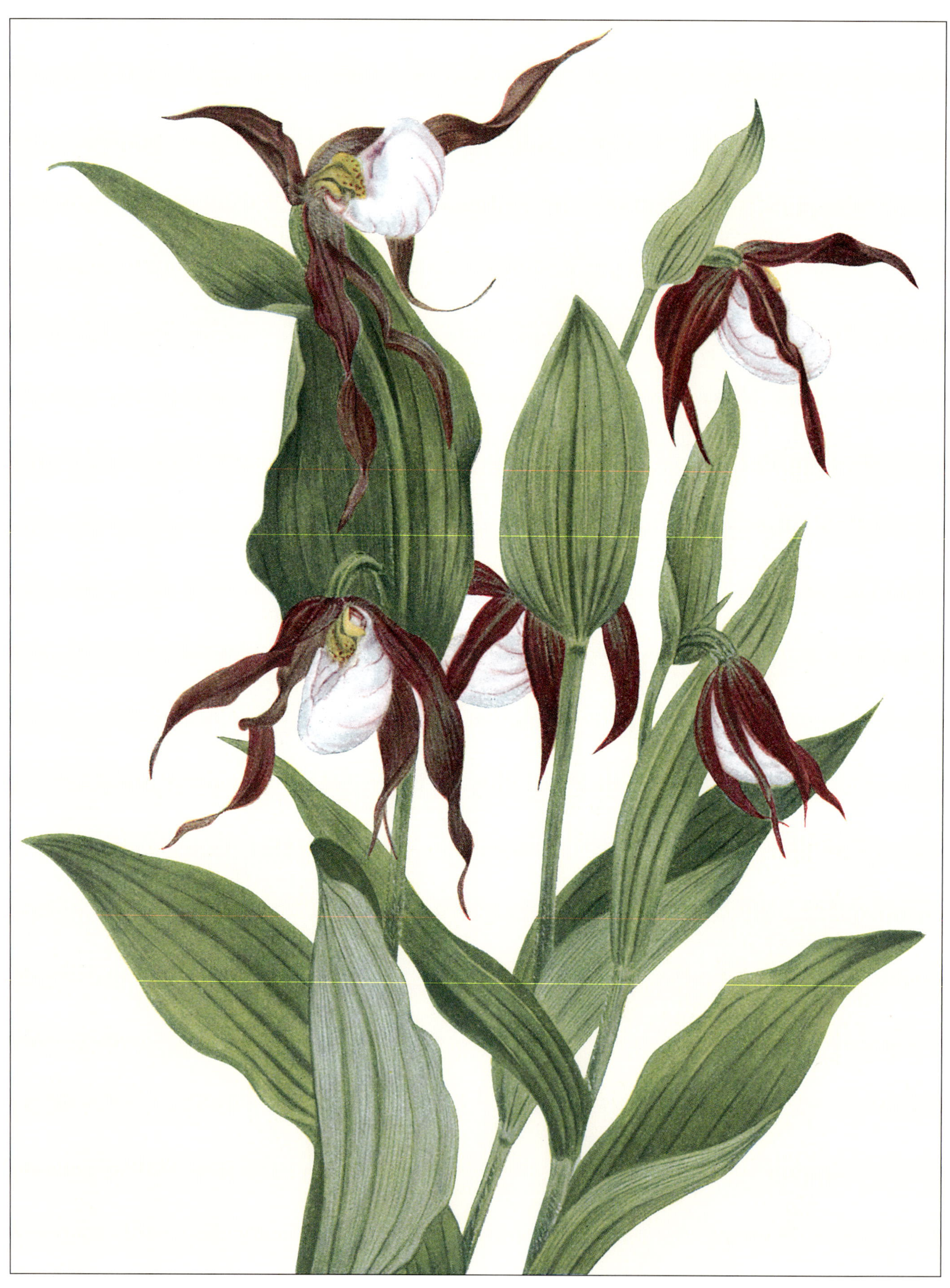

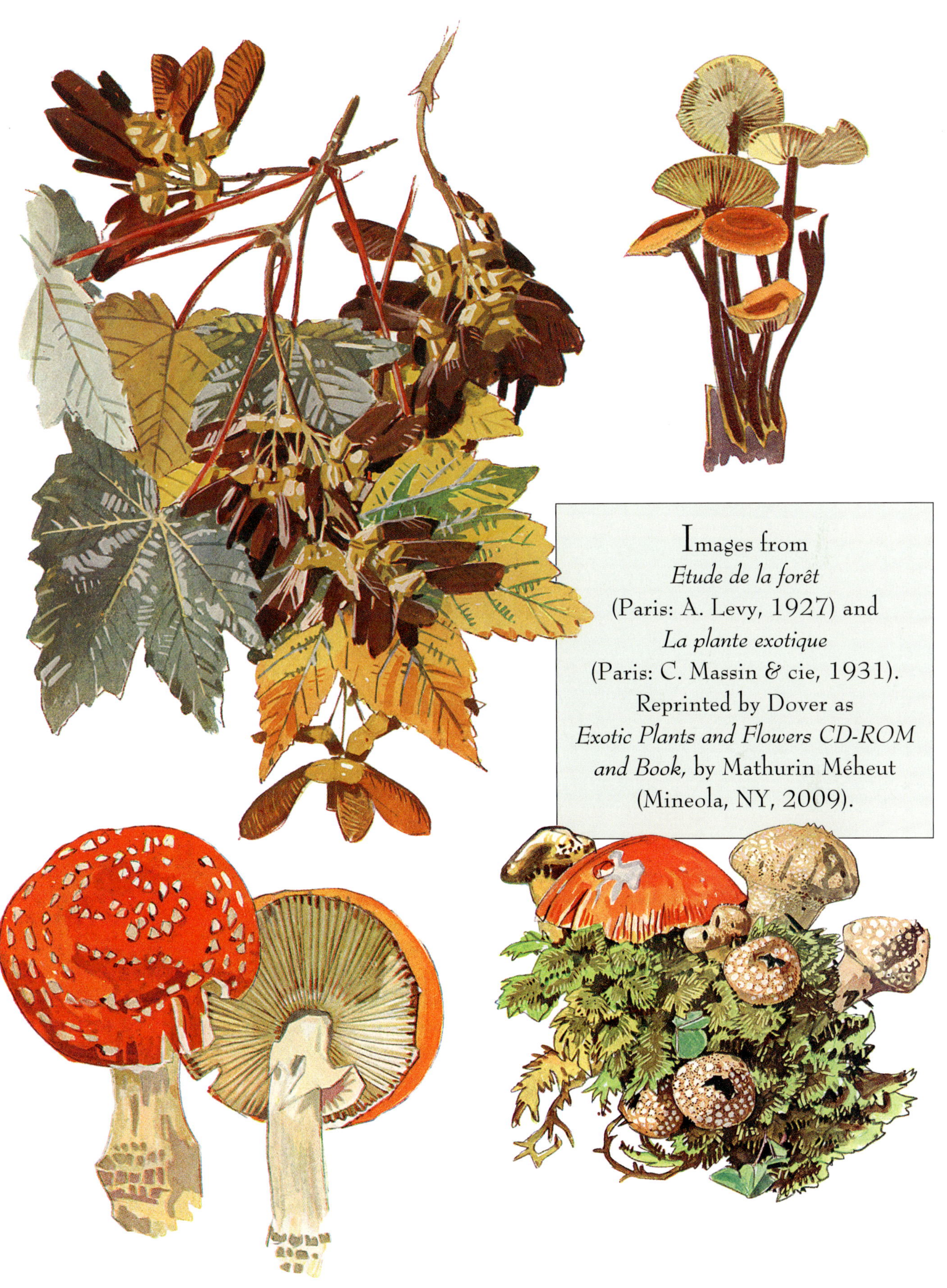

Images from
Etude de la forêt
(Paris: A. Levy, 1927) and
La plante exotique
(Paris: C. Massin & cie, 1931).
Reprinted by Dover as
Exotic Plants and Flowers CD-ROM and Book, by Mathurin Méheut
(Mineola, NY, 2009).

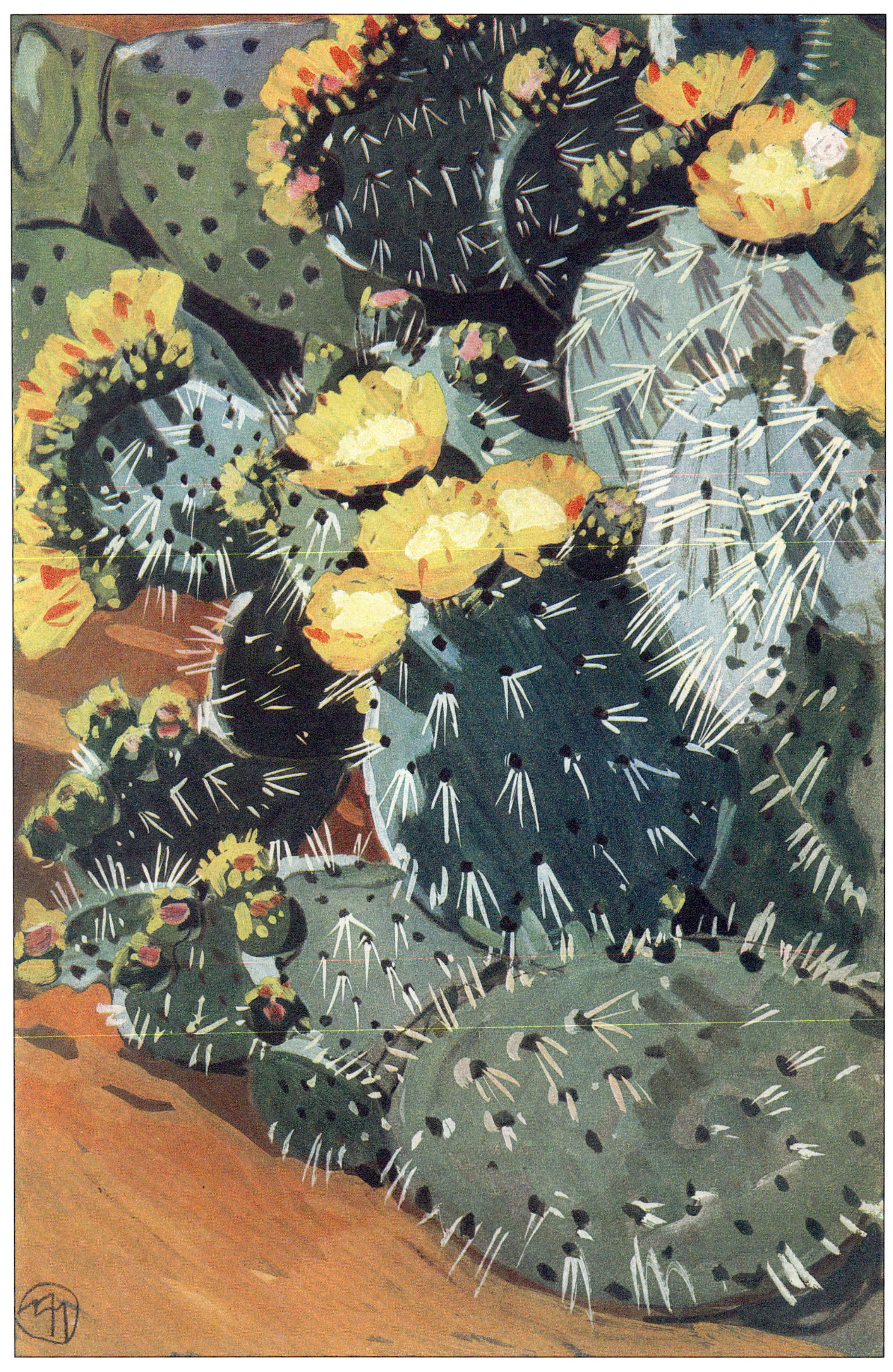

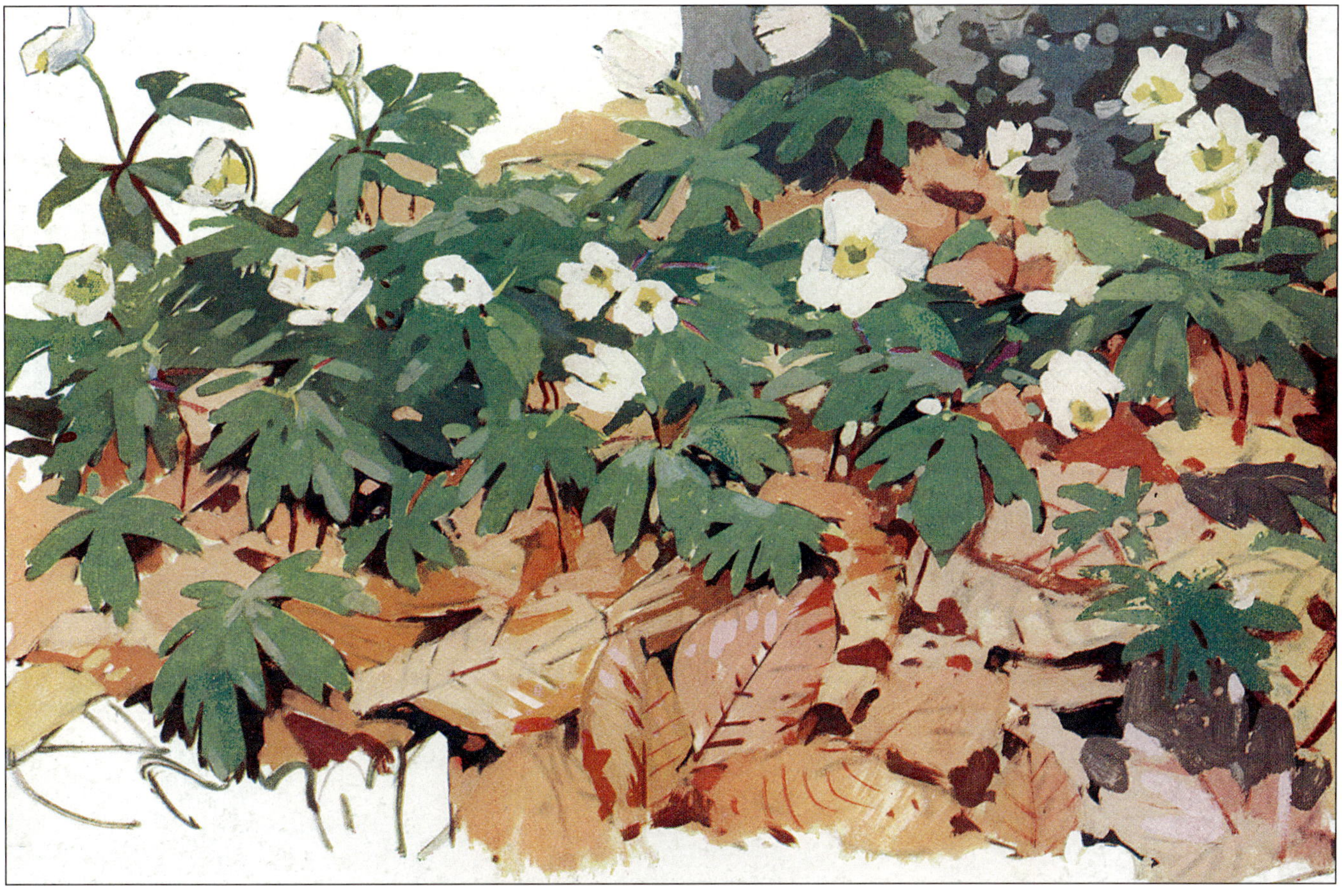

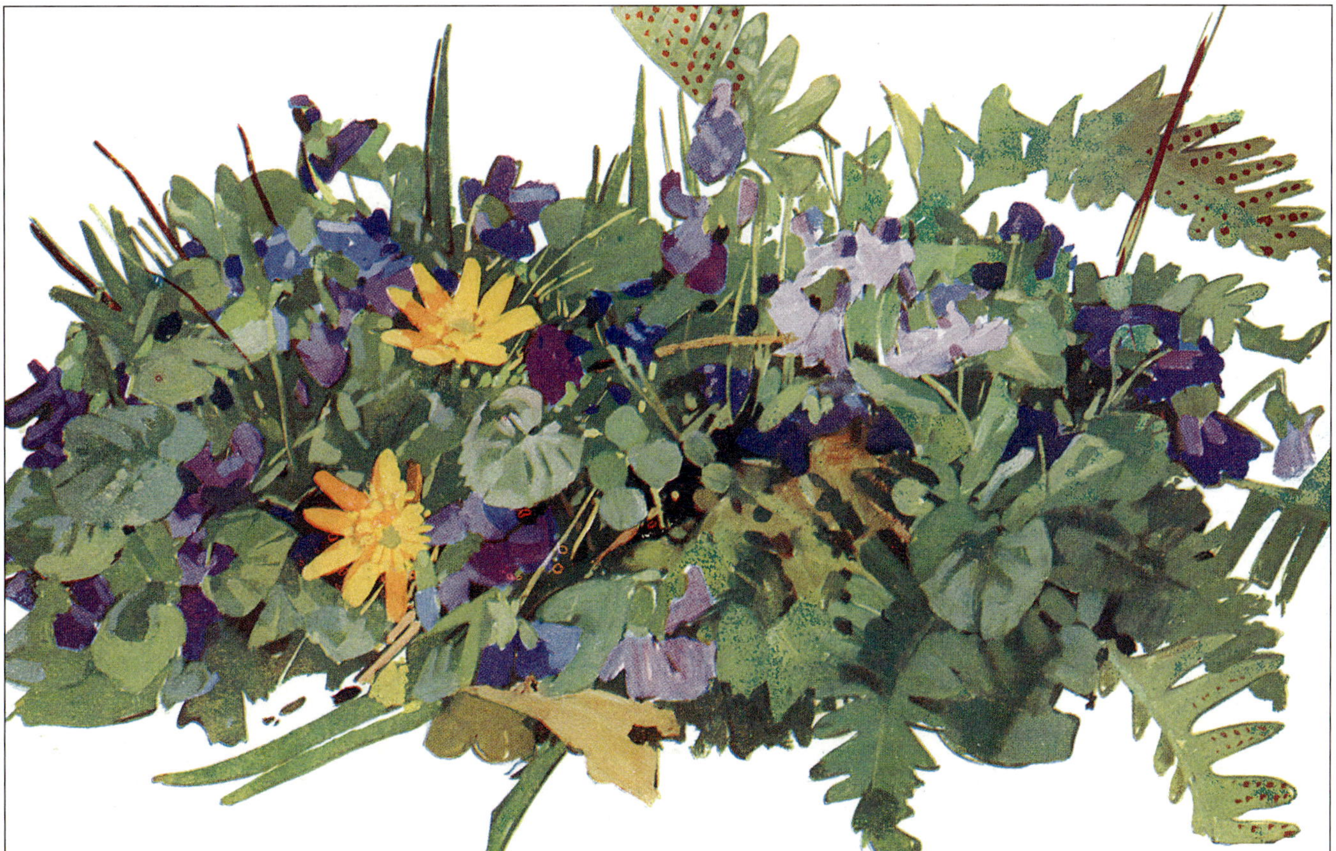

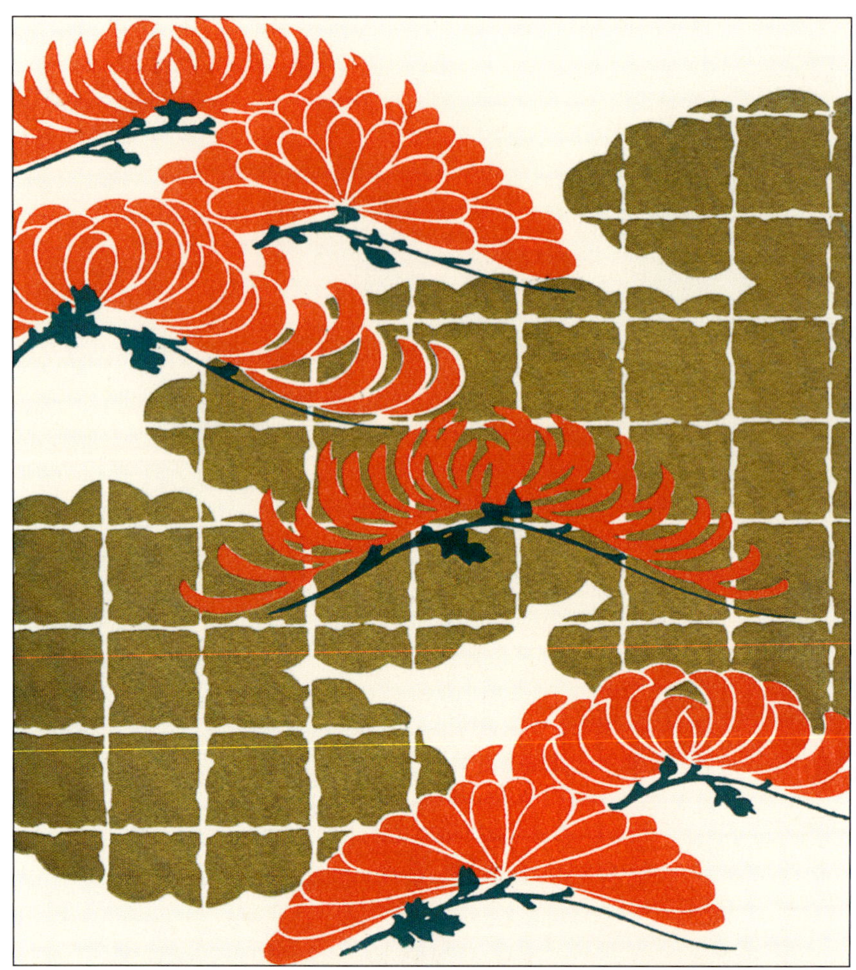

Images from
Kiku Hyakushu
(Kyoto: Uchida Bijutsu Shoshi, 1936).
Reprinted by Dover as
The Chrysanthemum in Japanese Design,
by Kawarasaki Kôtô
(Mineola, NY, 2012).

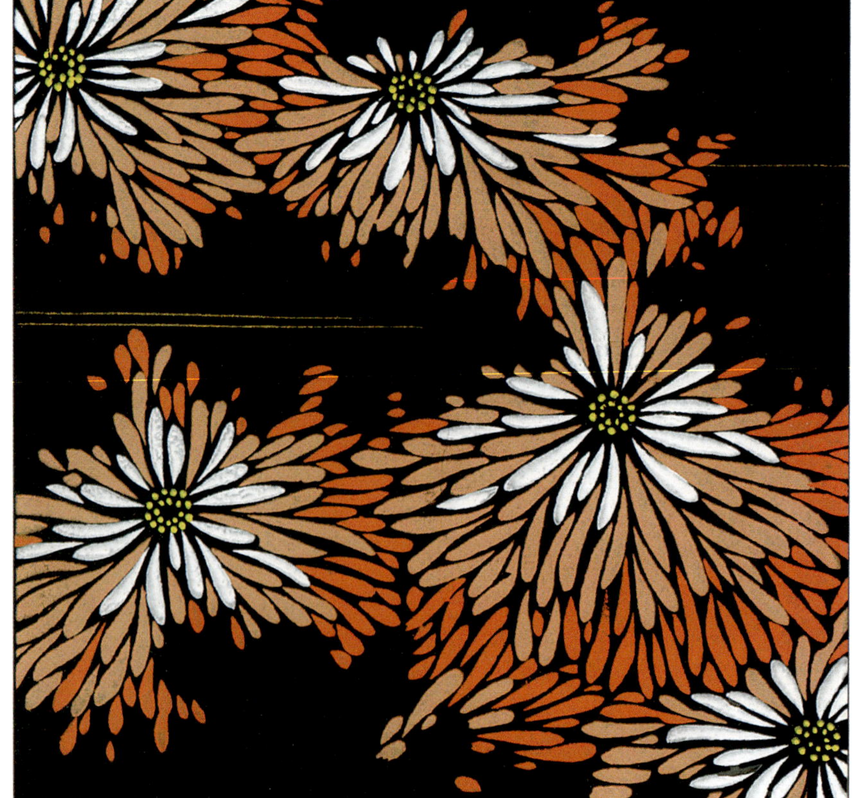

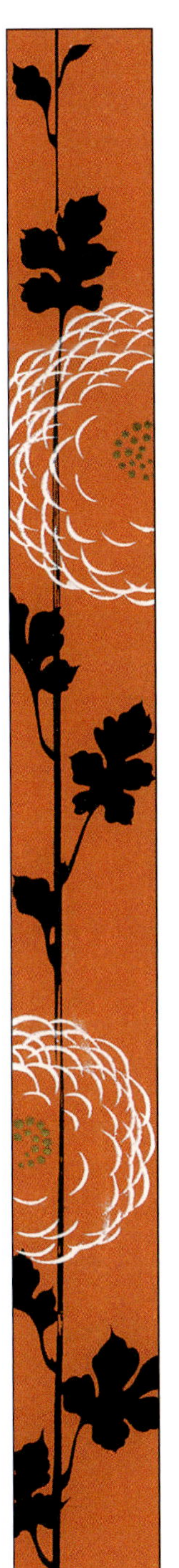
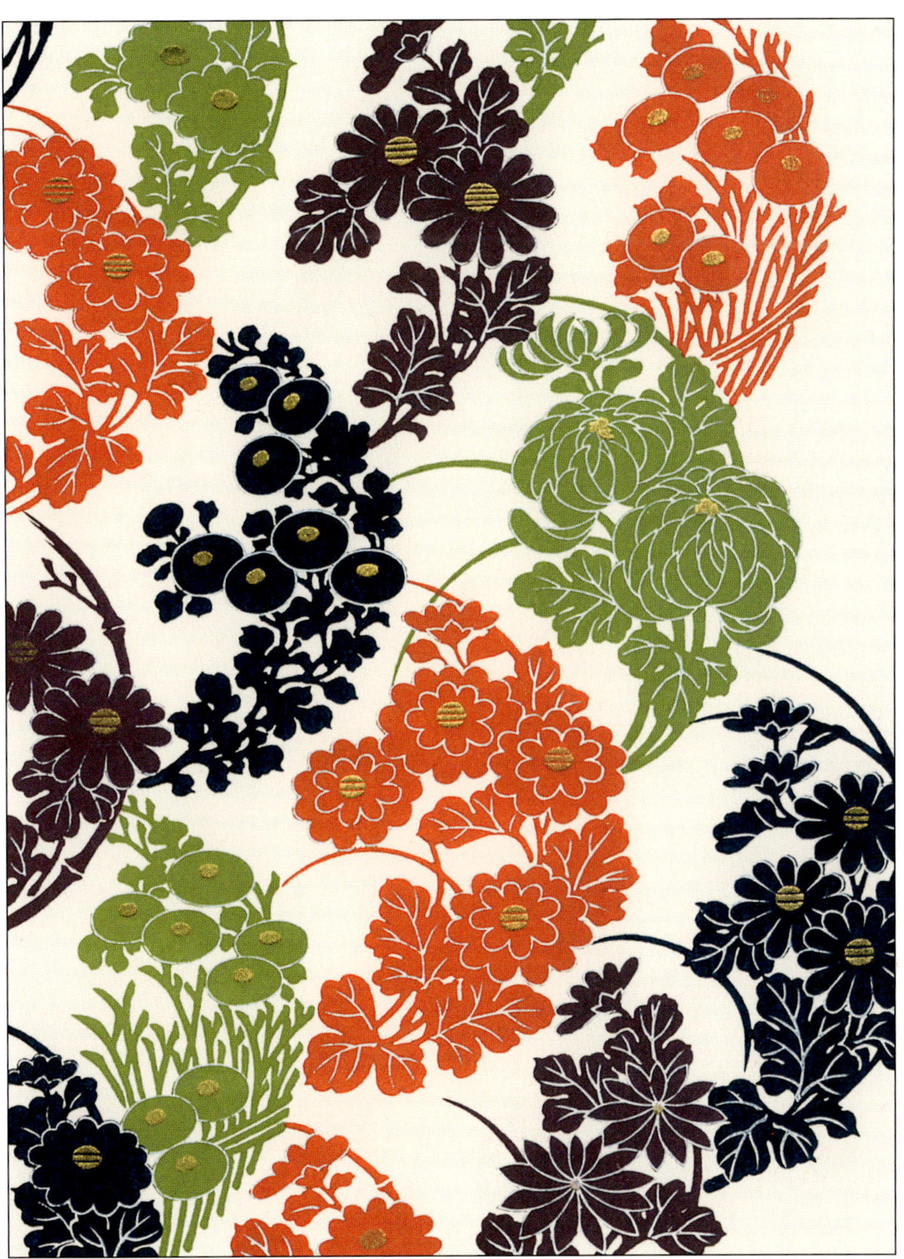
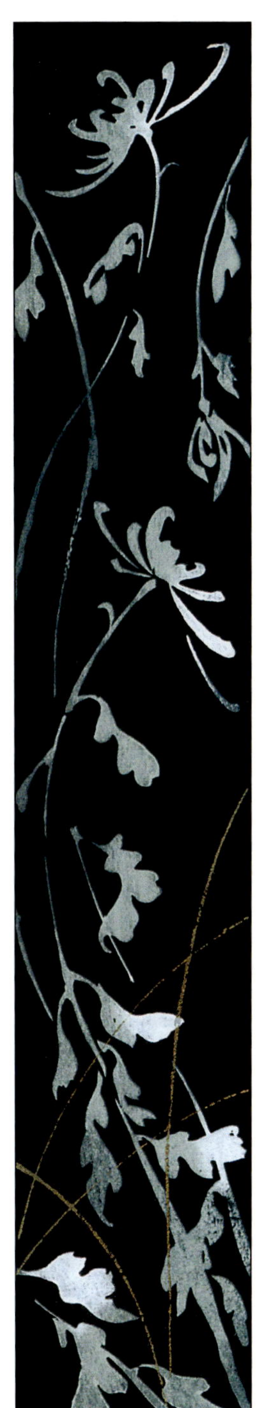
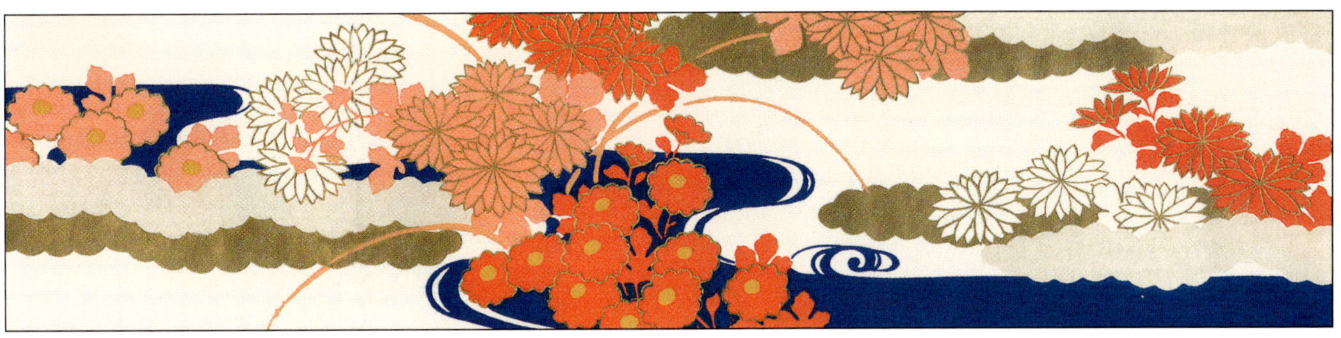

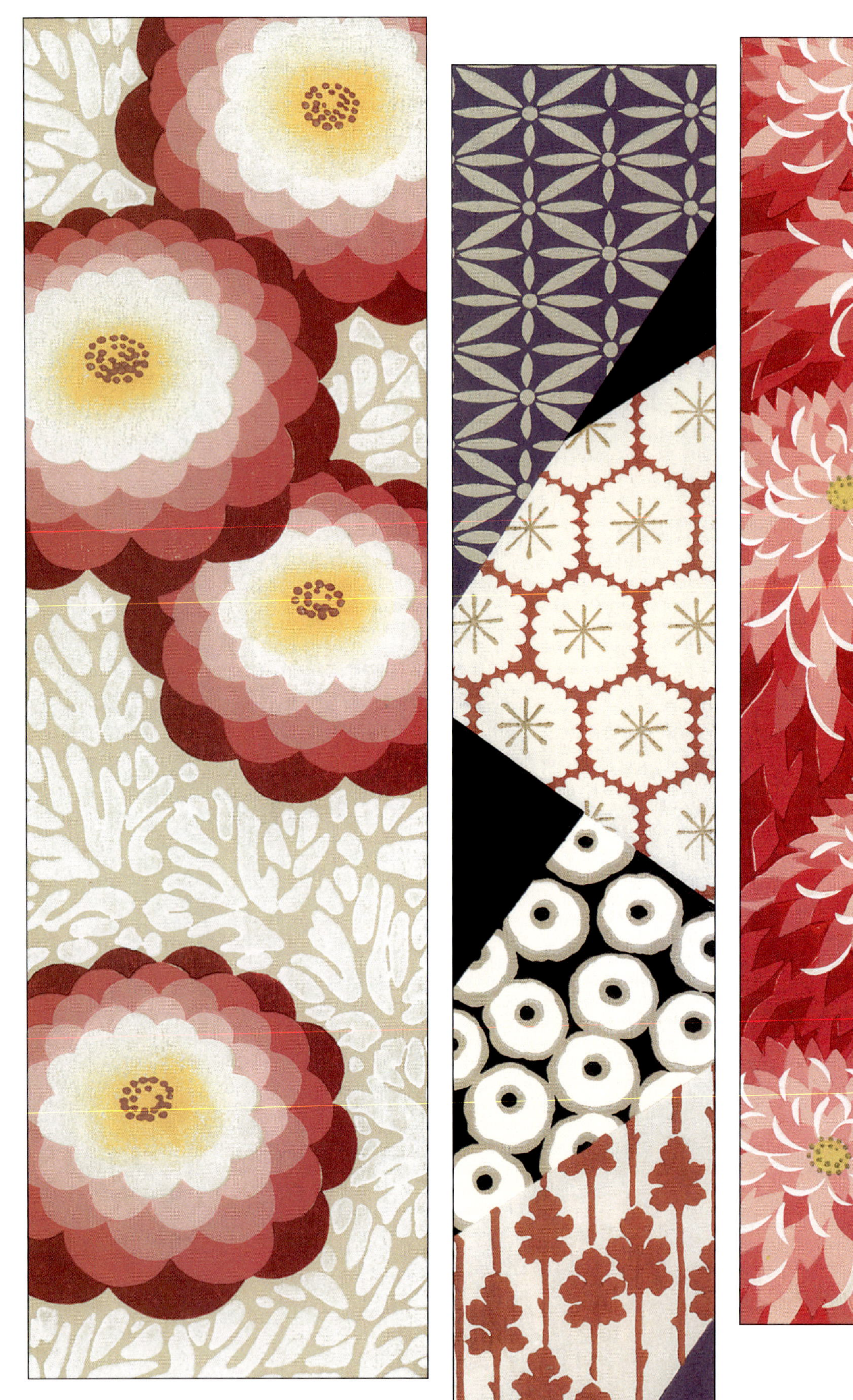

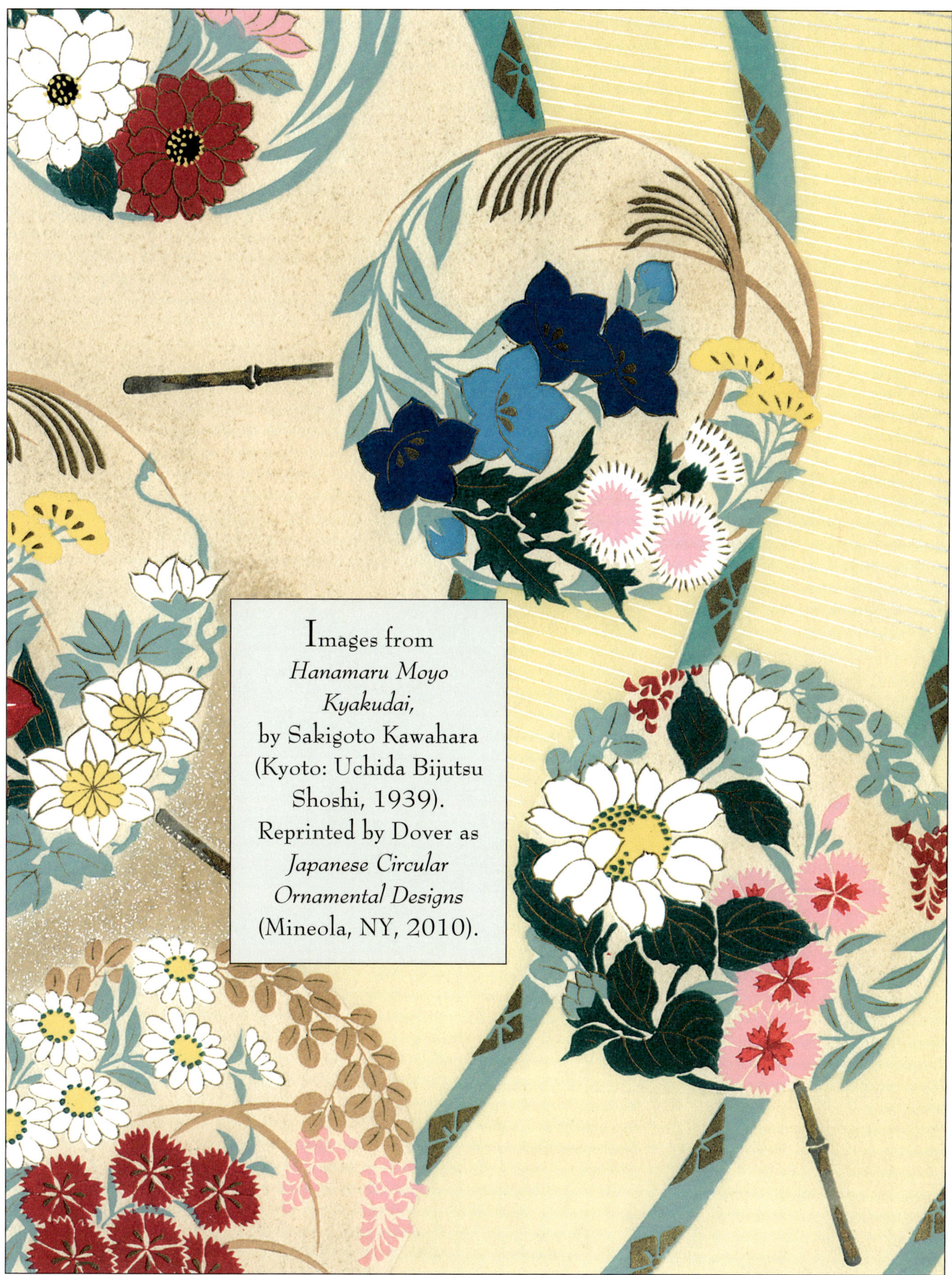

Images from
Hanamaru Moyo Kyakudai,
by Sakigoto Kawahara
(Kyoto: Uchida Bijutsu Shoshi, 1939).
Reprinted by Dover as
Japanese Circular Ornamental Designs
(Mineola, NY, 2010).

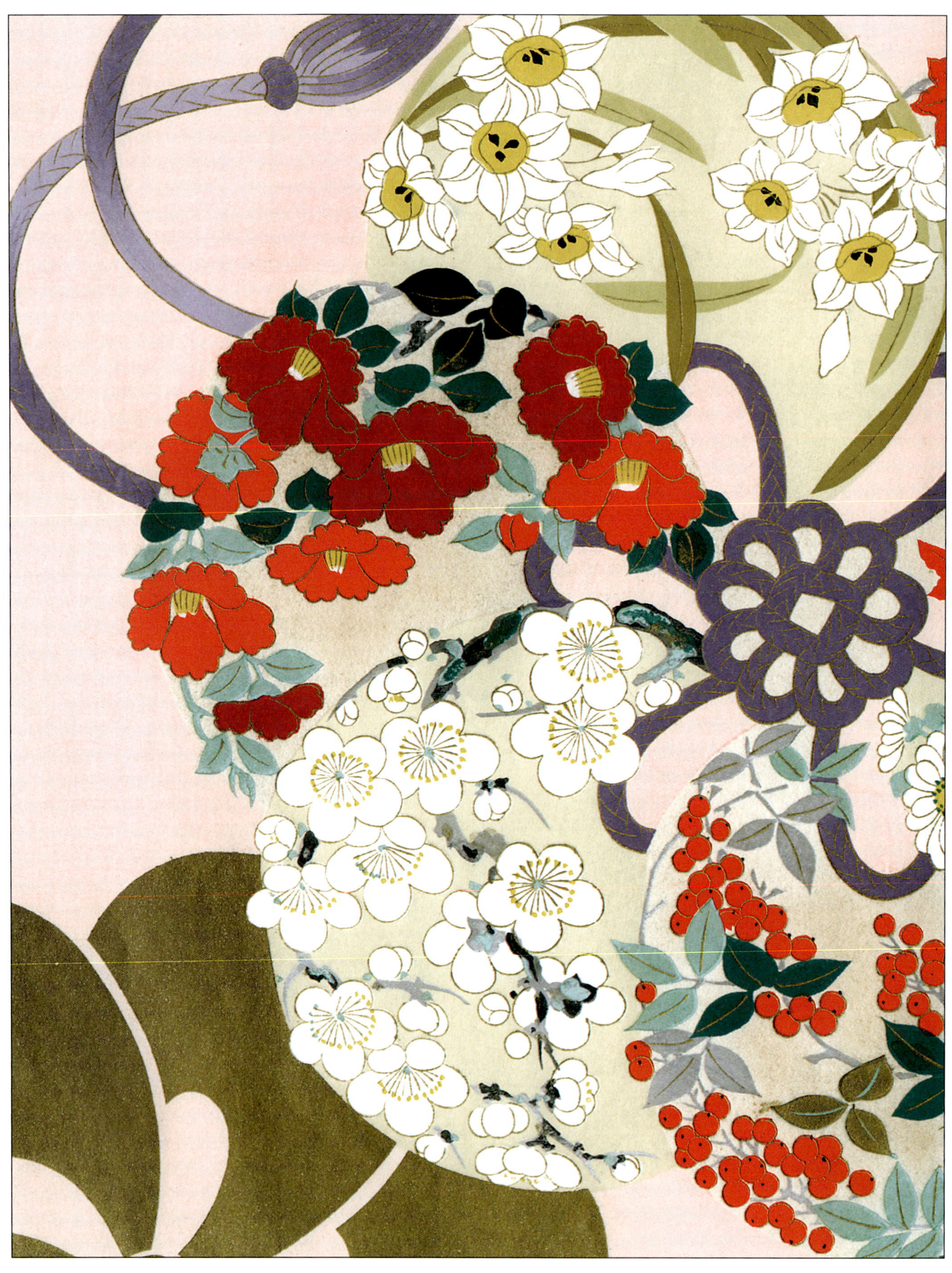

INDEX OF ARTISTS

Ferdinand Lukas Bauer (1760–1826)

Plate 44

Austrian botanical artist and engraver, served as botanical draughtsman on Matthew Flinders' 1801–03 expedition to circumnavigate Australia during which he produced drawings of more than 1,500 Australian plants and 300 Australian animals.

Basilius Besler (1561–1629)

Plates 8–10

German apothecary and botanist, created the great *Hortus Eystettensis* documenting the plants in the magnificent gardens at Eichstätt.

Abraham Bosse (1604–1676)

Plates 16–17

French artist and engraver, created depictions of French gardens.

Jean Bourdichon (1457/59–1521)

Plate 4

French miniature painter and manuscript illuminator, most famous for the *Grandes Heures of Anne of Brittany.*

Gustave Caillebotte (1848–1894)

Plate 94

This French Impressionist painter loved horticulture and produced many exquisite landscapes and floral pieces. He is, however, best known for his paintings of urban Paris.

Samuel Curtis (1779–1860)

Plate 50

Nurseryman and Proprietor of *The Botanical Magazine* founded by his father-in-law William Curtis. Published the classic flower book, *The Beauties of Flora* (1806–20).

Thomas W. Cutler [dates unknown]

Plates 70–71

Author of *A Grammar of Japanese Ornament* (London, 1880).

Georg Dionysius Ehret (1708–1770)

Plates 27–29

From his beginnings as a gardener's apprentice, went on, first in his native Germany and later in England, to become one of the greatest botanical artists in history.

Walter Hood Fitch (1817–1892)

Plates 62–63

Glasgow-born botanical illustrator, created 10,000 drawings in his lifetime, including almost 3,000 for *Curtis's Botanical Magazine.*

Hendrick Fromantiou (1633–after 1693)

Frontispiece

Dutch still life painter and, after 1670, conservator of the Royal collection at Potsdam. Exposed a famous episode of forgery in the 17th-century art world.

John Gerard (c. 1545–1612)

Plates 14–15

English botanist and herbalist, compiled the famous *Herbal, or General Historie of Plantes,* first published in 1597, and universally known as *Gerard's Herbal.*

Charles Gmelich (1875–1955)

Plates 98–99

German art instructor who studied in Paris around the turn of the nineteenth century. Collaborated with Gustave Kolb on a 1902 collection of Art Nouveau ornamental plates, *Von Der Pflanze Zum Ornament (From Plant to Ornament).*

Eugène Grasset (1845–1917)

Plates 82–83

Swiss designer, based in Paris after 1871, best known for his Art Nouveau graphic design. One of the pioneers of the Art Nouveau movement, several of his iconic posters are included in the famous collection *Les Maîtres de l'Affiche (Masters of the Poster)* (Paris: 1895–1900.)

Th. M. M. van Grieken [dates unknown]

Plates 72–73

Author of *De Plant in hare Ornamentale Behandeling* (Groningen, The Netherlands, 1888).

John Atkinson Grimshaw (1836–1893)

Plate 95

Victorian-era artist who specialized in landscapes and city scenes.

Ernst Haeckel (1834–1919)

Plates 106–109

German biologist, philosopher, and artist, supporter of Darwin and the teaching of evolution, and painter of hundreds of life forms.

Johann Elias Haid (1739–1809)

Plates 28–29

German artist and specialist in mezzotints, traveled widely throughout Europe.

Johann Jacob Haid (1704–1767)

Plates 28–29

German artist, father of Johann Elias Haid. Among his works is a mezzotint portrait of botanical artist Georg Dionysius Ehret based on a painting by A. Heckell.

Jan Davidsz de Heem (1606–1683/84)

Plate 7

Exquisite flower and table compositions were this Dutch Baroque artist's specialty. Balthasar van der Ast originally taught him in Utrecht.

Sir John Hill (c. 1714/21–1775)

Plate 30

English author and botanist. His compendium *The Vegetable System* was published in 26 volumes and illustrated with 1,600 copperplate engravings.

Jan van Huysum (1682–1749)

Plates 89, 91

Known for his floral scenes, this Amsterdam artist was referred to as "the phoenix of all flower painters," by fellow artists. His flower paintings were made up of blooms from different seasons in various stages.

Owen Jones (1809–1874)

Plates 67–69

Architect, designer, color theorist, and student of ornament and pattern design throughout history. Created the classic design sourcebook *The Grammar of Ornament* (London, 1856).

Sakigoto Kawahara [dates unknown]

Plates 127–128

Author of *Hanamaru Moyo Kyakudai* (Kyoto, 1939).

Johann Hermann Knoop (1700/1706?–1769)

Plates 32–33

German gardener and the father of pomology, the study of fruit varieties. His beautifully illustrated *Pomologia,* 1758, described more than a hundred apple varieties and 90 pear varieties.

Gustave Kolb (1867–1943)

Plates 98–99

See Gmelich, Charles.

Tanigami Kônan (1879–1928)

Plates 115–117

A master of the art of woodblock creation and color gradation, he is still celebrated as one of the finest artists of this highly specialized technique.

Kawarasaki Kôtô [dates unknown]

Plates 124–126

Author of *Kiku Hyakushu (One Hundred Aspects of the Chrysanthemum)* (Kyoto, 1936).

John Lindley (1799–1865)

Plates 45, 51–56

English botanist, prolific author and botanical artist with a specialty in orchids. Organized the first flower shows in England (1830) and was the first Professor of Botany at the University of London.

Jane Webb Loudon (1807–1858)

Plates 57–59

Author of fiction including *The Mummy: Or, a Tale of the 22nd Century,* published in 1827, and later the author of the first popular gardening books intended for a wide, general audience. These included *Botany for Ladies,* 1842.

Édouard Manet (1832–1883)

Plate 90

This French artist played an important role in the transition from Realism to Impressionism. While his interest focused on innumerable subjects for paintings, his great skill as a still life artist should also be remembered.

Jacob Marrell (1614–1681)

Plate 97

He was a pupil of Georg Flegel and is best known for his floral and still life paintings. This Dutch artist was the stepfather and teacher of Maria Sibylla Merian, the renowned naturalist and scientific illustrator.

Mathurin Méheut (1882–1958)

Plates 121–123

A native of Brittany, Méheut became an expert in painting marine life and other subjects in nature.

After World War I his interests turned to illustrating books.

Maria Sibylla Merian (1647–1717)

Plates 22–26

A major figure in the history of scientific illustration, Merian was a fabulously gifted artist who in 1699 received a grant from the city of Amsterdam to travel to Surinam, a Dutch colony in South America, for the purpose of studying and painting butterflies and other insects and related flora. This was probably the first publicly funded scientific/artistic expedition in history, and the plates Merian painted and published as a result are among the greatest masterpieces of botanical art.

John Miller (1715–1792)

Plate 31

German-born (as Johann Mueller) botanical artist, anglicized his name after coming to London in 1744. Miller painted and engraved the plates for the *Illustratio Systematis* (1770–77) of Carl Linnaeus and the great biologist described the plates as "more beautiful and more accurate than any that had been since the world began."

Henri Louis Duhamel du Monceau (1700–1782)

Plates 5–6

Versatile French botanist who was also a naval engineer and physician, published important books on fruit trees and other horticultural subjects.

Claude Monet (1840–1926)

Plate 93

One of the creators of the Impressionist movement, painted innumerable pictures of his famous gardens at Giverny.

Abraham Munting (1583–1658)

Plates 18–20

Dutch botanist and botanical artist, Professor of Botany and Chemistry at the University of Groningen, director of an extensive botanical garden and the moving force behind the publication of *Naauwkeurige Beschryving der Aardgewassen* or *"Accurate Description of Terrestrial Plants"* (1696). The remarkable and fascinating plates in this book were the work of Munting and artists Jan Goeree and Joseph Mulder.

F. W. Oliver (1864–1951)

Plates 51–53

English gardener and botanist, Professor at University College London.

Crispin van de Pass (c. 1564–1637)

Plates 11–13

Member of a family of Dutch engravers, largely responsible for the exceptional copperplate engravings in the *Hortus Floridus* (1614) on tulips and other plants, published at the height of the Dutch tulip 'bubble' in the 17th century

Sir Joseph Paxton (1803–1865)

Plates 51–56

English gardener, Member of Parliament, and designer of the Crystal Palace. From the 1830s on, he published several illustrated periodicals devoted to gardening including *The Magazine of Botany* (1834) and, beginning in 1841, *The Gardeners' Chronicle.*

A. Welby Pugin (1812–1852)

Plates 60–61

English architect, artist and designer, a leading proponent of the Gothic Revival in the early Victorian period. Pugin incorporated design elements based on Gothic floral forms into artistic designs for many purposes.

Pierre-Joseph Redouté (1759–1840)

Plates 21, 34–36, 38–40, 46–48

Perhaps the greatest flower painter of all time, most famous for his monumental works on roses and lilies. He was the official painter for the Musée National d'Histoire Naturelle, and also instructed generations of French aristocrats, including Napoleon's Empress Josephine.

Pierre-Auguste Renoir (1841–1919)

Plate 92

Among the founders of Impressionism, flowers are everywhere in his work, whatever the subject. Created a famous picture of Monet painting in his abundant garden at Argenteuil.

Nicolas Robert (1614–1684)

Plates 16–17

French flower painter, miniaturist and engraver, produced some of the finest botanical art of the 17th century.

Rachel Ruysch (1664–1750)

Plate 37

Born in The Hague, this artist was a student of Willem van Aelst. She is best known for her still life paintings of flowers and crystal vases.

Simon Saint-Jean (1808–1860)

Plate 96

Though his career was based in his native city of Lyon, Saint-Jean's flower paintings were prized by collectors throughout France and beyond. A meticulous craftsman who also worked as a textile designer, one of Saint-Jean's students recorded that he sometimes spent two days on a single rose.

Anton Seder (1850–1916)

Plates 79–81

Munich-born artist was the first Director of Strasbourg's College of Decorative Arts from 1890 to 1920 and a major figure in the Art Nouveau movement.

E. A. Seguy [dates unknown]

Plates 100–101, 112–114

French artist Eugène Alain Seguy published a series of unique and magnificent design portfolios starting about 1900 into the 1930s. A master of the pochoir technique, a printing process which yields dense, striking colors through the use of stencils, it is a great mystery that so little is known of Seguy's life apart from his art.

Gerard van Spaendonck (1746–1822)

Plate 1

A Dutch artist, he studied under Willem Jacob Herreyns and became the Professor of Floral Painting at the Jardin des Plantes in Paris. He was an important mentor to the great flower painter Pierre-Joseph Redouté.

Robert John Thornton (1768–1837)

Plates 41–43

English physician and author, the guiding light behind the greatest of all English flower books, *The Temple of Flora* (1799–1807).

Christoph Jacob Trew (1695–1769)

Plates 28–29

Physician and patron of the botanical artist Georg Dionysius Ehret. Some of Ehret's best work was published in Trew's *Plantae Selectae* (1750–73).

M. P. Verneuil (1869–1942)

Plates 84–85, 102–105

French artist and designer Maurice Pillard Verneuil studied with Eugène Grasset, and became a major Art Nouveau poster artist in the era of Jules Chéret and Toulouse-Lautrec. His work as a designer and graphic artist continued well into the Art Deco period.

Benedict Christian Vogel (1745–1825)

Plates 28–29

Professor of Botany at the University of Altdorf in Germany, Vogel completed the text for Christoph Jacob Trew's *Plantae Selectae* (1750–73) when Trew died before the last three parts had been written.

Mary Vaux Walcott (1860–1940)

Plates 118–120

American watercolor artist, her monumental *North American Wild Flowers,* including 400 plates and accompanying text, was published by the Smithsonian in 1925.

Nathaniel Wallich (1786–1854)

Plate 49

Danish surgeon and botanist spent much of his life on behalf of the East India Company in Calcutta where he assisted in the development of the Calcutta Botanical Garden, built a huge collection of botanical specimens, and worked with many botanists and researchers.

PLANT IDENTIFICATIONS

Plate 2: Helleborus viridis.

Plate 3: 1. Wild roses, pinks, daisies, stock, speedwell, borage, forget-me-nots and wood sorrel. 2. Rosa Gallica.

Plate 4: 1. Saffron crocus. 2. Sweet cherry tree.

Plates 5–6: 1. Matrimony vine. 2. Blue passion flower. 3. Common catalpa. 4. Rose of Sharon. 5. Cross vine, trumpet flower. 6. PawPaw. 7. Quince.

Plate 8: Common Sunflower.

Plate 9: White Rose of Sharon.

Plate 10: Green Dragon.

Plate 11: Crown Imperial with a double tier of flowers.

Plate 12: 1. The greater and lesser sunflower. 2. Double hollyhocks.

Plate 13: The great female paeone.

Plates 14–15: 1. Woolly St. James wort. 2. Double-flowered virgin's bower. 3. Broad-leaved-sweet William. 4. Double white and black poppy. 5. Mr. Hesketh's primrose. 6. Turkish peony. 7. Dock-leaved thistle-gentle. 8. Poppy windflower. 9. Kidney bean of Brazil. 10. Broad-leaved candy crowfoot.

Plate 16: Sunflower.

Plate 17: Mandrake.

Plate 18: Ricinus Americanus Major Rubicundus.

Plate 19: Sedum Maius Arborescens Radicabile.

Plate 20: Salvia Lutea Variegata.

Plate 25: Inflorescence of Banana.

Plate 26: Cocoa.

Plate 27: Frangipani.

Plate 28: Papaya.

Plate 29: Tulip Tree.

Plate 30: Imperial Gloriosa.

Plate 31: Sunflower.

Plate 33: Pears.

Plates 34–36: 1. Tiger flower. 2. Tulip. 3. Poppy. 4. Bellflower. 5. Pomegranate. 6. Fig. 7. Snapdragon. 8. Rose of Orleans. 9. Perennial sweet pea. 10. Blanket flower. 11. Peony. 12. Hyacinth. 13. Didier's tulip. 14. Lilac. 15. Cherry.

Plate 38: Lily-of-the-Nile.

Plate 39: Crown imperial.

Plate 40: Eating banana.

Plate 41: The Queen (strelitzia reginae Banks).

Plate 42: The Nodding Renealmia.

Plate 43: The Night-Blowing Cereus.

Plate 44: Albany Scarlet Banksia.

Plate 45: Cattleya labiata (orchid).

Plate 46: Rosa centifolia Bullata.

Plate 47: Rosa centifolia Anemonoides.

Plate 48: 1. Rosa Gallica Versiclor. 2. Rosa Eglanteria var. punicea. 3. Rosa centifolia foliacea. 4. Rosa alba Regalis.

Plate 49: Thomsonia napalensis.

Plate 50: Dahlias.

Plates 51–53: 1. Fuchsia nigricans, Lagetta lintearia, Drymonia cristata. 2. Abutilon insigne. 3. Echeveria bracteosa. 4. Tropaeolum deckerianum (nasturtium). 5. Common European hornbeam. 6. Brugmansia zipelli. 7. Jumping orchid. 8. Iris germanica. 9. Cuphea cinnabarina. 10. Leucojum vernum.

Plate 54: 1. The Box-Leaved Cantua. 2. The Splendid Aeschynanth. 3. The Thyrse-Like Billbergia.

Plate 55. The Morel Billbergia.

Plate 56. The Mysore Hexacentre.

Plates 57–59: 1. Mimulus. 2. Digitalis. 3. Salvia. 4. Gazania. 5. Tigridia, Rigidella, Ferraria. 6. Anemone. 7. Gentiana. 8. Paeonia. 9. Lilium. 10. Aconitum. 11. Dahlia. 12. Aster.

Plates 62–63: 1. Exanthemum palatiferum. 2. Lilium concolor. 3. Curly-fringed passion flower. 4. Single-flowered paranephelius. 5. Mrs. Benson's thunia. 6. Large-flowered oncidium. 7. Quito tacsonia. 8. Musa sanguinea. 9. M. Linden's tillandsia. 10. Allan Cunningham's blandfordia.

Plates 64–66: 1. Iris. 2, 16. Chrysanthemum. 3. Aster. 4. Rhododendron. 5. Oak tree. 6. Lily. 7. Carrots. 8. Pear. 9. Kelp frond. 10–11. Orchids. 12. Strawberry. 13. Mushroom. 14. Hydrophllaceae. 15. Tulip. 17. Water plant.

Plate 72: Crocus.

Plate 73: Crocus, narcissus, tulip.

Plate 79: Thistle.

Plate 80: Passion flower.

Plate 81: Tulip.

Plate 82: Wisteria.

Plate 83: Nasturtium.

Plates 84–85: 1. Dandelion. 2. Fuchsia. 3. Lily of the valley. 4. Lady's slipper. 5. Horn poppy. 6, 7. Cyclamen. 8. Snowdrop.

Plates 98–99: 1, 9. Honeysuckle. 2. Mistletoe. 3, 11. Daisy. 4. Vetch. 5, 6. Holly. 7, 12, 13. Bindweed. 8. Forget-me-not. 10. Snowball bush.

Plates 100–101: 1. Arum. 2. Arrowhead. 3. Buttercup. 4. Anemone. 5–8. Orchids.

Plate 102: Iris.

Plate 103: Sunflower.

Plate 104: Rhododendron.

Plate 105: Anthurium.

Plate 106: Liverworts (related to mosses).

Plate 107: Orchids.

Plate 108: Malaysian pitcher plant.

Plate 109: Various species of mosses.

Plate 111: Tulip.

Plates 115–117: 1. Begonia. 2. Dahlia. 3. Schizanthus, gladiolus. 4. Tulip. 5. Water lily. 6. Canna.

Plate 118: Parrot Pitcherplant.

Plate 119: Franklinia.

Plate 120: Mountain Ladyslipper.

Plate 121: Mushrooms, leaves.

Plate 122: Cacti.

Plates 124–126: Chrysanthemums.

Chapter Opening Paintings

Plate 1: Gerard van Spaendonck (1746–1822) / *Flowers in a Stone Vase on a Carved Ledge*

Plate 7: Jan Davidsz de Heem (1606–83/84) / *Vase of Flowers,* c. 1660

Plate 21: Pierre-Joseph Redouté (1759–1840) / *Flower Still Life,* 1796

Plate 37: Rachel Ruysch (1664–1750) / *Flower Still Life,* c. 1726

Plate 89: Jan van Huysum (1682–1749) / *Vase of Flowers on a Garden Ledge,* c. 1730

Plate 97: Jacob Marrell (1614–81) / *Flower Piece,* 1647

SOURCE INFORMATION

Bauer, Ferdinand Lukas. *Illustrationes florae novae hollandiae*. London: 1813.

Besler, Basilius. *Hortus Eystettensis*, 3 vols. Nuremberg: 1613.

Bosse, Abraham and Robert, Nicolas. *Memoires pour servir a l'histoire des plantes* by Denis Dodart. Paris: Imprimerie Royale, 1676.

Bourdichon, Jean. Illuminations. French: early 16th century.

Codex Bellunensis. Illumination. Italian: early 15th century.

Curtis, Samuel. *The Beauties of Flora*. Gamston, Notts., U.K.: 1820.

Cutler, Thomas W. *A Grammar of Japanese Ornament and Design*. London: B. T. Batsford, 1880.

Duhamel du Monceau, Henri Louis. *Traité des Arbres et Arbustes qui se cultivent en France en pleine terre*, 2 vols. Paris: 1755.

Ehret, Georg Dionysius. *Plantae et Papiliones Rariores*. London: 1748–59.

Fitch, Walter Hood. *Curtis's Botanical Magazine*. London: 1868–72.

Gerard, John. *The Herbal or General History of Plants: The Complete 1633 Edition as Revised and Enlarged by Thomas Johnson*. London: Adam Islip Joice Norton and Richard Whitakers, 1633.

Grasset, Eugène, editor. *La plante et ses applications ornamentales*, second series. Paris: Librairie Centrale des Beaux-Arts, c. 1898.

van Grieken, Th. M. M. *De Plant in hare Ornamentale Behandling*. Groningen, The Netherlands: J. H. van de Weijer, 1888.

Haeckel, Ernst. *Kunstformen der Natur*. Leipzig and Vienna: Verlag des Bibliographischen Instituts, 1904.

Harter, Jim. *The Plant Kingdom Compendium*. New York: Bonanza Books, 1988.

The Hastings Hours. Illuminations. Flemish: 1475–83.

Hill, Sir John. *Exotic Botany, illustrated in thirty five figures of Curious and Elegant Plants explaining the Sexual System and Tending to give some New Lights into the Vegetable Philosophy*. London: 1759.

Jones, Owen. *Examples of Chinese Ornament Selected from Objects in the South Kensington Museum and Other Collections*. London: S. & T. Gilbert, 1867.

Kawahara, Sakigoto. *Hanamaru Moyo Kyakudai*. Kyoto: Uchida Bijutsu Shoshi, 1939.

Knoop, Johann Hermann. *Pomologia*. Nuremberg: Johann Michael Seligmann, 1760.

Kolb, Gustave and Gmelich, Charles. *De la Plante à l'Ornement*. Göppingen, Germany: Jllig & Müller, 1902.

Kônan, Tanigami. *Seiyô Soka Zufu*. Kyoto: Unsôdô, c. 1917.

Kôtô, Kawarasaki. *Kiku Hyakushu*. Kyoto: Uchida Bijutsu Shoshi, 1936.

Lindley, John. *Collectanea Botanica; or, Figures and Botanical illustrations of rare and curious exotic plants*. London: R. and A. Taylor, 1821.

Lindley, Professor John and Paxton, Sir Joseph. *Paxton's Flower Garden*. London: Bradbury and Evans, 1850–53.

Loudon, Jane Webb. *The Ladies' Flower Garden*. London 1840–44.

Méheut, Mathurin. *Etude de la forêt* and *La plante exotique*. Paris: C. Massin & cie, 1931.

Merian, Maria Sibylla. *De metamorphosis insectorum Surinamensium*. Amsterdam: Gerard Valk, 1705.

Merian, Maria Sibylla. *Erucarum Ortus, Alimentum et Paradoxa Metamorphosis*. Amsterdam: 1718.

Miller, John. *Illustratio systematis sexualis Linnaei—An Illustration of the Sexual System of the Genera Plantarum of Linnaeus*. London: 1777.

Motivenschatz für Modernes Kunstschaffen Studienblatter für Kuenstler. Dresden: Verlag von Gerhard Kuehtmann.

Munting, Abraham. *Naauwkeurige Beschryving der Aadgewassen*. Leyden, Holland: Pieter vander Aa, 1696; Utrecht, Holland: François Halma, 1696.

Oliver, F. W. *The Natural History of Plants: Their Forms, Growth, Reproduction, and Distribution*. London: Blackie & Son, Limited, 1902.

van de Pass, Crispin. *Hortus Floridus*. Utrecht, Holland: Salomon de Roy, 1615.

Pugin, A. Welby. *Floriated Ornament: A Series of Thirty-one Designs*. London: Henry G. Bohn, 1849.

Redouté, Pierre-Joseph. *Les Liliacées*, 8 vols. Paris: Didot Jeune, 1802–16.

Redouté, Pierre-Joseph. *Les Roses*. Paris: Firmin Didot, 1817–24.

Seder, Anton. *Die Pflanze in Kunst und Gewerbe*. Vienna: Gerlach & Schenk, 1890.

Seguy, E. A. *Les fleurs et leurs applications décoratives*. Paris: Librairie des Arts Décoratifs, A. Calavas, c. 1902.

Seguy, E. A. *Primavera: Dessins & coloris nouveaux*. Plauen, Germany: Christian Stoll, n.d; *Floréal: Dessins & coloris nouveaux*. Paris: A. Calavas, c. 1914; and *Samarkande: 20 compositions en couleurs dans le Style oriental*. Paris: Ch. Massin, c. 1920.

Thornton, Robert John. *The Temple of Flora*. London: T. Bensley, 1807.

Trew, Christoph Jacob; Ehret, Georg Dionysius; Vogel, Benedict Christian; Haid, Johann Jacob and Haid, Johann Elias. *Plantae selectae*. Nuremberg: 1750–73.

Verneuil, M. P., editor. *Encyclopédie artistic et documenter de la plante*. Paris: Librairie Centrale des Beaux-Arts, 1904–08.

Verneuil, M. P. *Étude de la Plante: son application aux industries d'art*. Paris: Librairie Centrale des Beaux-Arts, c. 1900 and *L'ornementation par le Pochoir*. Paris: Schmid and Laurens, n.d.

Walcott, Mary Vaux. *North American Wild Flowers*, 5 vols. Washington, D.C.: The Smithsonian Institution, 1925–.

Wallich, Nathaniel. *Plantae asiaticae rariores; or, descriptions and figures of a select number of unpublished East Indian plants*. London, Paris, Strasburgh: 1830–32.